RIVER OF LOST SOULS

THE SCIENCE, POLITICS, AND GREED
BEHIND THE GOLD KING MINE DISASTER

RIVER OF LOST SOULS

THE SCIENCE, POLITICS, AND GREED
BEHIND THE GOLD KING MINE DISASTER

JONATHAN P. THOMPSON

TORREY HOUSE PRESS

Salt Lake City • Torrey

First Torrey House Press Edition, March 2018
Copyright © 2018 by Jonathan P. Thompson

Published by Torrey House Press
www.torreyhouse.org

Portions of this book originally appeared in the *Silverton Standard & the Miner*, *Silverton Mountain Journal*, and *High Country News*.

International Standard Book Number: 978-1-937226-83-1
Ebook International Standard Book Number: 978-1-937226-84-8
Library of Congress Control Number: 2017930158
Cover design by Alisha Anderson and Kathleen Metcalf

For
Wendy, Lydia, and Elena,
who give me a reason to write all the words.

In memory of
Ian M. Thompson, Allen Nossaman, and Stanton Englehart,
who taught me that art, inspiration, beauty, and ideas are
abundant right here in our home.

Contempt for the natural world is contempt for life.
The domination of nature leads to the
domination of human nature.

—Edward Abbey

Acknowledgments

The reporting for this book took place over 20 years, much of it for stories that originally appeared in the *Silverton Standard & the Miner*, the *Silverton Mountain Journal*, or *High Country News*, and I had a great deal of help and support along the way, from Wendy, Elena, and Lydia, who put up with living with a small-town newspaperman, to the people who actually paid money to read the *Mountain Journal* and my friends who contributed art, photos, knowledge, and text to the *Mountain Journal*, usually for free; from the folks who shared their stories with me, to my colleagues at *High Country News*, who have selflessly dedicated themselves to chronicling the important issues of the American West, and who continue daily to push me to be a better journalist, writer, and pursuer of the truth. I owe a special debt of gratitude to Paul and Mary Beaber, who were by far our biggest supporters in our various Silverton ventures and beyond, as well as to Dick Jones, without whose generosity the *Mountain Journal* would have collapsed after a few months. Thanks to Peter Schertz of the fabulous Maria's Bookshop in Durango for reading the text and giving feedback, and to Torrey House Press and Kirsten Johanna Allen. Of course I couldn't have done any of this without my parents: Ian Thompson, Jan Thompson, and my stepfather Gary Matlock, all of whom supported me through my various zany pursuits. And last but not least, the Yeti of Hematite Basin, for keeping me the word factory fueled with Zia tacos and Wine Merchant goods.

A Note on Terms

River of Lost Souls, or Rio de las Animas Perdidas: As you read the text, you'll discover that this is not the name given to the Animas River by Juan Maria Rivera in 1765. He called it *Rio de las Animas* (River of Souls). However, in the late 1800s, someone appended "perdidas" to the name and it stuck. As far as I'm concerned, River of Lost Souls is as good a name as River of Souls. After all, Rio de las Animas was not the first name of the river—the Ute and Navajo people had their own names for it as well.

Animas Valley and Animas River valley: I use Animas Valley to refer to the U-shaped valley just north of Durango. I use Animas River valley to refer to the entire length of the drainage.

Contents

PART I

Headwaters

Blowout

Instead of a pure, sparkling stream of water, an opiate for tired mind and jaded nerves, what do you see? A murky, gray stream of filthy, slimy, polluted water, a cesspool for the waste of man.

—Durango-area farmer, 1937

BONITA PEAK'S ROCKY CREST GIVES WAY TO A SLOP-ING CARPET OF GREEN. The tundra, spattered with blue, red, yellow, and lavender wildflowers, is particularly verdant this summer of 2015, helping obscure the violent origins of these mountains, the San Juans of southwestern Colorado. Here are huge plates of quartzite bent upward; a land of ancient lakes of bubbling lava, eruptions, and volcaniclastic mudflows. Twenty-seven million years ago, a vast chamber of magma collapsed, leaving behind what geologists now call the Silverton Caldera, rife with fractures that were later filled with minerals to become veins of gold, silver, and zinc ore. The caldera is shaped roughly like a human heart, with Mineral Creek running along the west side, the upper Animas River the east, Cement Creek slicing through its center, and the small town of Silverton on the southeast end, where the three major streams converge before continuing southward like a massive vein linking mountain peaks with the high desert.

Bonita Peak rises up just above the center of the caldera. Piles of yellow-ochre earth that look like a giant gopher colony cling to the slope here and there, the remnants of mining prospect holes and piles of waste rock mined from the earth years ago.

On one of those piles, on the morning of August 5, a yellow CAT excavator paws gingerly and jerkily at dirt and tundra as workers in orange hard hats and neon-green vests watch. At approximately ten-thirty a.m. a stream of water spurts from where the excavator digs. It looks a lot like that opening scene in the Beverly Hillbillies when Jed strikes oil with a gunshot to the ground, only this isn't oil and it doesn't even look like water—it's bright orange. The excavator operator pulls away from the slope. One of the workers pulls out his phone and starts filming.[1]

Within minutes, the little spout grows into a fountain and then a roiling torrent of thick, Tang-colored water. As the workers look on, stunned, the water roars over the edge of the mine waste-rock dump, carrying tons of the metal-laden material with it, crashing into the gently gurgling stream of the north fork of Cement Creek, far below, but not before a fair amount of it inundates one of the work vehicles, a black Suburban, filling it up with orange muck.

"Should we get out of here?" one worried worker asks.

"Oh, he's going to be pissed," another answers. "This isn't good."

"What do we do now?" someone else asks, shocked yet oddly calm, as though a household plumbing project had gone awry.

The workers are staffers and contractors with the Environmental Protection Agency who, in the moments before the catastrophe, were investigating the Level 7 portal of the Gold King Mine, which had been drilled into the side of Bonita Peak back in 1900. The agency will later estimate that three million gallons of water—enough to fill four and a half Olympic-sized swimming pools, or to supply twenty-one families for a year—blasted out of the mine over the course of minutes. Only this isn't just water. It carries with it some 880,000 pounds of metals: zinc, cadmium, aluminum, arsenic, and, mostly, iron hydroxides, giving it the electric-orange color that will captivate and horrify onlookers near and far. It has been backing up underground behind debris for years, the pressure building, until, finally, on a sunny day in August, a heavy equipment operator facilitates its escape.

A wall of water and sludge, we'll call it the slug, careens into Cement Creek, swelling it into a raging cataract. It blasts past the ghosts of the old Gladstone townsite, rushes through Silverton and into the Animas River's chilly, clear water, instantly staining it orange.

Forty-five miles downstream, in the town of Durango, hundreds of people frolic on or beside the Animas River's green waters, which ply the town in two. Stand-up paddle boarders skim the smooth, deep water on the north end of town. Anglers, resembling wader-clad symphony conductors, rhythmically swing their oversized batons in the boulder-studded, trout-rich water south of town.

In the middle of town, back behind the high school, a couple dozen bikini- and shorts-clad teens and twenty-somethings lounge about in the grass of "Paradise Cove," drinking Pabst Blue Ribbon from cans as a stereo blasts pop tunes and tubers float by, holding bologna sandwiches high to salute their fellow revelers.

They are oblivious to the orange menace creeping toward them from the mountains. During the first hours after the blowout, EPA officials that know about the event apparently think that the slug will dissipate as it travels downstream, that the sludge will drop out en route, and the terrible color will become diluted. They are wrong.

The prow of the slug moves quickly through the deep canyon that the Animas has carved through the gorge below Silverton, moving alongside the narrow gauge tourist railroad whose tracks sit just above the normally emerald green and frothy whitewater of the river's class four and five rapids. Some twenty-four hours after the orange spurt of water appeared up at the Gold King, the slug charges out of the narrow granite gorge into which Robert Redford and Paul Newman jumped in *Butch Cassidy and the Sundance Kid*, passes under Baker's Bridge, and creeps into the Animas Valley above Durango. At about the same time, word of the disaster reaches the general public in Durango—or at least that's when I notice it on my Twitter feed as I sit in my home office on the morning of August 6, pounding away on a story about the methane pollution emanating from the San Juan Basin gas fields south of here.

"I gotta see this," I say to my half-empty coffee cup. I run out to my car and drive to the nearest bridge over the Animas in Durango. The water here is its usual placid green. A handful of boaters and tubers float by obliviously. So I continue north into the broad, flat-bottomed Animas Valley, carved and scoured of rock and boulders by a glacier some ten thousand years ago. I pass by my second cousin's ranch and constructed wetlands, my aunt and uncle's house, my cousin's house, and my grandparents' old farm, where I spent a good portion of my childhood. It's been a good year for rain, and the fields are all green, the cottonwoods lush.

About six miles north of town, I turn onto Trimble Lane. When I was a kid, this part of the Animas Valley was a big, open field. Now there's a golf course here, and Dalton Ranch, a community of McMansions stacked up between the river banks and the highway. I drive past them to a little turnout by the bridge and stroll towards the river. Turbid, electric-orange water, utterly opaque, sprawls out between the sandy banks, as iron hydroxide particles thicken within the current like psychedelic smoke.

At about that same moment, unbeknownst to me, Bill Simon, who probably understands the mining-related pollution problems in this watershed better than anyone, is scurrying down to the river a few miles upstream, at Baker's Bridge, to take some water samples. "What struck me was the intense color," he says, later. In the days to come, that distinctive shade of orange will strike a lot of other people—millions of them, in fact—too.

Within a few hours, the river through town is empty, an eerie sight on a hot August afternoon. The bridges across the river, on the other hand, are crowded with people milling about, waiting for the slow-motion disaster to unfurl in the dark green water below them. I amble among the little clusters of people, eavesdropping. Everyone is aware that something bad happened upstream, and that the result is headed our way, but their understanding of it is unclear. One guy says a hazardous waste truck tipped over on an entirely different tributary of the Animas, spilling its load. Someone else says a plume of cyanide is coming our way. People are angry, sad, befuddled.

A television news helicopter flies over, which seems odd, since the nearest TV stations are in Albuquerque, and in my naïveté I can't imagine why people way down there would be interested in our orange river.

In the six or so miles between Trimble Lane and the north end of Durango, the river drops fifteen feet or so in elevation, thanks to that old glacier that crept through here with so much force millennia ago. As a result, the river runs slow through the broad floodplain, taking any path except for the straight one, so the slug takes far longer to reach town than anticipated. The sun lingers on the western horizon, and the river is still green. I leave to eat dinner and when I return the crowd has grown even larger. My phone dings with various news organizations asking to use my photos. The slug still hasn't arrived as darkness falls, and most of us go home.

Late that night, the slug sneaks into town, and by morning the river is like a bright orange incision slicing its way through green Durango. The sheriff has closed the river to any kind of activity, but it probably isn't necessary. No one is going in or even near that water; we still aren't sure what's in it. Downstream, Aztec and Farmington officials shut off their municipal water intakes and start calculating how long they can continue to run their taps, water their lawns, flush their toilets on storage. The Animas and the slug join the San Juan River on the edge of Farmington, promptly turning it orange, too, before slowly sliding onto the Navajo Nation. Water—life—is cut off from hundreds of small Diné farms where crops are grown for sustenance and corn for ceremony. "When we heard about this yellow plume coming down the river toward us, we didn't know what to do," said Duane "Chili" Yazzie, a Shiprock-area farmer, activist, and politician. "We were at a loss. It was right in the middle of the growing season, when our crops have to have water on the regular basis. To be told that our water is ruined, it is utter devastation, particularly to our elders."[2]

Farmers will lose crops, and rafting companies in Durango will miss out on hundreds of thousands of dollars of potential revenue. In coming months, Republican congressmen will hold a half-dozen hearings in Washington, D.C., where, for the first time in many of their political lives, they'll rail against an alleged polluter—in this case the EPA—and demand prosecution. The state of New Mexico and then the Navajo Nation will sue the agency over what they will call one of the worst environmental disasters of our time.

As shocking and heartbreaking as the Gold King spill and its aftermath may be, however, it's merely the tip of the proverbial iceberg. The disaster itself was the climax of the long and troubled story of the Gold King Mine, staked by a Swedish immigrant back in 1887. And it was only the most visible manifestation of a slow-moving, multi-faceted environmental catastrophe that had been unfolding long before the events of August 5, 2015.

For thousands of years, humans and this river and the landscape through which it flows have been intimately entangled. The land shaped the humans, their cultures and their religions, and the humans returned the favor by building settlements, cultivating fields, hunting game, and even burning underbrush to make for better game range.

In the 1870s, however, this relationship shifted. The white settlers that arrived then were no less dependent on the land than their indigenous predecessors, and their culture, too, was shaped by this place. Yet they tended to derive less of their identity from the land itself than from its exploitation. They shaped the land, not the other way around. Silverton was not a mountain town, but a mining town. My grandparents were not people of the dirt and the river, but farmers. They pulled and pulled the riches from the earth and for so long didn't give back. That which fuels our existence fouls our home. Our history is a history of pollution.

The history of human settlement along this river, from its headwaters high in the San Juans, down to the confluence with the San Juan River, and into Utah, has been rich, full of struggle, hardship, beauty, and triumph. It has also been one of desecration, death, poison, and blight. This land and water is sacred, and it is sacrificial.

Holy Land

The farmers along the Animas River are sitting down and permitting the waters of that river to be so tainted and polluted as that soon it will merit the name of Rio de las Animas Perdidas, *given it by the Spaniards. With water filled with slime and poison, carrying qualities which destroy all agricultural values of ranchers irrigated therefrom, it will be truly a river of lost souls.*

—Durango Wage Earner, 1907

'M MAYBE SIX YEARS OLD and it's June, just after the first cutting of hay, so that pungent aroma still lingers in the early afternoon air as we walk down past my grandparents' milk barn and the hay barn and through the dank human-sized culvert that passes underneath the new highway, which isn't so new anymore but that's what we call it anyway.

"Maybe we can find some asparagus," I say, darting toward the fence.

"It's too late," my dad says, his voice deep. "All gone to seed."

So I pick butter and eggs—yellow toadflax—instead, bunching a bouquet up in my little fist, no idea it's some sort of noxious scourge, already overrunning the Animas Valley. We're going down to the Sandbar, which is what we call the place on the river below the Farm where we fish and picnic and camp. Used to be, all the farms stretched to the river and beyond, but the new highway sliced all the old homesteads in half, so a lot of the fields down below went fallow. Then my grandparents retired and sold off the lower part, anyway, but the new owners still let us go down there so it makes no difference to me.

We called it the Farm because back then it was a farm— that's how my grandparents made a living. They had dairy cows and sheep, they had fields of hay. They had rows of corn, apple orchards, peaches, strawberries and raspberries, spinach and lettuce. What they didn't eat, they sold. My mom and her sisters, hair in ponytails, picked raspberries for a nickel a quart and folks would come by on the old road on their way back up to Silverton and pick up some of the bounty.

The valley floor here is wide and flat. The glaciers pushed all the rocks downstream or ground them into coarse sand, so the river runs slow here, meandering between steep and sandy banks, nearly twisting back on itself at times like a giant, murky green umbilical cord. In the spring, when the water's big and red and brown, listen and you might hear it eating its way through the soft earth. At the Sandbar, the banks were softened into a beach by the current. As we get close, I run off ahead of my father and brother. I take off my shoes. The sand burns my feet. The water whispers.

I stare at the old, crushed cars all lined up against the opposite bank, their front ends underwater.

"That was a drive-in theatre," my towheaded, freckle-nosed brother tells me, again. "And one day the bank collapsed and they all fell in the river and died."

Maybe I believe him, maybe I don't, but I do wonder what

movie they were watching when it happened. Upstream from the Sandbar, around the next corner, an ancient-looking rowboat sits half buried on the gravelly shore. Sometimes we try to get it out so we can float down the river on it, but it won't budge. An ancient boxelder tree grows at the edge of the sand, its canopy so dense and low that we can crawl under there and sleep and stay dry even in a downpour.

Just downstream from the Sandbar, polished and crooked cottonwood branches jut out from the murky deep green swirling water. Suckers and carp and brown trout so big you don't want to catch them lurk down there. The lost souls, the *animas perdidas* of the river's name, linger there, too. And if you venture in, my grandmother says, the undertow will pull you down into the cold, deep, and dark, and you will join them. Sometimes, my brother coaxes me into wandering over to that place, and to stand close enough to the edge to peer into the depths. Look hard enough, he says, and you'll see a big brown trout coming up for a meal. But when I dare to look in there, I see only darkness and my reflection gazing back, both curious and scared.

TEN MILES DOWNSTREAM AND 210 YEARS EARLIER, Spanish explorer Juan Maria Antonio de Rivera stood on the banks of the river and gave the river its soulful name.

Rivera had headed out from the Pueblo of Santa Rosa de Abiquiu, in the New Mexico province of Spain, in June 1765 at the order of the governor. Abiquiu, some fifty miles from Santa Fe, was the northwest outpost of the Spanish empire. Though the conquistadors and missionaries had invaded this land 167 years earlier, very few of the colonists had dared venture beyond Abiquiu, in part because the Crown forbid it. The extensive San Juan mountain range, along with the rugged valleys, mesas, and basins that spread out from it, was the domain of the Weenuchiu, Tabeguache, Caputa, and Mouache bands of Ute, and Spain didn't want to provoke them any more than necessary. It had made that mistake before: In 1637, Spanish conquistadors took eighty Utes as slaves, then suffered a barrage of brutal retaliatory raids (and got their horses stolen, which were then used against them). And in 1680 more than a dozen Pueblo tribes up and down the Rio Grande and stretching west all the way to Hopi in Arizona revolted, killed at least four hundred Spaniards, and drove the colonists back to El Paso, where they stayed for more than a decade before returning, somewhat humbled. The best way to keep a shaky peace was to keep Spaniards out of Ute territory; if Utes wanted to trade with the colonists, they could come to Abiquiu to do so.

On one such occasion, a Ute, whose name has been lost to time, reputedly paid an Abiquiu blacksmith for his services with an ingot of silver that came from somewhere in the San Juan country. It gave the New Mexico governor a pretense—find the source of the precious metal—to send Rivera into the forbidden territory. This first official European expedition into the San Juan River watershed was really more of an undercover conquistador mission to scout the region for possible future colonization, and to confirm the existence of the mythical Rio Tizon, now known as the Colorado River.

Rivera never found the source of the silver ingot. He thought he reached the Colorado River near what is now Moab, but recent scrutiny of Rivera's diaries by historian Steven Baker reveals that the explorer actually stood on the bank of the Gunnison River near present-day Delta, Colorado.[3] Utes, suspicious of his motives, led him astray. Still, he earned a reputation as a blazer of trails and namer of places throughout the terra incognita of the Four Corners country. Eleven years after Rivera's journey, Franciscan priests Atanasio Domínguez and Silvestre Vélez de Escalante would follow Rivera's approximate route, as would a host of Spanish and then Mexican travelers over the next century.

In fact, Rivera merely followed well-established routes through a land that had been inhabited for millennia, and that had been intimately mapped in the collective consciousness of oral histories. Rivera probably wasn't even the first Spaniard to tread these paths; mavericks defied the travel and trade ban to acquire deerskins or to try their luck in the mineralized slopes of the high San Juan Mountains, or *Sierra de la Grulla*—Mountains of the Crane. The Spanish mavericks, in turn, were merely following paths already well trodden by Utes, Diné, Pueblos, and nomadic hunters long before that. Almost all of the country that Rivera traveled through was not just the homeland, present and past, to a number of tribes. It was also holy land.

After leaving the Chama River, as he headed toward the Continental Divide, Rivera passed by the deep-green lake from which the people of Jemez Pueblo emerged into the Fourth World.[4] He passed under the shadow of *Piedra Parada*, now known as Chimney Rock, an ancient lunar observatory, and he forded the chilly Pine River a dozen miles upstream of *Tó Aheedlí*, the residence of the Diné Hero Twins and the heart of *Dinetah*, the Diné ancestral homeland.

On July 4, with Utes guiding them, the explorers crossed *el Rio Florido* and followed a path through sagebrush, piñon, juniper, and ponderosas to the valley south of present-day Durango. Here, near a Ute encampment, Rivera stood on the steep and cobbled bank of the river the Utes called *Sagwavanukwiti*, or Blue River. As the Spaniard pondered the swift, cold current swirling around the boulders as big as bulls that the glaciers had pushed down from the high country so many years before, he decided to give it his own name: *Rio de las Animas*, or River of Souls. Contrary to current legend, the souls in the river were not *perdidas*, or lost, though some historians believe that it was originally implied. That adjective wouldn't be tacked on to the name for another century or so, for reasons unknown, but it has stuck—along with an apocryphal but false origin story.

Rivera's journals are infamously terse, and he doesn't explain to whose souls he referred. Maybe his Ute guides had told him stories about people drowning in the river or its propensity to flood cataclysmically. He may have thought that the river had a lot of spirit, or soul. More likely, he sensed the presence of the many that had treaded this ground for centuries before he arrived.

Rivera and his men had to go several miles downstream before they could find a place to safely ford the Animas River, and still the water was up to the horses' bellies. The Spanish explorer then made his way back upstream and climbed up into Ridges Basin, a gentle valley that runs from east to west between Smelter Mountain, Durango's southern backdrop, and the Hogback Monocline, one of the region's most geologically distinctive landforms. Here, Rivera encountered the remnants of a large pueblo atop a hill in the middle of the basin.[5]

This was most likely what archaeologists today refer to as Sacred Ridge, a small village within the larger Pueblo community of Ridges Basin, a sort of eighth-century boomtown that rose up quickly, flourished for a relatively brief period, and then—after a horrific incidence of violence—was left empty, despite the local abundance of resources.

TEN THOUSAND YEARS BEFORE RIVERA WANDERED THROUGH HERE, when the scars were still fresh from the last wave of glaciers pushing aside mountains like battleships, nomads known as Paleoindians roamed these valleys and mesas, chasing down wooly mammoth and other megafauna. They were followed by Archaic people, who most likely camped in and around the Animas Valley in the summers, subsisting on game and wild nuts, plants, and berries.

Yet it wasn't until about the time a prophet named Jesus was born in another Holy Land on the other side of the globe that people started settling down permanently in the Durango area and farming the fertile soil. These ancestors of today's Hopi, Zuni, and Rio Grande Pueblo people built and lived in dwellings scattered around on the mesas of current-day Durango, in Ridges Basin, and at Talus Village and the Dark-mold site on the red-dirt hillside above where my grandparents would one day set up their Animas Valley farm. They also lived in rock shelters that they constructed under a vast, overhanging layer of sandstone in Falls Creek, just west of the Animas Valley.

The Basketmaker II, as these people are known in archaeological parlance, lived here for five hundred years or more. They grew corn and squash, but not beans; they used their atlatls to hunt deer and rabbits for protein. They ate wild plants, such as amaranth. They wove baskets, sandals, and other items, but did not have pottery.

During the fifth century temperatures cooled, and farming at these relatively high altitudes must have gotten even tougher. People began bailing on the Animas Valley, and by the sixth century AD, the population of the area had shrunk almost to zero. It may have been the first natural resource bust to hit this terminally boom-bust region. Or perhaps the people who lived here just decided it was time to move on, to let this particular place rest for a while and recover from a half-millennium of human occupation.

If you want to understand Place, with a capital *P*, in the Four Corners country, it makes sense to begin with the Pueblo people. They've been in this region for thousands of years, interacting with the landscape, adapting to vagaries of climate, creating cultures and religions, developing languages. They've moved around, but have never abandoned, or been displaced from, their ancestral homeland. Their cultures continue to flourish in the Place from which they emerged.

During the summer of 2016, in hopes of getting a better understanding of the Pueblo sense of Place, I embarked on a trip around the Four Corners, visiting Hovenweep, Cedar Mesa, Chaco, Tsegi Canyon. On Pueblo Revolt Day, the 336th anniversary of the uprising against the Spanish colonizers, I drove my tiny 1989 Nissan Sentra across the high northern Arizona desert from Tuba City to Hopi's Second Mesa. There, I sat down with Leigh Kuwanwisiwma in the living room of his small home.

Kuwanwisiwma has been the Hopi tribe's cultural preservation officer for nearly three decades. When an oil company wants to drill public lands that overlap Pueblo ancestral lands, Kuwanwisiwma is called in during the "consultation" process. He fought to get Hopi ritual objects back from a Paris auction house. And he continues to search for leads on the theft, years ago, of a crucial ceremonial altar—he thinks maybe it's serving as a headboard for some Aspen millionaire's bed.

We talked about growing corn and about his tribe's connections to the lands farther north. He let me taste salt he had gathered from deposits down near where the turquoise-hued waters of the Little Colorado merge with the Colorado River in the Grand Canyon, and also gave me a sample of chili pepper he had grown on a dryland field nearby.

He told me that when his ancestors emerged from the Third World into the Fourth World, the holy people instructed them to "place their footprints" across the region's landscape. Each clan was sent on its own multi-generational migratory path—the Parrot, Badger, and Greasewood clans settled at Mesa Verde, he said, and the Rattlesnake, Fire, and Coyote clans at Kawestima in Tsegi Canyon. All paths ultimately converged on the northern Arizona mesas, reaching like fingers off of Black Mesa, where the clans reside today. The other pueblos have similar migration narratives, with common themes of movement, rest, and renewal.[6] After emerging from the "Sandy Place Lake," in the mountains north of their current homeland, the Tewa people were directed to take twelve "steps" in each direction, live in each place until it is time to move on, and finally settle for good along the Rio Grande in New Mexico, writes Alfonso Ortiz, a renowned anthropologist from Ohkay Owingeh (San Juan Pueblo).[7]

A footprint was placed in the Durango area in Basketmaker times, then another beginning right around the turn of the eighth century, during the early part of the Pueblo I period. Humanity trickled in at first, a few families making their way to Ridges Basin or, about a mile away, Blue Mesa. Word that this was a desirable place must have gotten out, because right around 750 AD, the migratory trickle turned into a human flash flood, and by the turn of the ninth century 200 people lived in Ridges Basin and another 250 at Blue Mesa. Considered on their own, each complex would have been the largest community of its time in the Four Corners region; taken together they blew every other Pueblo I settlement away.[8]

THE SMELL OF CIGARETTE SMOKE, OF THE PAGES OF OLD BOOKS, OF SAGE. They mingle together in my memories of my father, of his tiny home in Cortez, Colorado, of the beaten-down old cars he drove. He was a writer, a journalist, an intellectual jack of all trades. But for the last couple decades of his life—he died in 1998—his focus was on archaeology, on the Pueblo culture, past and present.

My father was particularly interested in something called AWUF, or architecture with unknown function, such as big earthen berms that arced around prehistoric structures or alignments of huge boulders with no apparent utility. The most famous AWUF of the Southwest are the Chacoan "roads," which are not roads nor are they exclusively connected to the pueblos at Chaco Culture National Historical Park in northern New Mexico. The Great North Road stretches at least thirty-five miles directly north from the rim of Chaco Canyon out across the plateau toward the San Juan River. This was no ordinary foot path, beaten into the earth by repeated use. It was deliberately constructed to a degree that segments are still clearly visible more than one thousand years later. Rather than ebbing and flowing with the contours of the land, or veering around canyons and buttes, as a path would, it never deviates from a nearly straight, northward course. No one knows its purpose.

When I was in my late teens and early twenties I'd accompany my father on his journeys. We'd get up early, drink some instant coffee, and drive west from Cortez on some washboarded road that rattled dashboard screws free and caused dust to rise like smoke from the car's floorboards. We ambled through sage, piñon, and juniper to the site, typically a structure from the Pueblo III period, which usually revealed itself as no more than a pile of hewn stones covered with lichen. In the heat of summer, cicadas screeched in the trees. In the winter, the silence was overlain by the distant hum of infrastructure sucking carbon dioxide from the McElmo Dome. As jays and magpies eyed us curiously we'd walk in circles or a rough grid-like pattern until we found the AWUF. It's subtle but, to the practiced eye, unmistakable.

For most of my life I've been surrounded by archaeology and archaeologists—my brother's one, my stepfather was an archaeologist working around the West for the federal government for decades, and my mom wanted to study archaeology in college but was shot down because she was a woman. As a young man, though, the field left me cold (an ailment of which I've since been cured). I couldn't see how excavating the tangible remains of material culture could ever get at the juiciness of what life was really like—what people felt, thought, how they interacted, and what philosophical or religious forces motivated them. Nor could it answer the question that always gnawed at me: Why here? Why did they choose this place, despite the hardships, to build a civilization? Sure, there were concrete, practical reasons: Ridges Basin is a gentle valley with a southward-slanting slope on one side, a stream, and even a marsh, where tasty waterfowl often alighted. But bigger factors must have been in play. Just consider Chaco's elaborate pueblos, which rose up in a landscape so austere that the early builders had to drag unwieldy ponderosa pine trees from the Zuni Mountains and Chuska Mountains, each fifty miles distant, for architectural uses, and may have even imported corn. It was a pragmatist's nightmare on par with modern-day Las Vegas.

"Here, the human landscape is meaningless outside the natural context—human constructions are not considered out of their relationship to the hills, valleys, and mountains," Rina Swentzell, a Santa Clara Pueblo scholar and an architect, wrote with my father and two archaeologists, Mark Varien and Susan Kenzle, in a 1997 paper. "Puebloan constructions are significant parts of a highly symbolic world. Even today, that defined 'world' is bounded by the far mountains and includes the hills, valleys, lakes, and springs." That suggests that places like Chaco, and Ridges Basin, became communities or political centers not only due to tangible factors, but also because of where they fit into the symbolic world. Perhaps the "roads" and other AWUF were bridges of sorts, linking the built architecture with the symbolic world, a sort of architectural map of the Pueblo cosmos.

The Great North Road, for instance, points toward 14,252-foot Mt. Wilson, the highest peak in this part of the San Juan Mountains. If one were to follow the road's trajectory—or what archaeologist Stephen Lekson calls the Chaco Meridian—toward Mt. Wilson, she would first pass through the Aztec Great House on the banks of the Animas River and then, right where the meridian transects the Hogback Monocline, Ridges Basin.[9] The monocline is not only dramatic looking, but its coal outcrop has been known to ooze methane, spontaneously combust, and even "erupt," particularly where waterways slice through the monocline. Surely the ancients witnessed these phenomena. We can only guess as to whether it influenced their decision to settle nearby, or the tragedy that followed.

It's especially ironic, then, that the remains of those same corn fields at Ridges Basin are now inundated by a reservoir, Lake Nighthorse, the end product of an anything-but-humble, decades-old dream to plumb the watershed, to lift up a portion of the Animas River and send it over the ridge to the La Plata River, where arable land is plentiful but water scarce. The plan for the Animas-La Plata Project, which initially included several reservoirs, a coal power plant on the Southern Ute reservation, and hundreds of miles of canals, pipes, and tunnels, was diminished over the years, finally ending up being no more than one pumping plant lifting Animas River water hundreds of feet uphill into Ridges Basin, where it currently sits, stagnant, in order to fulfill Southern Ute and Ute Mountain Ute water rights. Someday the water will be piped to distant fields, or to another power plant, or even to a golf course in the desert.

In advance of the reservoir's creation, archaeologists were sent in to catalog what forever would be entombed by Lake Nighthorse. The most intriguing, and disturbing, finds were made at a village the archaeologists called Sacred Ridge. Atop this knoll sat a little hamlet made up of several structures. Another dozen pit structures, with associated surface dwellings, were situated on the knoll's slopes, oriented toward the top of the knoll like people sitting around a fire. The pit structures tended to be larger than those found elsewhere in the region during this time, and some were surrounded by "stockades" or fences of a sort—possibly an early form of AWUF. The entire knoll-top hamlet was similarly fenced in, and its pit structures seem to have been used not just for living in, but also for community ceremonies. Perhaps most notable was the tower, made of wood and adobe in the jacal style, on top of the knoll. Though masonry towers would become commonplace at pueblos hundreds of years later, this appears to be the only one from this particular time period.[11] Its function is also unknown.

Archaeologists who excavated the sites in Ridges Basin theorize that the architecture and prominent location suggest that Sacred Ridge was home to the upper class, the community's elite.

In the early 800s the clouds were offering less rain than they had a few decades earlier, and the dense population was beginning to put pressure on local resources. It was nowhere near a crisis, yet something must have gone awry. The community, the landscape, or both were somehow out of balance.

And over a short period of time, maybe even in just one day, someone came in and overpowered nearly three dozen of Sacred Ridge's residents—men, women, children, even domestic dogs. Some of the captives were hobbled, their feet, ankles, or toes broken to keep them from running and to scare others from doing the same. Then the perpetrators tortured, scalped, and finally killed the victims, butchered the corpses, tossed the thousands of pieces into the Sacred Ridge pit structures, and then lit the structures on fire.

The dehumanizing stereotype of the Pueblo people as "peaceful farmers" was long ago debunked. Archaeological evidence and oral history reveal that violence, whether it was one-on-one murders, mass killings, or warfare between different tribes or groups, was not unheard of in prehistoric or historic times. Like every other society throughout history, these ones had their moments of darkness. Yet evidence suggests Sacred Ridge was among the most brutal, particularly for that time period. Archaeologists have a handful of hypotheses. It appears as if neighbors massacred neighbors. Maybe it was ethnic cleansing, a populist revolt, or a reaction to suspected witchcraft.

Soon thereafter, everyone in the Durango area up and left. By 820, the place was devoid of humanity. "What is intriguing about the abandonment of the Durango area is the suddenness and totality of the exodus," writes archaeologist James M. Potter. "Even with a climatic downturn and depleted local environment, the Durango area could have continued to support a smaller population."[12]

Over the following centuries, the Chaco region bloomed and the population ballooned. When that society waned, new ones grew up along the Animas River near present-day Aztec, New Mexico, in the Mesa Verde region, and in southeastern Utah. Yet no Pueblo people ever came back to the Durango area to live, despite the reliable water sources, fertile soils, and abundance of low, farmable mesas. The trauma from the Sacred Ridge massacre not only must have rippled throughout the Animas River valley, but also reached down through the generations, leaving a dark pall over this place, its spot on the symbolic map forever tainted.

THE PUEBLO PEOPLE TENDED TO GENTLY PULL UP THE ROOTS AND MOVE in response to broad climatic shifts. The Utes, who probably arrived in the Four Corners country from the West at the tail-end of the Puebloan era, moved with the seasons. They were nimble, light on the land, mindful of subtle shifts in flora and fauna. If the Pueblo people's calendar was marked by a shaft of sunlight touching the center of a spiral carved in stone, the Utes' was imprinted by the first bear emerging from hibernation or bucks shedding their antlers or the skunk cabbage's hue transforming from green to rust.

After the Animas River swelled up with snowmelt, the

Weenuchiu band followed well-worn trails up the river and into the high country, following the deer, collecting osha, feasting on tart wild raspberries and tiny, sweet alpine strawberries. When the aspen leaves turned yellow and they'd awake to lace-like frost clinging to the grass, they'd pack up and head back down to the lowlands, gather into larger groups, and stay in one place for the winter. They followed the annual cycle in the San Juan Mountains and the surrounding lowlands for three centuries before the Spanish arrived in 1598. Even then, the Ute people were mostly left alone; when in the early 1600s an escaping band of Ute captives managed to get away with some Spanish horses, they became even more formidable warriors and hunters.

When Rivera arrived at what he called the Animas River, he encountered a Ute *rancheria,* or encampment. He plied the people there with tobacco, corn, and pinole, in hopes of finding a man named Cuero de Lobo, who purportedly knew the source of the silver. Instead, Rivera was sent on a goose chase of sorts; while the Utes were willing to help Rivera find his way, they seem to have suspected his motives, and purposefully sent him astray more than once. When he finally found Cuero de Lobo, Rivera was led to a "mountain of metal" in the range west of Durango. Rivera referred to this branch of the San Juans as *Sierra de la Plata,* because he thought it was where the silver had come from. Again, he was disappointed; the samples taken from the mountain didn't have much in the way of precious metals. While Spanish and then Mexican travelers would continue to come into the Animas River country, they only passed through, oblivious of the mineral bounty hidden away in the nearby mountains and, most likely, their ceremonial significance, as well.

"In the north, First Man placed the Dark Mountain (Dibé Ntsaa)," writes Diné, or Navajo, historian Clyde Benally. "He planted it with a Rainbow and covered it with Darkness, Dark Mist, Female Rain, and Blue Water. He sent Darkness Boy and Girl there, to what is known now as Hesperus Peak in the La Plata Mountains of Colorado." And so, the northern boundary of Diné cosmology, one of its most sacred places, was established. Diné oral history refers to the builders at Chaco, which would have meant the Diné were in the Four Corners country as early as the 900s. Archaeologists generally believe, however, that the Diné came much later—in the 1400s or 1500s—from the North, crossing through the San Juan Mountains into the lowlands along what would become their sacred river of the North, *Bits'íís Doo ninít'i'í*, or the San Juan River, and beyond. They lived, farmed, and hunted in the lower Animas River watershed, and *Totah*, where the Animas and La Plata rivers join the San Juan, is a significant region. To this day they continue to make pilgrimages to their sacred mountain of the North.

When Rivera stood on the steep banks of the river, he was undoubtedly oblivious to the thousands of years of indigenous history that had already unfolded there. He didn't know the Diné name for the Animas River, *Kinteeldéé' 'Nlíní*, or "Which Flows from the Wide Ruin." And he must not have cared about the Ute name, or any of the many names before. Maybe on some intuitive level, though, he felt that presence in the water, the trees, the mountains, and that is why he said the river was full of souls.

Awful in Their Sublimity

It is ever thus; when you feel you are treading a path never trod by a living thing before, and your imagination begins to build for itself a romantic picture, if some such vile, worldly thing as a paper collar or a whisky-bottle does not intrude itself on the sight, some beastly quadruped needs must break the precious solitude and scatter your airy castle to the winds.

—Franklin Rhoda, upon encountering a grizzly bear on Mount Oso in 1874

FRANKLIN RHODA, WEARING A WIDE-BRIMMED HAT AND A PONCHO-LIKE TOPCOAT, clutched his leather-bound sketchbook to his side. His older half-brother, A. D. Wilson, had a surveyor's tripod slung over his shoulder as the two men made their way up the craggy, rocky slope of fourteen-thousand-foot-high Sunshine Peak in the "great mass" of mountains known as the San Juans. It was August 1874, and a violent thunderstorm loomed on the horizon. Wilson was the topographer and director of the San Juan Division of the U.S. Geological and Geographical Survey, or the Hayden Survey. Rhoda, just twenty years old at the time, was his assistant. Along with geologist Frederic M. Endlich, a chef, and a support crew, they had been tasked with taking stock of some of the last territory to be invaded by Euro-Americans in the United States.

After Rivera had skirted the foothills of the San Juans a century earlier, Escalante and Dominguez came through, giving a much more complete accounting than their Spanish predecessor of what lay there. Other Spaniards followed, usually on their way westward, but none stuck around; the same was true after Mexico had wrested independence from Spain. Any eighteenth-century conquistador dreams of expanding the empire northward were dashed upon Ute resistance and the impenetrability of the mountains—the San Juan country remained firmly in Ute hands.

In 1859, John N. Macomb led the first official American expedition into the San Juan country, generally following the Old Spanish Trail, but throwing in a few side trips along the way. Macomb was somewhat baffled, sometimes disgusted, by the land he passed through. His geologist, J. S. Newberry, was more sagacious. He predicted that the hot springs at Pagosa, east of Durango, would someday become a resort, and he described the San Juan Mountains as a "thousand interlocking spurs and narrow valleys, [which] form a labyrinth whose extent and intricacy will at present defy all attempts at detailed topographical analysis. Among these are precipices, ornamented with imitations of columns, arches, and pilasters, which form some of the grandest specimens of nature's Gothic architecture I have ever beheld. When viewed from some nearer point they must be even awful in their sublimity."

Macomb and company never did view the daunting mountains from up close. The following year, Capt. Charles Baker made his way into the San Juans and the Animas River watershed from the river's headwaters. His promises of oodles of gold and silver lured hundreds of would-be prospectors to the high country. They based themselves in a little cluster of cabins they called Animas City, located next to today's Baker's Bridge, at the north end of the Animas Valley, and traveled and prospected upstream to Baker's Park, the valley in which Silverton sits today. The rush lasted for maybe a year before folks got discouraged, heeded the warnings from local Utes and Diné to get out, or went back home to fight in the Civil War. By late 1862, Animas City was empty. Boom. Bust.

The next wave arrived in Baker's Park in 1870 to mine in nearby Arrastra Gulch. This time, the Utes let the prospectors be, despite the fact that the white men were trespassing on their land. In 1873, the Brunot Agreement was signed, taking the mineral-rich San Juans and the surrounding foothills and valleys from the Utes. The various bands reserved the rights to hunt in and roam through the mountains "so long as the game lasts and the Indians are at peace with the white people."

By the time Rhoda and friends arrived for their peak-bagging extravaganza, hundreds of miners had oozed into the mountains and were staking claims and digging prospect holes by hand. Silverton was founded that same year, and consisted of no more than a dozen homes spread out near the confluence of Cement Creek and the Animas River. Rhoda wasn't impressed, but had he looked a bit more closely he would have seen that this was no mere fly-by-night mining camp. Rather, it was already gaining some permanence, even in its infancy. The first white woman to settle in this part of the San Juan Mountains, Amanda Cotton, had come that year from Salina, Kansas, with her husband, John. They set up a store and restaurant in Howardsville, just upstream, before moving to Silverton and building one of the first structures there, which they would run as a lively boardinghouse for years and which still stands. They were also social dynamos, organizing parties and often supplying the music, with John on the fiddle and Amanda on the melodeon. Downstream from the ruins of Baker's cabins, in the broad, fertile Animas Valley, farmers had just started tilling the land, growing potatoes, melons, and corn.

Even these early white settlers left a deeper footprint on the land than their Native American predecessors had. Still, their impact was limited to a few valleys. Most of the high country, its log-choked valleys, tundra-covered slopes, cascading streams, and wildflower-spackled meadows, remained, if not pristine, then at least wild, primal, alive.

Rhoda, a born adventurer with a way with words, reveled in it. On climbing Uncompahgre Peak, the highest, but certainly not the most difficult, in the San Juans, he wrote: "We were terribly taken aback, when, at an elevation of over 13,000 feet, a she grizzly, with her two cubs, came rushing past us from the top of the peak. We found that the bears had been all over the summit of the peak, though how they got up over one or two short but steep passages in the ascent, puzzled us not a little."

When again they ran into a grizzly above thirteen thousand feet, Rhoda became frustrated with the bruins' ubiquity. "To show our utter disgust for all animate things that could not live below this altitude, we yelled and threw stones after the bear till he finally was lost to sight far down the mountainsides. After this experience, we named the peak Mount Oso . . ."

Finally, on the ascent of Mt. Sneffels, probably the most challenging climb, Rhoda surrendered to the bears: "Everything seemed to conspire to make a beautiful day, and we lacked only time to let our imaginations run on and make a sublimely-romantic picture of sunrise at a high elevation. The claw marks on the rocks, on either side of the summit of the pass, showed that the grizzly had been before us. We gave up all hope of ever beating the bear climbing mountains."

They encountered black bears, more grizzly, huge stampeding flocks of mountain sheep, and, near Lizard Head, "a few cranes, which, with their long legs and unearthly noises, only served to add to the funereal aspect of the scenery."

By Rhoda's reckoning, the feral bounty of the San Juans, unspoiled and indigenous, was invulnerable to the invaders. The swarms of settlers that looked like insects far below as he climbed peak after peak were mere irritants to this grand place, and the nascent towns would never amount to much. It was too hard to get to the isolated valleys, the climate too severe, there was no nearby coal for fuel, and nothing would grow here. Little did he know to what lengths greed and Manifest Destiny, fueled by the General Mining Act of 1872 that literally gave federal land away on a first-come, first-serve basis, would drive men. "No natural obstacles," wrote Frederick Ransome, another USGS surveyor, in 1901, "have ever long withstood the restlessness and indomitable perseverance of the seekers after precious metals."

The whole region in the mid-1870s teetered on the precipice between the old world and the new, between wildness and human restlessness. Hordes of people would pour into the mountains from Kansas, Missouri, Sweden, Italy, China. Within a couple of decades, every mountainside near every mining camp—Gladstone, Howardsville, Silverton, Eureka—would be shorn of all of its trees. Massive mills and boarding-houses would perch where sheep once roamed, and hundreds of miles of tram lines would be strung across hillsides. Tunnels would be blasted and drilled into mountains until their innards resembled Swiss cheese, the streams would run grey, yellow, or orange on a daily basis. The Utes would be pushed farther and farther out of their hallowed and sustaining mountains, crammed onto a tiny sliver of land where the federal government would try to force them to become farmers. The San Juan hunting rights that were guaranteed to the Utes in the Brunot Agreement were quickly usurped, and would not be reinstated for another 130 years. All those grizzlies, so plentiful in Rhoda's time as to be almost pesky, would be murdered systematically, their pelts paraded down Silverton's Greene Street, until they were all gone.[13]

Several years after his San Juan adventure, Rhoda would go to the Bay Area and become a radical preacher. One can't help but wonder if his journey toward God didn't begin on the rocky slope just below the summit of Sunshine Peak, where he had his most intimate and frightening encounter with nature's grandeur. The dense, dark, swirling clouds sped towards them like freighters on a choppy sea as Rhoda and Wilson set up their instruments. They rushed their work, taking measurements and sketching the skyline, not because of any danger in the clouds, but because they'd affect visibility.

"We had scarcely got started to work when we both began to feel a peculiar tickling sensation along the roots of our hair, just at the edge of our hats, caused by the electricity in the air," wrote Rhoda, in a remarkably detached way. "By holding up our hands above our heads a ticking sound was produced, which was still louder if we held a hammer or other instrument in our hand . . . and presently was accompanied by a peculiar sound almost exactly like that produced by the frying of bacon. This latter phenomenon, when continued for any length of time, becomes highly monotonous and disagreeable."

Surely a sane person today would at that point launch himself down the slope, scrambling to lower and perhaps safer ground. Rhoda and Wilson, however, continued their work, marveling at the phenomenon that enveloped them.

The instrument on the tripod began to click like a telegraph-machine when it is made to work rapidly; at the same time we noticed that the pencils in our fingers made a similar but finer sound whenever we let them lie back so as to touch the flesh of the hand between the thumb and forefinger. The effect on our hair became more and more marked, till, ten or fifteen minutes after its appearance, there was sudden and instantaneous relief, as if all the electricity had been suddenly drawn from us. After the lapse of a few seconds the cause became apparent, as a peal of thunder reached our ears. The lightning had struck a neighboring peak, and the electricity in the air had been discharged.

The clouds soon began to rise up and approach us. As they did so, the electricity became stronger and stronger, till another stroke of lightning afforded instantaneous relief; but now the relief was only for an instant, and the tension increased faster and faster till the next stroke. By this time, the work was getting exciting.

All around the two young men, the stones sang, each producing its own peculiar note. Finally they decided it was time to go. Wilson folded up his tripod and got a nasty static shock when he hefted it to his shoulder. When the brass lens protector fell clanking to the stones, he didn't bother to pick it up. Maybe it's still there, sitting amongst lichen-covered stones, a tiny reminder of a world that was.

Dandelion Brew

A FEW YEARS AFTER RHODA PASSED THROUGH, my maternal great-great-great-grandmother, Julia Mead, her daughter Emily, and son-in-law Harry Hathaway, joined the fledgling Animas Valley community. They came from Bourbon County, Kansas, leaving shortly after the death of Julia's husband, Joseph, making the arduous trek by wagon from Kansas to the San Luis Valley, east of the San Juan Mountains, and over Cumbres Pass to Chama, New Mexico. From there they followed roughly the same well-trodden path that Rivera had taken a century earlier.[14]

Our family creation story does not explain why a sixty-seven-year-old widow would venture into a land so fraught with uncertainty and danger. But by most accounts she was strong-willed, independent, and adventurous. Nor do we know why she and her companions chose to stop here in the Animas Valley. I suspect they had heard news of the San Juan rush and the flood of opportunity spilling out of the mountains. Or maybe they knew that any westward journey would soon get more rugged as they passed into Utah's canyon country and then into Latter-day Saints territory, where just two decades before more than one hundred gentile travelers had been massacred by a group of Mormons.

I like to think that they came down the little gulch south of the not-yet-born Durango in the early evening, just after the sun had settled behind Carbon Mountain. That's when the water gets dark and smooth and wrinkles up against the rocks as if it is made of molten glass. Nighthawks boom through the lavender sky hunting insects. Mayflies bounce across the river's surface, and metallic-looking trout shoot skyward in pursuit, momentarily blemishing the big, moving mirror. Maybe in the uncanny calm of that moment between light and dark, Julia, a spiritualist who spoke with the dead, heard the river's souls speaking to her, beckoning her to remain.

They headed upstream on the east side of the river, across the low, sagebrush-covered mesas on which Durango's residential neighborhoods would sprout several years later, past a new Animas City that was taking root on the glacial moraine at the Animas Valley's south edge, and onward several miles more to a place where towering red cliffs watched over ponderosas and scrub oak. They carved a cave out of the sandy river bank, and lived there until they upgraded to a small cabin nearby, which Julia described as a "well insulated chicken house." Henry made a claim on a 160-acre homestead on the east side of the Animas River, adjacent to the confluence with Hermosa Creek.

Some called Julia a witch. And it's true that, being of a spiritualist bent, she attended séances. More importantly, she was a healer. Still a largely unsettled land, the valley lacked the professional medical resources to serve the growing population. Julia Mead filled in the gaps, serving as doctor, nurse, and, most notably, midwife. She supervised the births of countless babies in Hermosa and its surroundings and she tended to the sick with elixirs made from roots and flowers gathered from the fields and hillsides. A half century after her death, old-timers still spoke of the healing powers of Julia's pitch plaster and her Oregon grape root and dandelion brews. Some even blamed her for spreading noxious dandelions throughout the valley. I hope it's true.

After a year or two, Julia's son, Ervin Washington Mead, his wife Emily, and their son Ervin (Lyman), followed mother, sibling, and in-laws west. The Hathaways eventually went back to Iowa, and apparently sold the homestead, but Julia and the others stayed. With the money she had earned from her medical practice, Julia bought forty acres of land south of Hermosa Creek, a tributary of the Animas that runs in from the northwest side of the valley, and started a small farm there.

As she grew older, Julia liked to sit in the shade of a towering ponderosa pine on a corner of the farm on warm summer afternoons. She asked her son Ervin to bury her under the tree, so that her body could mingle with the old giant's roots, but when she died in 1894 he went against her wishes, and she was interred in the staid and manicured cemetery above Durango, instead. Legend has it that some years after Julia died, Ervin heard a voice telling him to dig under the ponderosa. When he did so, he found a box full of money left by his mother.

Olaf and the Gold King

IT'S APRIL 1891 AND OLAF ARVID NELSON IS DYING. He lies in his bed in the little house in Howardsville, a few miles upriver from Silverton. When he tries to stand he's gently pushed back to the pillow by Louisa, his wife. His lungs are filling up with fluid, his body drowning itself. Whenever he moves, or breathes too deeply, it feels and sounds as if nutshells are rattling around in his lungs.

"The Mighty Swede" does not complain. Even before he was sick he didn't talk much. Words don't have much to them. They flitter away forgotten as soon as they leave your lips. Work is everything. And damn did he ever work. Six days a week drilling, blasting, and hauling ore out of the Philadelphia Mine, which he leased. And nights and Sundays up at his own claim on Bonita Peak.

NELSON FIRST EMERGED INTO THE HISTORICAL RECORD, and was nearly wiped right off of it, as a twenty-two-year-old wannabe miner in search of opportunity.[15] During the winter of 1878–79, he and fellow Swede Jonathan Peterson headed up Cement Creek on the brand new wagon road to the nascent camp of Gladstone. From there they continued up the canyon to Brown Mountain, where they set up a prospecting camp in a rickety cabin dug into the south-facing slope. During a normal winter, the mountainside would be covered with several feet of snow, but it had been unusually warm and dry, making life easier for the miners. One February evening, after a long day of digging, the miners retired to their hut, kicked off their soggy boots, and settled in for the night. Meanwhile, the mountain slope was doing some settling of its own as melting snow oozed into the earth, softening and lubricating things. Soon, a chunk of the slope broke free, and a torrent of rocks, dirt, and ice rained down on the cabin, crushing it.

Both men survived the calamity, though both were pinned under debris, with no one nearby to come to their rescue. Peterson was able to free himself, then went to work on Nelson, who was more thoroughly stuck. He had little more to work with than his hands, a straight razor, and his stubbornness. Eleven hours later, Nelson, too, was free and virtually unscathed. The two walked down Cement Creek, barefoot, to Gladstone and caught a ride back to Silverton.

The February warmth that had loosened the earth and nearly taken Nelson's life continued into the spring. Today that sort of climatic anomaly would be considered a threatening drought; the newspapers at the time hailed the mild weather as yet another reason to put down roots in the San Juan Mountains. By then, the main route in and out of Silverton via Stony Pass to the east was being replaced by the Animas Toll Road that followed the Animas River to the south, opening up the Silverton market to Animas Valley farmers and ranchers. The farmers, Julia Mead among them, put seeds in the ground in mid-March that year, two months ahead of time. By May, most of the snow had melted off of even the highest mountain passes, and the relentless high-altitude sun had turned the forests to tinder.

During the first days of June 1879, somewhere near present-day Purgatory ski resort, a spark or flame or hot ember leftover from a traveler's campfire ignited some ponderosa pine needles on the forest floor. The flames jumped to the gambel oak, then to the spruce trees, their canopies exploding into fire. The conflagration marched steadily up the Lime Creek drainage toward Silverton, charring everything in its path.

L. W. Pattison was working just south of Silverton at the Molas Mine as the flames approached, and wrote this account:

One of the most terrific fires that has ever come under my observation occurred yesterday down the Animas Trail. We had noticed the heavy columns of smoke from the South and southwest for some days but anticipated no danger until after dinner yesterday, when the air became so heavy with smoke and the flames appeared to be moving so rapidly, that we began to pay attention to the matter.

Pattison and his fellow miners buried their explosives and shored up the cabin against the flames. A big, cinnamon-colored bear barreled through the camp, followed by several deer, oblivious to the humans there. Too late to outrun the flames, the men bolted to the mine tunnel. From that place of relative safety they watched in dismay as one of their burros wandered directly into the inferno.

The Lime Creek Burn, as this "scene of unusual and weird magnificence" would become known, charred twenty-six thousand acres of high country before subsiding. It would stand as the largest fire to burn in Colorado until the mega-fires of the early 2000s blackened hundreds of thousands of acres of the state's forests. The Burn forever altered the landscape south of Silverton. Before the blaze, the area around Molas Lake and Molas Pass was densely forested with conifers; today, it's mostly wide open meadows studded by blackened stumps, a smattering of aspen trees, and incongruously green Scotch pines, a non-native species that was planted by the U.S. Forest Service beginning thirty years after the fire.

The flames stopped just short of Silverton, due, perhaps, to the fact that all the surrounding slopes had been clear-cut. But ash and smoke rained down on the town for days. For a few settlers, Nature's terror had crept a little too close to home, and they pulled up stakes and moved elsewhere. Most, however, dug in their heels and stubbornly vowed to stay.

The blaze was likely caused by the unattended campfire of one of the many mountain-roaming cowboys or hunters who were out and about at the time. But a few months later, a more useful scapegoat would emerge. In September members of the White River band of Utes in northwestern Colorado rose up and killed Indian agent Nathan Meeker and his staff and kidnapped his family, an event that came to be known as the Meeker Massacre. Meeker was a racist, and one who endeavored to convert the White River band from nomadic "savages" to sedentary Christian farmers. He kept pushing the Utes, who had already been squeezed out of much of their homeland, until finally they stood up to him. Meeker called in the cavalry, leaving the Utes little choice but to fight. The isolated incident inflamed a statewide Ute-phobic rage.

"Indians are off their reservation, seeking to destroy your settlements with fire," warned Colorado Governor Frederick Pitkin, who had enriched himself with San Juan Mountain mine investments. "The Utes must go!" Someone should have reminded Pitkin that the Brunot Agreement explicitly gave the Utes free rein to roam, hunt, and forage "off the reservation" in the San Juan Mountains; to take that freedom away was equivalent to robbing them of their identity. Silvertonians took up arms and prepared for a fight. My ancestors, in the Animas Valley, joined with others at a hastily constructed sod fort on the north end of the valley. Extremists ached for a provocation, so they could settle the "Ute Question" once and for all. "Here in Silverton we have received 40 stand of arms and have perfected a military organization," noted the *Miner* newspaper, describing a sort of nineteenth century version of today's right-wing "militias." "We say bring on your Utes—the Johns and Joes can soon exterminate them."

The attack never came, however, leaving the settlers and their representatives in Denver and Washington to resort to more subtle forms of extermination—like labeling the Native Americans as terrorists. The Lime Creek Burn was retroactively attributed to the Utes. A La Plata County resolution forwarded in 1880—a year after the blaze had gone out—claimed that the Utes set the fire to roust game or "to maliciously injure the settlers and miners . . . destroying millions of dollars worth of timber and a vast amount of private property."

For the next twenty years, every skirmish that involved one of the "Rabid Reds" was framed by newspaper accounts and politicians as a precursor to the next Indian War. Every Ute was deemed a potential terrorist, aching to launch another Meeker Massacre, regardless of the fact that the southern bands, under the leadership of diplomatic peacekeeper Chief Ouray, put up little resistance to the encroachment on their homeland. The persecution was part plain-old racism, and fear of the "other." Mostly, though, it was a calculated campaign designed to give the white newcomers more land and resources. By 1880, the game populations were already dwindling, thanks to over-hunting by the newcomers, and the Utes competed ably for that scarce resource. In the lowlands, the farmers and ranchers were outgrowing the land that had been stolen on their behalf in earlier treaties, and they wanted more. Meanwhile, the people who had established businesses in Durango had saturated the market. They needed more customers, and a new land rush for Ute reservation lands was just the ticket.

Portraying the Utes as a threat provided a justification for the feds to push them further and further into the margins in the hope that they just might go away. Meanwhile, whites who were truly violent and threatening were allowed, quite literally, to get away with murder, so long as some of their violence was directed toward the Utes.

A LATE SUMMER CHILL SETTLED OVER THE YOUNG TOWN OF SILVERTON as the sun fell behind Anvil Mountain on the evening of August 24, 1881. The light faded, and the saloons—the Tivoli, the Senate, the Blue Front, the Golden Star, the Rose-bud, the Star of the West—filled up with miners, merchants, and travelers. It was a rowdy night. Every night was a rowdy night in Silverton.

The crews building grade and laying tracks for the Denver & Rio Grande Railroad had yet to make it into Baker's Park, but by now their arrival was imminent, and in anticipation the little smattering of houses Rhoda had witnessed had blossomed into a bona fide town with stately residences and a lively commer-cial district, replete with two bakeries, a furniture-making and undertaker business, and two shoemakers. A man could get his dingy clothes cleaned at the Quong Wah or Sing Lee laundry, stop in at the Tennyson Bath House, and get shorn next door at the Merrifield Barber Shop. The *San Juan Herald* had emerged that summer to compete with the *Miner*, making Silverton a two-rag town. Law offices nearly outnumbered saloons. There was just one church.

Olaf Nelson had not been scared away by his brush with death, nor by Silverton's close call with wildfire. He was here to stay, along with hundreds of others like him, folks from Italy, Austria, Wales, Poland, and China, looking to reinvent themselves on the rugged but quickly civilizing frontier. A few months earlier, Nelson's wife Louisa had given birth to their first child, Anna. Nelson worked hard but played little, his Lutheran upbringing keeping him above the bawdy fray.

That night, in a sleeping room in the back of the Senate Saloon on 13th and Greene (in the now-vacant lot north of the Teller House), Town Marshal David Clayton Ogsbury was trying to do the same. He was dead-tired, but unable to sleep.[16]

Ogsbury, born in New York, had come to the San Juans in the early 1870s. He had been a saloon owner, prospector, bridge designer, and store clerk. But his real calling was law enforcement, and as Silverton's marshal he was one of the area's most respected lawmen. On nights like this, however, he would just as soon be prospecting.

Young Silverton was boisterous, but some semblance of law and order tended to keep the stew from boiling over into bloodshed. The same could not be said for Silverton's junior, downstream neighbors, Durango and Farmington. Ogsbury's colleagues in the lower Animas River country had been dealing with cattle rustling, highway robbery, and theft, much of it perpetuated by two warring gangs, the Farmington-based Coe-Hambletts and the Stockton-Eskridge gang, led by Ike and

Port Stockton, cattlemen who had come up from Texas, and Harg Eskridge, who owned a Durango saloon.

In late 1880 the simmering tension between the two gangs boiled over into outright war when a Coe ally was killed and, in retaliation, the Coe-Hamblett boys shot and killed Port Stockton. The Stockton-Eskridge faction retreated to Durango, the Coe-Hambletts pursued them, and in April of 1881 the two gangs clashed in an intense firefight on the edge of town. A stray bullet made its way into the office of the *Durango Record*, the young town's first newspaper, where it just missed hitting publisher, editor, reporter, and writer Caroline Westcott Romney. Romney, a forty-year-old seasoned journalist, came to Durango from Chicago via Leadville the previous year, and printed the first issue of the *Record* on a "job press" in a canvas tent on a frigid, snowy December 29, 1880. Romney wasn't one to be cowed by gangs of rustlers or anyone else: During her three-year tenure in Durango she was a champion for women's rights, rallied against prostitution, and held a special disdain for opium dens and their patrons. And as soon as the dust from the firefight had settled, she stood up to the Stockton-Eskridge gang and demanded they be run out of town.[17] And they were, sort of. Town leaders asked the bunch to leave, and even paid them $700 as an incentive, which was enough to get them to skedaddle, for a while.

But a couple months later, the Stockton-Eskridge boys were instrumental in chasing down and killing "bands of renegade Indians" who had allegedly killed three ranchers near Gateway, Colorado. Ute-phobia festered at a fever pitch among the white newcomers, and they not only forgave the gang of recidivists and murderers for their past deeds, but elevated them to the status of Indian-fighting heroes. Even Romney, who thought the scant amount of land left to the Mouache, Caputa, and Weenuchiu bands would be more productive in white hands, was swayed, becoming one of the gang's most vocal defenders. When the criminals moseyed back into town, lawmen like La Plata County Sheriff Luke Hunter turned a blind eye, allowing them to continue their lawless ways.

On that late-August afternoon, gang members Bert Wilkinson, Kid Thomas, and Harg Eskridge's brother Dyson went on a robbing rampage on the Animas Toll Road, and were rumored to be headed toward Silverton. Ogsbury waited anxiously, though there was little he could do once they arrived, since he had yet to receive a warrant from La Plata County.

Typically, Ogsbury had to grapple with slightly more benign crimes. Two days earlier, for example, he had tossed Bronco Lou—the barkeep at the Diamond Saloon—into jail for enticing a man into her bar then robbing him blind. Bronco Lou (aka Susan Warfield, Susan Raper, Susan Stone, Bronco Sue, Lou Lockhard, and Susan Dawson) was one of the more colorful characters of the time, and had she been a man would surely have gone down in history as one of the West's outlaw folk heroes along with Jesse James and Billy the Kid. Instead, she was maligned as a "prostitute and thief." Lou was no prostitute. She was a skilled larcenist, but also so much more. Bronco Lou could outshoot and outride just about anyone in the region and was "fierce as a fiend in her ferocity or as gentle as a lamb or as soft as an angel in her devotion to those she liked."[18] When she and a group of her cohorts got tangled up with a southern Colorado posse, Lou not only nursed the outlaws back to health while they were in jail, but then planned and carried out their escape. When they were recaptured, and about to be hanged, Lou again rescued the men. She allegedly killed two husbands prior to her arrival in Silverton, and singlehandedly saved a third husband's life from an Indian attack (he left her shortly thereafter). On that August night, Lou would be the least of Ogsbury's troubles.

At about eleven p.m., Ogsbury was roused from sleep by a knock.

"Clayt, wake up," said a familiar voice. Ogsbury opened his eyes and saw Charlie Hodges, a local businessman. He was accompanied by Luke Hunter, sheriff of La Plata County, who had finally arrived with the warrants. Ogsbury quickly got dressed, fighting the temptation to ask Hunter what in the hell had taken him so long. He suspected Hunter of going easy on the Stockton gang. As far as Ogsbury was concerned, they should have all been behind bars already.

Little did Ogsbury know that Hunter, after arriving in Silverton, had taken his time finding the marshal, and in the meantime had indirectly warned the outlaws that the local law was on to them. "We'll need help," said Ogsbury. "I'll send for Thorniley [San Juan County Sheriff George Thorniley], and we can round up a few others, just in case there is trouble."

"That won't be necessary," replied Hunter. "I know these men. They'll give in peacefully."

So the three of them, Ogsbury, Hodges, and Hunter, set off toward the Diamond Saloon, aka Lower Dance Hall, Silverton's rowdiest drinking establishment.

As they drew near, they saw the silhouette of a man in the street and stopped. Ogsbury instinctively reached down and lightly touched the handle of his pistol. He peered into the darkness in an attempt to identify the still, silent figure.

A flash of light, a crack in the night, and then a sickening thud as Ogsbury's body hit the dusty street.

The shooter was one Bert Wilkinson, a tall, skinny, freckle-faced nineteen-year-old from a prestigious family, who had taken up with a rough crew. He and his companions took advantage of the chaos that ensued. Wilkinson and Eskridge headed for the hills, while Kid Thomas, an African American, tried to hide out in town. It didn't work and Thomas, "The Copper Colored Kid," was captured and tossed in the small town jail. The next day, a mob of vigilantes broke him out and hanged him in the streets of Silverton.

Thomas's companions, meanwhile, managed to head up Mineral Creek, over into the San Miguel River drainage, and then into the Dolores, before crossing back to the east, ending up at the home of Ellen Louise Wilkinson, Bert's mother, just south of where Purgatory Ski Resort sits now. Ellen Louise sent her son and his companion several miles east, to a less-traveled place on Missionary Ridge. A couple of days later, she summoned gang leader Ike Stockton, and asked him to go help her son escape to Mexico. Stockton ambled into the fugitives' camp, sent Eskridge away, then marched Wilkinson right into the hands of the law, betraying his young protégé for the $2,500 reward on his head.

Wilkinson was tossed into the Silverton jail, and less than a week later vigilante justice reared its ugly head once again. A mob broke into the jail, ordered the guard to leave, and put a noose around Wilkinson's neck.

"Do you have any last words?" a voice asked from the crowd.

"Nothing, gentlemen. Adios," replied Wilkinson, and he kicked the chair out from beneath himself.

Such are the violent pangs felt by a frontier community, awash with wealth from the mines, in its adolescence. Contrary to how today's peddlers of the wild, wild west, with their fake gunfights, might portray the history of Silverton and Durango, the reality is, this sort of lawless, highway-robbing, gun-slinging, and frontier justice were a mere blip on the region's record.

The murder of Marshal Ogsbury and the lynchings that followed were not just the climax of this short period in history, but also the dying gasp. In Silverton, the Diamond Saloon was shut down and demolished and Bronco Lou run out of town. Ike Stockton was gunned down in the streets of Durango, not because he was an outlaw, but because he betrayed his young friend. Stockton's gang disintegrated and the Coe-Stockton feud evaporated. Communities moved to end the lawlessness, and even implemented gun control statutes that are far stricter than today's. "Firearms in the daily walks of life have no place in our modern civilization and should not be carried," noted a Durango mayor in 1903. The communities of the San Juan country, though still brand new, were maturing.

ELEVEN MONTHS AFTER THE SILVERTON SHOOTING, a far more cataclysmic sound than a gunshot would echo through Baker's Park: the whistle of the first steam locomotive. The railroad had finally arrived, marking a huge pivot in the region's history.

Prior to that fateful day in July 1882, mail and supplies were brought into Baker's Park by horse, mule, or wagon on rugged trails over high mountains. Throughout the 1870s, the most traveled route to the outside world was a seventy-mile journey to Del Norte, in the San Luis Valley. The trail crossed the Continental Divide at Cunningham Pass, elevation 12,090 feet (currently part of the Hardrock Hundred ultramarathon course). During the winter, which at these elevations can last six months or more, the horses and burros were traded for wooden skis, ranging from six to twelve feet in length, known as snowshoes.

Heroic and hardy mail carriers—mostly Nelson's fellow Scandinavians—plied the long boards, usually tag-teaming the route and braving avalanches, frostbite, hypothermia, and snow blindness to keep Silverton running through the winter. One mailman once carried sixty pounds of newsprint over the route in order to keep the local rag in print. Astoundingly, only one mail carrier perished. On November 27, 1876, John Greenell, née Greenhalgh, set out from Carr's Cabin on the other side of the divide on the return trip to Silverton. He never arrived. A group of searchers found his body a few days later, frozen to death near the top of the pass, his hand rigidly clutching his mailbag.

The train was challenged by snow, as well, but it opened up a thick artery connecting Durango, rich with coal, timber, cattle, and crops, with the mineral-rich veins around Silverton.[19] The miners got access to heavy equipment that would have been almost impossible to haul over the passes with mules, and they could then send their ore by the railcar-load back down to Durango and the new San Juan & New York smelter built along the Animas River's banks. Potential investors in the mines no longer had to brave sphincter-puckering wagon rides over steep passes to see future prospects.

The rails stretched from Denver down to Alamosa, in the San Luis Valley, then further south to Chama, New Mexico, where they picked up the old Ute and Spanish trail to Durango before following the Animas River to Silverton. The railroad's advent didn't just impact the mining camps. The pair of steel ribbons and the coal-eating, smoke-belching locomotives that rode on them rapidly transformed the entire region's land-scape, cultures, and economy. The locomotives sucked up water from rivers and streams, and new coal mines were opened to feed the chugging beasts. Glades of tall, straight, and wise old ponderosas near Chama, on the Tierra Amarilla Land Grant, were sheared down en masse now that there was an easy way to haul them to market. Once-isolated villages along the old Spanish trail, settled in the 1870s by members of the New Mexican Penitente Brotherhood looking to flee religious persecution from mainstream Catholics, were suddenly linked to the outside world.

Towns and sawmills and cattle-loading chutes popped up along the tracks; subsistence farms and ranches morphed into commercial-sized operations. And in the high country, the mostly entrepreneurial mining trade slowly transformed into an industrial-scale concern, funded by outside capital. In 1881, approximately six hundred tons of ore were pulled out of Silverton-area mines. A couple of years later, it had jumped to fourteen thousand tons and climbing. The population of Silverton and surrounding towns ballooned into the thousands.

By then, Olaf Nelson had another mouth to feed, a son named Oscar. Freelance prospecting wasn't paying off, so he got a real job up at the Sampson Mine, located on the upper slopes of Bonita Peak. It was one of the upstart mines in the area, first staked in the early 1880s. In 1883 its owner, Theodore Stahl, had a mill built in Gladstone along with a tram to link mine and mill, one of the first in the San Juans. Nelson's job was to run the tram, which carried ore down to the mill and served as a sketchy, primitive chairlift for miners, adding to the long list of ways to die while in the trade. Nelson and his family moved into the mine's boardinghouse, perched at twelve thousand feet above sea level near the mine portal, in 1885.

That is where Louisa, Olaf, Anna, and two-year-old Oscar found themselves on a January evening in 1886. A blizzard had raged outside since late the previous night and even during the light of day the flakes came down so thick that Olaf couldn't see beyond the second tram tower. As they sat in the dim light of lanterns they occasionally heard a deep and eerie *whoomph* as slabs of snow tumbled from the roof. But inside, with a stoked stove and the deep snow providing insulation, they were warm, at least. The baby slept, Anna read, and Louisa knitted. Olaf felt another *whoomph*, only deeper, louder. He heard a hissing, and noticed that a stream of smoke was blowing out of the stove door. Then the crashing, the world moving, the wall rushing towards them: Avalanche.

A baby was crying. Louisa called out: "Anna. Anna." Olaf Nelson moved silently and quickly through the darkness. Amid the wreckage he found the pipe from the stove, still hot, and used it as a shovel. He dug frantically through the snow toward the cries, tears rolling down his face.

Once again, Olaf Arvid Nelson had cheated death. Louisa, Anna, and Oscar made it out of the catastrophe with nothing worse than a few scratches, bruises, and a lot of fear. The time-line gets fuzzy here, but it seems that the family relocated down the slope to Gladstone, where Louisa operated a store while Nelson stayed on at the Sampson, now working underground.

Nelson was no geologist, but he had spent enough time poking around in these rocks to get a gut sense of how mineral-loaded veins operate, and what sorts of trajectories they tend to follow through a mountainside. Every day that he stepped into the Sampson Mine and hammered and drilled and blasted at the stope, he was also calculating. He deduced that he and his coworkers were mining in the wrong place; the vein would be richer, thicker, riper elsewhere. He kept his thoughts under wraps, though, and on April 11, 1887, he acted on his hunch, quietly staking a 1,500-foot by 300-foot lode claim on Bonita Peak's slope, not far below the Sampson workings. He called it the Gold King.

Nelson quit the Sampson and he and the family—he now had five children—moved to Howardsville. Louisa started up another store, while Nelson leased the Philadelphia Mine, a proven producer, so that he'd have a semi-reliable source of income. It was a success; he was pulling out ore that netted two hundred dollars (equal to $5,000 today) per ton, a relatively high grade. He also was appointed constable of Howardsville in 1890, adding to his workload. But what Nelson really wanted was to build a mine from the ground up, to strike it rich on his own, and he spent all of his spare time up on Bonita Peak at the Gold King, working at night, on Sundays, in storms, and in sunshine.

This wasn't the way mining worked anymore. You were supposed to stake a claim then go out and promote it and bring in some venture capital to finance development. That's the kind of large-scale capitalism that had turned San Juan County into a mining powerhouse, with the industry employing more than 1,200 people at 176 mines, thirteen mills, and two electric plants. But no, that wasn't Nelson's way. He kept his find quiet, working surreptitiously and alone. He endured cold and rain and the dank and dusty underground air for more than three years, sometimes working all night long, ultimately sinking a fifty-foot shaft and a fifty-foot drift. Then he became so sick that he could work no more. They called it pneumonia, a common affliction of the day. It might have been silicosis, or miner's lung, which had yet to be classified. Maybe Nelson had just worked himself into his deathbed.

Nelson's breathing is shallow and useless. Outside, huge, lacy flakes of snow catch the soft, late-afternoon light as they fall slowly to the earth. It is April 1891 and Olaf Arvid Nelson is dying. "And for what?" He asks in a raspy voice, speaking to no one in particular. Then he says no more. His obituary will remember him as an "honest and hard working man." It won't even mention the Gold King Mine.

Perfect Poison

ACID MINE DRAINAGE MAY BE THE PERFECT POISON. It kills fish. It kills bugs. It kills the birds that eat the bugs that live in streams tainted by the drainage. It lasts forever. And to create it, one needs no factory, lab, or added chemicals. One merely needs to dig a hole in the earth.

The hole, or mine, exposes once-buried, sulfide-bearing rocks such as iron pyrite ($FeS2$) to oxygen. As the hole gets deeper, it will penetrate aquifers or intersect groundwater-carrying faults and fractures, and even draw groundwater to it since it provides the path of least resistance. Put those three in-nocent ingredients—oxygen, water, and iron pyrite—together, and they engage in an atom- and ion-swapping molecular-level orgy. Hydrogen, sulfide, and oxygen come together to form sul-furic acid ($H2SO4$).[20] Thus, the water becomes acidic, or its pH drops. Iron and oxygen hook up to form iron oxide ($Fe(OH)3$). The iron oxidizes, or rusts, giving the Gold King slug, and acid mine drainage in general, that striking ochre hue.[21]

As the now-acidic groundwater moves through the mine, it dissolves and picks up naturally occurring metals in the rocks over which it flows, a process known as metal loading. Mine drainage is typically loaded with iron, zinc, cadmium, lead, copper, aluminum, arsenic, and silver. Mercury can get mixed in, too, sometimes even uranium.

It gets worse. As the pH level of the water drops below 4.8, acidophilic bacteria begin feeding off the metals, releasing more acid into the solution and causing metal loading to occur up to one million times faster than in water with higher pH. The result is acid mine drainage, mining's most insidious, pervasive, and persistent environmental hazard. The water trickling, gurgling, and sometimes gushing out of a mine portal can have a pH equal to that of battery acid or worse. This concoction can carry hundreds of pounds per day of toxic heavy metals with it, picking up even more as it courses over or through the mine-waste rock dump piled outside nearly every mine portal.

"Probably all the waters met with in the mines of the Silverton quadrangle . . . are meteoric waters variously modified by the materials through which they have passed," noted Frederick Ransome, in a 1901 U.S. Geological Survey report about the region. "The descent of the meteoric water through masses of pyrite and other ore minerals is often sufficient to give it a strong acid reaction and render it highly ferruginous." The water at the Yankee Girl Mine, just over the ridge from the Gold King, was so acidic that "Candlesticks, picks, or other iron or steel tools left in this water became quickly coated with coppers (sulfate salts). Iron pipes and rails were rapidly destroyed, and the constant replacement of the piping and pumps necessary to handle the abundant water was a large item in the working expenses."

Acid mine drainage is ubiquitous in mining country, from Idaho's contaminated Coeur d'Alene River basin to the eerily colored mine pool of the Berkeley Pit in Butte, Montana, where thousands of migrating snow geese perished in one fell swoop after landing on the contaminated "lake." The waters flowing from the Richmond Mine in California are more corrosive than battery acid and will devour a shovel in twenty-four hours. Left alone, the mine will continue to spew into the Sacramento River watershed for thousands of years to come. An ancient mine in southern Spain, abandoned four millennia ago, continues to ooze acid mine drainage into the aptly named Rio Tinto to this day.

A "normal" and healthy stream will have a pH of 6.5 to 7.5. Drop below that (or go above it), and the creatures that live in or rely on the stream begin to struggle. Mayflies, stoneflies, and caddisflies can't survive below pH 6; rainbow trout perish at pH 5.5. Hardier fish species can hang on in water with a pH as low as 4.5, but their health will be impacted, their eggs won't hatch, and their food sources will be diminished. When a stream's pH drops below 4, all deals are off for aquatic life. Water draining from the Gold King Mine prior to the blowout had a pH ranging from 2 to 3. Since the Silverton Caldera's geology offers up no natural buffers such as limestone, Cement Creek retains its high acidity (pH 3.5, similar to Mountain Dew) all the way to its juncture with the Animas River. Cement Creek (and, presumably, Mountain Dew) is uninhabitable, extremophiles notwithstanding.

After the waters of Cement Creek, Mineral Creek, and the Animas River come together, and as the now combined streams leave the Silverton Caldera, the pH rises quickly thanks to dilution and natural geologic buffering. Even the Gold King slug's acidity diminished as it moved downstream, measuring in at a healthy pH 6.8 as it slithered through Durango. Acid, however, is not the only, or even most harmful, element of acid mine drainage. The metals contained in that water can be far more deleterious in the long run. And those metals remain in the river, either in solution or as tiny, suspended particles, for miles and miles downstream, even as the acidity dissipates.

Zinc, copper, and cadmium, in both dissolved and solid states, are particularly toxic to trout and other fish and the bugs on which they depend. In very high concentrations, these dissolved metals can bring death in a fell swoop; a single high runoff event at California's Richmond Mine killed forty-seven thousand fish. At lower concentrations, it's a slow ecocide. The metals accumulate in the food chain, hindering fish growth, stifling reproduction, and wiping out more sensitive species altogether. Some metals are more persistent than others, and aren't broken down by natural processes. So they bioaccumulate, building up in a fish's organs over time without killing it, making the fish toxic to whatever eats it, including humans. Mercury is especially pernicious in this regard, because it tends to build up in the fish's muscles, the part most commonly eaten, and mercury is also biomagnified as it moves up the food chain. That's why tuna, near the top of the chain, is likely to have higher mercury concentrations than sardines. Changes in water chemistry and temperature can make metals more or less bioavailable and toxic. Zinc and cadmium have a synergistic relationship, meaning in combination they are more pernicious than alone. Relatively benign iron becomes toxic at lower concentrations when the pH drops below 5, and warmer water temperatures generally increase metals' toxicities, yet another reason to fear climate change.

Metals in solid form are not as easily ingested or absorbed, so pose less threat to bugs or fish as toxins. Yet they can snuff out a stream's oxygen and light, they can build up on and kill plants, and accumulate on or abrade a fish's gills. Iron is not especially toxic, but it is abundant in acid mine drainage and as it precipitates out of solution it settles onto the stream bed and hardens into ferricrete, thus damaging bug habitat and cementing over gravel in which fish spawn. Cement Creek probably got its name from the ubiquitous coating of ferricrete throughout its length.

Acid mine drainage spews into western watersheds daily from thousands of abandoned hardrock, coal, and uranium mines. It amounts to a round-the-clock defilement of aquatic ecosystems. Yet except on rare occasions—such as when three million gallons of it got backed up in the Gold King Mine, then came blasting out over just a few hours—acid mine drainage is invisible, and goes mostly unnoticed. When mines are active in a region, however, a far more apparent form of pollution, mill tailings, or slimes, can cause even more damage—call it acid mine drainage, supersized.

Slime Wars I

66 **THE ANIMAS RIVER WAS ONCE A BEAUTIFUL, CLEAR AND SPARKLING FLOW** of wholesome water, and the home of the finest specimens of mountain trout in the state," wrote *Durango Democrat* editor David F. Day in the spring of 1900. "The flow of the Animas River is rapidly being destroyed as a beverage and agency for irrigation by the absolute and unlawful recklessness of Silverton mill men and steps should be taken at once to force the mill operators to either impound their tailings or cease to run."

With this blistering editorial targeting the Silverton-area mines and mills, Day had yanked the communities along the Animas River into a statewide row over the dumping of mill tailings into Colorado streams. By that time, Front Range farmers had been battling upstream mines and mills for decades, trying to get state lawmakers to clamp down on mine-related pollution. Mostly it was for naught. But with the irascible Day in the fray, the anti-pollution crowd had gained a potent weapon.

IF THE RAILROAD WAS THE CATALYST FOR INDUSTRIAL-IZATION of the region's landscape, then large-scale milling had an even more profound effect on the mines around Silverton and, consequently, on the water that spills out of the mountains here. When Olaf Nelson and Jonathan Peterson were hit by their first landslide in 1879, San Juan mines were mostly small-scale operations. Nelson and his colleague followed the vein using hand tools and dynamite, then sorted through the ore by hand, picking only the chunks with the highest concentrations of metals, which they took by wagon or burro to the nearest smelter, where the metals would be cooked out of the rock.

While the miners could scale up their side of the operation by adding more laborers or using more efficient means of transporting ore, they were still limited by the smelting process. Smelting only works on high-grade ores, those containing relatively high concentrations of valuable metals. That meant that the miners had to leave the low-grade ore in the mountain or toss it aside in waste dumps. For the first decade or so, that wasn't a problem; there was an ample supply of high-grade ore. But there was a lot more low-grade ore to be had, if only it could be smelted. This is where milling—an intermediate step between mining and smelting—comes in.

Milling ore is simple in concept: You grind up the rocks and separate the valuable stuff out from the "chaff." But in the late 1800s, engineers still struggled to make it work on a large scale in the San Juans. Mills were constructed at various mines in the Silverton Caldera throughout the 1880s, but none really achieved the desired economies-of-scale until Edward and Lena Stoiber built their revolutionary mill.

Stoiber and his brother Gustav, German engineers, came to Silverton in the early 1880s to get a foothold in the nascent mining boom. They acquired a group of claims on the shores of Silver Lake, a classic, high alpine gem northeast of Silverton in a hanging basin ringed on three sides by steep, rocky peaks.

In 1888, Edward was married to Lena Allen, a young divorceé whom he met in either Silverton or Denver. Soon after, Lena bought into the Silver Lake Mine, becoming an equal partner in the venture with her husband.

The veins were not especially rich at the Silver Lake, but Stoiber figured he could make a profit there anyway, with proper engineering. In 1890 he had a mill constructed on the shores of the lake, designed specifically to go after low-grade ore, along with a hydropower plant far below on the Animas River to supply the juice to run the thing. While it wasn't the most efficient operation, it worked well enough to turn a profit from rock that had once been considered worthless, and soon other mines were following the Stoibers' lead.

The mills that emerged during this era were enormous, dangerous, noisy structures, usually built up a slope so that gravity could help move the ore through the byzantine process. At the Silver Lake mill, the high-grade ore was sorted out by hand to go directly to the smelter. The rest of the rock went through two crushers before it was further pulverized by fifty stamps, each of which weighed hundreds of pounds, crashing down at high repetitions. The crushed ore was ground down even further by four sets of cylindrical rolls. The resulting fine-grained material was then mixed with water and moved through shaker tables and jigs in order to separate the valuable metals from the rest of the powdered rock. Some mills used mercury-coated plates to capture the gold via amalgamation.

Put a ton of ore in one side of a mill and, after a bunch of crushing, stamping, screening, shaking, and amalgamation, several pounds of concentrates—a sandy form of high-grade ore that can be smelted—emerge from the other end. That leaves hundreds upon hundreds of pounds of sludge-like left-overs, or industrial waste, known as fines, tailings, or "mill slimes." The slimes are not benign. Mills in the Silverton Caldera kicked out wastes containing mostly iron pyrite, the main ingredient of acid mine drainage; large quantities of zinc, which wasn't marketable until about 1916 and is toxic to aquatic life; and other toxic metals, such as copper and lead, that didn't shake out in the inefficient milling process.

Nearly all of the slimes—tons each day—along with their acid-generating sulfides and toxic metals, were dumped without second thought into the nearest creek, river, lake, or flood-plain. Mills, like slaughterhouses and sawmills and power plants, were built near rivers to utilize the water for power or processing raw materials, and because rivers made handy sewers: Dump your crap in there and watch it wash downstream into oblivion or, in this case, to Durango, Farmington, the Navajo Nation, and southeast Utah's Mormon country.

Even if it doesn't contain otherwise toxic materials, the turbidity from the tailings is harmful. The thick sediment clogs and cuts up fishes' gills, reducing oxygen uptake, it can coat eggs and hurt their viability, and it blocks sunlight from reaching aquatic plants and algae that are an important part of the aquatic food chain. The silt can clog up farmers' ditches, town water pumps, and hydropower turbines. And tons of this was dumped into the rivers. It was like the Gold King spill, of a less vivid hue, repeated day after day on nearly every water-course in the state of Colorado and across the mining country of the West. Naturally, the downstreamers weren't happy about it, and that ignited a region-wide cold war that would simmer for decades.

COLORADO MINING GOT ITS START AT THE END OF THE 1850S ON THE FRONT RANGE of the state, in the mountains west of what is now Denver and Colorado Springs, and pollution problems cropped up there first. Clear Creek, a stream that gets its start up on the Continental Divide above what is now the Eisenhower Tunnel on Interstate 70 and then follows the freeway through Georgetown and Idaho Springs, was the initial battleground. The mining-turned-gambling towns of Black Hawk and Central City sit on North Clear Creek, which joins the main stem above Golden. Today, the gargantuan Coors Brewery straddles Clear Creek's waters in Golden, and the stream joins the South Platte River in an industrial part of north Denver.

Mines, and then mills, swarmed the upper reaches of Clear Creek, and farms sprouted along the lower sections out in the foothills and plains, drawing water from the stream for irrigation. By the 1880s, Clear Creek no longer lived up to its moniker, and in 1882, the *Colorado Transcript* ran one of the first articles about an attempt to get the miners to clean up their act, and the water:

> *Farmers of Jefferson County are interested in securing legislative action for the purpose of preventing the pollution of the waters of Clear Creek by the mills and mines of adjoining counties . . . the condition of the waters in Clear Creek is becoming more damaging to the farming lands along the creek; that the large amount of sediment carried in the water, coming from the quartz mills along the creek in such quantities and being of a mineral character, whereby it covers and chokes the soil wherever it settles, suffocating vegetation and preventing all growth of any plants, while the pyrites and other minerals contained therein when spread out and exposed to the action of the air, decom-*

pose, chemical action occurs in connection with the alkali and salts of the earth, and the copper, arsenic and other deadly and poisonous elements are set free, rendered soluble, and thus with every rain and use of water spreads the destruction over a wider domain of the lands.

The farmers' representative, engineer E. L. Berthoud (for whom the Colorado pass and town were named), even offered a partial solution: build a series of settling ponds along North Clear Creek just below the mills. Berthoud acknowledged that this would merely get rid of the particulates, not the acidity and dissolved heavy metals. But it was a start, or it could have been had anyone acted on the suggestion. They did not. Colorado lawmakers made no move to stop the sullying of the state's waters for years, and the mine managers weren't about to fix the problem themselves.

Finally, in 1887, the state gave those battling pollution a foothold, albeit a tiny one: it passed a statute making it unlawful to kill any "food fish" in public waters except for the purpose of eating the fish right away. The new statute didn't mention tailings or pollution, however, and was premised not on the intrinsic value of water or wildlife or even food, but on the notion that food fish are a type of game, and therefore belong to the state. A decade later the state expanded and sharpened the statute by passing the Forestry, Game, and Fish Law. It read, in part: "Proprietors of saw mills, stamp and reduction mills, and placer mines are notified to so dispose of their sawdust and tailings as not to pollute the waters containing food fish."

That same year the legal case for impounding tailings was further bolstered by a state court ruling. The owners of the Ames hydroelectric plant near Telluride had sued an upstream mill operator because the latter's tailings were mucking up its operations.[22] A district court judge ruled in favor of the electric company, and in 1897 the Colorado State Court of Appeals upheld the decision, further ruling, "The operators of stamp mills must use reasonable means to prevent the flow of tailings into streams where others would be materially injured nearby."

The law and ruling seemed to be of little concern to the mill operators, however, who did virtually nothing to clean up their mess. Still, local news outlets across the state gave the issue plenty of ink. "Owners of stamp mills concentrating works and placer mines, situated along the Roaring Fork in the Aspen neighborhood, have defied the authority of Commissioner Swan of the Fish, Forestry, and Game Department in his efforts to purify the waters of that stream," noted the *Fort Collins Courier* in June 1897. The *Aspen Tribune*, in November 1898, had a more dire take: "Upon examination of river water, sufficient arsenic, together with other poisonous minerals, was found to kill a human being. . . . Ores treated at the new Smuggler and Gibson concentrator are largely zinc, with a heavy showing of arsenic, and tailings have been dumped into the river regardless of danger to human life. . . . All summer long ranchers living on the banks of the Roaring Fork have reported the death of cattle from poisoning."

THE ANIMAS RIVER DID NOT BECOME A REAL FRONT OF THE TAILINGS WAR until 1900, when *Durango Democrat* editor David F. Day got involved. If anyone was equipped to face down the powerful mining interests, it was Day. The Ohio native signed up with the Union Army in 1862, when he was just fourteen years old, to fight in the Civil War. He was captured, wounded, and sent into seemingly hopeless situations multiple times, only to emerge as a war hero—all before he turned eighteen. When he heard about the raucous mining towns in Colorado, Day headed west in 1879 and started the *Solid Muldoon* newspaper in Ouray. He quickly became notorious for his irreverent, pointed prose, and for the dozens of libel suits against him.

After riling up folks on that side of the San Juans for more than a decade, Day was lured across the mountains to Durango, a Republican stronghold, where in 1892 he fired up the presses of the *Durango Democrat*. In photos, Day, a stout, mustachioed man with a cowboy hat and round-rimmed spectacles, resembles Teddy Roosevelt. The two seem to have shared some personality traits as well. Day, with an iron will, was once described as "a mingling of the chivalry of the South and the broad-minded, free-heartedness of the West."[23]

In the pages of the *Democrat*, Day kept flogging at the mine owners for months, but the pollution only grew worse. Finally, in 1902, officials from the City of Durango couldn't ignore the problem any longer. Nearly all of the citizens' household water came from the river, and the water in it was growing nastier and nastier by the day. The City considered taking legal action against the miners; after all, the law was clearly on the downstreamers' side. Tailings weren't the only offensive pollutant in the river. Silverton's town dump was in the Animas River floodplain, boardinghouse toilet vaults were perched over streams, and much of the county's sewage eventually made it to the river.

Up until this point, Silverton mining interests had mostly ignored Day's concerns. But now that he had gotten an official audience, they lashed back, with the *Silverton Standard* as their mouthpiece. That May, the *Standard* ran a piece headlined, "Would Kill the Goose That Laid the Golden Egg":

As to mill tailings, there can be no controversy except that no one but the law of gravitation has committed an open 'violation of the law.' It is true that the tailings from the half-dozen mills in San Juan County, and the impregnated water therefrom, eventually reaches the Animas River.

But there is reason in all things. We do not deny the proposition that the pollution of the waters of the streams of the state in any manner is contrary to law. Neither do we deny that mill tailings in a stream to a certain extent pollutes it—not of course the pollution that sewage is, but rather a filling of the water with mineral matter that makes its use extremely obnoxious if not positively dangerous to health.

But is the practice, under the existing conditions, a willful violation of the law, as Colonel Day suggests? Here are a half-dozen mills giving employment directly and indirectly to 1,000 men, whose work in turn gives employment to another 1,000 men in Durango. They are public benefactors to the extent that perhaps 5,000 people are and have been depending on their operation for a living. To compel the owners to build settling tanks and handle the settlings would be at best but a costly experiment and would result in ruining the mining industry of the San Juan County, as her ores are essentially a low grade milling proposition.

This bizarre twist of logic was a common refrain, heard all over the West. Mine owners and their surrogates admitted to poisoning the waters. But they argued that any ill effects felt by those downstream are offset by economics. Jobs are more important than health, gold is more valuable than water, and profit trumps everything. Day had numerous allies in this fight, and his pen was potent. The mine owners and managers he was fighting against, however, were far more powerful. They not only carried the economic heft of their industry, which at the turn of the century directly employed some thirty-five thousand Coloradans, or five percent of the population, but also clout from personal wealth or political position. Take the San Juan power couple of Lena and Edward Stoiber. While Edward Stoiber wrangled with the technical details of the Silver Lake mine and mill, Lena, aka "Captain Jack," handled the business side. The "buxom, handsome, talkative, and self-willed" woman, who became an associate member of the American Society of Mining and Metallurgical Engineers in 1894, managed personnel—a workforce that grew to several hundred—and ran the mine's relatively luxurious boardinghouse.[24] By the turn of the century, the Stoibers were millionaires; they weren't about to give that up for the sake of some fish or downstream farmers. And Lena was not one to be bullied by the likes of Day. She's known to have pioneered something called a "spite fence" at one of her Silverton homes: a massive structure on her property line having no other function except to block the sunlight and view of a neighbor with whom she had a feud.

Even game commissioner Swan, who had gone on a bit of a crusade to save the state's fish, backed off or perhaps was bought off. After the Roaring Fork ranchers had risen up, Swan told them, in writing: "Fishermen and ranchmen should not be given such preferences as to destroy the state's greatest industry . . . I am in sympathy with the mining men of Aspen. If the reduction works are closed down, several thousand people will have no means of support, as the mines would be obliged to close." And then the kicker: "Clear Creek belongs to a class of streams which have been abandoned as fishing streams and for good reason, too. The Roaring Fork is of a similar character. The valley is too narrow for the use of settling basins and if the water is to be made pure the mines must close."

Swan was referring to the notion of industrial sacrifice zones, still used as justification for wholesale and unfettered oil and gas or other development. It's the idea that once a stream or a landscape is polluted, there's no reason to protect it or try to clean it up. Better to abandon the stream or the forest to industry, and redefine it as a dumping ground.

Durango, where the economy was inextricably tied to the upstream mines, also abandoned the Animas River to the sacrificial altar. Near the end of 1902 the City switched tactics. Rather than try to get the mines and mills to clean up their act, the City Council surrendered the river to them. Durango would get its drinking water from elsewhere.[25] It bought water rights on the Florida River, several miles and a ridge away, and diverted water from that drainage into a mesa-top reservoir above Durango, from which it could then be gravity-fed to the city. The city spent more than one hundred thousand of the taxpayers' dollars in order to allow the upstream mining companies to continue polluting without restraint.

Day didn't give in so easily, though. As the Florida River option gelled, he wrote, "We are violently antagonistic to allowing the Animas River to be destroyed by mill tailings and polluting agencies that should be cremated instead of floated . . . and if there is a law to prevent pollution of the Animas, in God's name let it be enforced regardless of any other source of supply." By thus championing the intrinsic value of the river, Day may have emerged as the first white environmentalist in the region, though an imperfect one: there's no record of him getting on the case of the Durango smelter, which day after day belched thick, sulfurous coal smoke out over the city—particularly neighboring Santa Rita, the Hispanic neighborhood otherwise known as "Mexican Flats." He didn't go after the

Durango sawmills or slaughterhouses or coal power plant that had parked themselves on the river's banks so as to more easily dispose of their waste.

The new municipal water source was of little comfort to the many farmers who had no choice but to draw irrigation and even drinking water from the Animas River. As the tailings continued downstream past Durango, they crossed the Southern Ute reservation and its myriad homesteads, into New Mexico and through the communities of Aztec and Farmington, which also depended on the Animas.[26] It's likely that the tailings continued into the San Juan River and downstream to Utah. After all, in 1892 there had been a gold rush to Bluff City, Utah, on the San Juan's banks. The target was not local gold, but "flour gold" in the riverbed that had been washed down from the San Juan Mountains. If gold can make it that far, fine tailings can, too.

By 1900, the Stoibers' Silver Lake Mine consisted of more than seven miles of underground workings, and the couple had used a piece of their fortune to build a mansion on the banks of the Animas River that they called Waldheim. The lake itself paid the price. Every grain of tailings from Stoiber's revolutionary mill ended up in the once-emerald waters of Silver Lake, and by the turn of the century, some five hundred thousand tons of slimy mill tailings had piled up in the water. "The original beauty of this little sheet of water has been marred by mining operations," noted Frederick Ransome, USGS geologist, in 1901, "particularly by a partial filling with tailings from the Silver Lake Mill."

WHEN WE LOOK BACK AT PAST ATROCITIES, ENVIRONMENTAL OR OTHERWISE, we tend to do so in a generational-centric way. We pardon our forebears for wrongdoing based on the belief that they just didn't know any better, or that moral and ethical standards were lower back then. They couldn't even imagine that hollowing mountains out would wreck the waters on which we all depend. They had no clue that burning millions of tons of coal and blackening the skies over towns and cities would sicken and kill people, wildlife, crops, and the climate. After all, how could a handful of men, hacking away at a giant mountainside, have any lasting impact on God's creations?

Except that they did know, and had understood for many centuries before mining came to the Rocky Mountains exactly what destruction they sowed with their picks, drills, crushers, and mills. In 1556 a German named George Bauer, under the pen name Georgius Agricola, wrote a voluminous tome called *De re metallica*, the first writing to consider mining a science, rather than just a brute trade. Mining was already an ancient art by then, its environmental effects clear. Agricola writes: ". . . the fields are devastated by mining operations, for which reason formerly Italians were warned by law that no one should dig the earth for metals and so injure their very fertile fields, their vineyards, and their olive groves." Forests were chopped down to supply fuel to the smelters, and "when the woods and groves are felled, then are exterminated the beasts and birds . . . Further, when the ores are washed, the water which has been used poisons the brooks and streams, and either destroys the fish or drives them away."

Stoiber learned his trade at the Freiberg University of Mining and Technology, a school founded in part upon the work of Agricola. There, Stoiber and his classmates would have been steeped in *De re metallica* and similar works that elucidated the science of mining and its effects on the world around

Vertical Integration

The success of a few encouraged extravagance in the incompetent, and opened a rich field to unscrupulous and dishonest promoters. Smelting plants and mills were erected before the presence of ore was ascertained. . . . Thus in 1876 Animas Forks was a lively town of some 30 houses and 2 mills, and in 1883 boasted of a population of 450. But there was never any real justification for its existence. Built upon hope never realized, its decline was almost as rapid as its rise, and the town is now ruined and desolate. . . . Capital thus invested serves only to build monuments of failure, folly and dishonesty.

—Frederick Leslie Ransome, 1901

ONLY TWO MONTHS AFTER OLAF ARVID NELSON BREATHED HIS LAST BREATH, his widow, Louisa, patented the Gold King claim, effectively privatizing the ten-acre parcel of public land. The cost to Louisa Nelson and the hundreds of others who were patenting claims throughout the San Juans and the West? Virtually nothing, thanks to the General Mining Act of 1872, which not only gave land away to whoever staked a claim on it, but also allowed for unlimited, royalty-free extraction from said claims.

Louisa Nelson was too busy to bother with that, though.

She had six kids to raise on her own (though the youngest died in early 1892) as well as the Howardsville store to run.

In 1894, Louisa married Henry Forsyth, a respected Silverton businessman, in the Silverton home of Forsyth's friend, Willis Z. Kinney. Kinney had come to the San Juan Mountains twenty years earlier and served as Silverton's postmaster. But he was far better known for his skills at running mines, and at reeling in outside cash to fund such ventures. Within weeks of the Forsyths' wedding, Kinney—or rather his New England backers, Cyrus W. Davis and Henry Soule—had bought the Gold King claim from Louisa for $15,000.[27]

That wasn't exactly pocket change, but now it's clear that Louisa would have been better off in the long-term had she held onto the claim and followed the example of her contemporary, Amanda Cotton. Cotton owned the Minnehaha claim not far from the Gold King, as well as a number of other area properties. None would be nearly as lucrative as the Gold King, but by leasing them out or hiring someone to mine the properties, Cotton was able to make a decent livelihood for herself and her husband. Even if Louisa didn't have the business acumen for that approach, it's quite likely that she could have gotten a higher price had she shopped the Gold King around a bit. After all, outside capitalists were aching to buy into the San Juans. In 1891, for example, a Shanghai- and Hong Kong-based syndicate bought the minimally developed Belmont Mine above Telluride for $150,000. That claim was the seed of the Tomboy Mine, which sold five years later to the British Rothschild group for $2 million, or about $50 million in 2017 dollars.

Davis, a career politician from Maine, and Soule, with Kinney as mine superintendent and partner, soon got their money back and then some. The capitalists formed the Gold

King Mining & Milling Company, and went to work developing the claim, combining it with the nearby Harrison Mine. By the summer of 1895, Nelson's one hundred feet of workings had grown to five hundred feet; in 1896 the Harrison mill at Gladstone reportedly pounded out more than $10,000 from Gold King ore. In 1897 the company built a mile-long tramway reaching from the new Gold King mill to the mine portal and the neighboring boardinghouse and blacksmith shop. It also began work that year on the Level #7 adit, originally planned as a long haulage tunnel that would provide lower-elevation access to the mine's workings.[28] This is the level that would blow out in 2015.

"I may be pardoned the apparent egotism of the assertion, when I affirm that the Gold King, situated at Gladstone, is a property in which this city takes delight, and a property whose future is not behind it," wrote Davis to the *Silverton Standard* in May 1898. He claimed that he and his colleagues paid sixty thousand dollars per year in labor, that they were doubling the capacity of the mill, and were adding a cyanide plant to extract the gold. He continued: "The $500,000 of capital stock of this corporation which is organized under fifteen men, all capitalists of Massachusetts, Maine, and New Brunswick; men whose combined personal wealth exceeds tens of millions."

The company was a prime example of vertical integration, and the antithesis of the romantic vision of miner as lonely entrepreneur. The Gold King Consolidated Mines Company owned the mine—made up of thirty-six claims—the tram, and the mill. It also owned the Rocky Mountain Coal Company in Durango, which included the City Mine in Horse Gulch southeast of Durango and the Champion Mine to the west, from which it got fuel for its operations. In 1899 it built and operated the Silverton, Gladstone, and Northerly Railroad so it could more efficiently haul ore and concentrates back to Silverton, where they could be loaded onto the Durango train. And by 1900 it owned the Anglo-Saxon Mining & Milling Company, with operations in the Cement Creek drainage.

The mine reportedly grossed around $4 million per year, with more than $1 million in dividends paid out to the New England investors annually. The owners' substantial geographical remove from the mine itself spared them from seeing the horrendous costs others were paying. As one of the biggest ore processors around, the Gold King mill also belched out a lot of tailings, most of which ended up in Cement Creek and, ultimately, the Animas River. And as one of the largest employers in the county, it was also one of the deadliest.

Mining is and always has been a difficult and hazardous vocation. In 1898 alone, Silverton-area miners froze to death, were poisoned, and got caught in the belting at a mill to gruesome effect. Frank Deputy and Gail Munyon figured it would be a good idea to thaw their powder on their cookstove in a cabin near the Yukon Tunnel along Cement Creek. They were both blown to bits. Miners were swept into oblivion by avalanches, large and small, while they were getting to and from the mines or even while sleeping or dining in the boardinghouses, built with no respect whatsoever for geologic hazards. On St. Patrick's Day 1906, following a massive multi-day storm, nearly two dozen people, mostly miners, lost their lives to snow slides in the county. Local newspaper editors called repeatedly for county-wide zoning aimed at preventing such tragedies. They were ignored.

The Gold King was as perilous during its heyday as it was profitable. The litany of dead and injured near the turn of long it boasted a membership of hundreds, and by the turn of the century had become the most powerful institution in the county. Unions did far more than just agitate for better working conditions. The Silverton union built and ran the Miners Union Hospital, hosted community-wide parties and balls, and started the Labor Day celebrations (that live on as Hardrockers' Holidays). When a miner died, the union stepped in to help his widow and children, and in the days before the New Deal, the unions generally cared for the destitute, the elderly, and the ill.

The Gold King had a few brushes with organized labor, both directly and indirectly. In 1899, the whole operation had to shut down because the workers at Durango's smelter went on strike over hours worked and wages paid. In 1905 all 175 of the Gold King complex's workers walked off the job after the manager barred the president of the Silverton Miners Union from coming on the property to collect dues. And just weeks later, the miners again went on strike—very briefly—because the boardinghouse cook, who was of French descent, printed the menu in his own language and the miners couldn't read it. Management ended the strike by getting a bilingual waiter to translate. When another Gold King cook refused to join the union in 1907, all 180 boarders escorted him on foot to Silverton and told him to keep going. "Silverton is a strong union camp," wrote Dave Day admiringly in the *Durango Democrat*, "and it looks like an unhealthy place for non-unionists to visit."

The boardinghouses, each of which housed dozens of miners, could feel like testosterone-fueled pressure cookers. So, during the woefully short, high mountain summers, they'd blow off steam on the ball field. The Gold Kings, stocked with a ringer or two from the Colorado School of Mines, batted against the Silver Lakes. Silverton's "Slattery's Slobs"—named after the longtime team manager and owner of the Hub Saloon, Jack Slattery—did battle with Durango, Ouray, Montrose, and Leadville. The Slobs wore sharp uniforms of pearl gray with black trim, the letter *S* over the pocket, as they stepped up to the mound or the diamond in the shadow of Kendall Mountain. When the "idolized invincibles of the Animas slope" traveled to Durango to play, Silverton fans crowded onto the baseball special train to support their team in Smelter City.

Even a young Harold Ross, founder of *The New Yorker*, witnessed the mining-country baseball phenomenon in the form of an epic but snowed-out Silverton game on July 4, 1902. "At the end of the third the snow started and by the first of the fifth it was all off, despite the bonfire near the pitcher's box," he wrote, in a letter to an acquaintance. The high-altitude sun had burned off the snow by the next day, allowing the resumption of the Independence Day athletic contests, which included a six-mile bike race, a pony race, and a quarter-mile run. The ball game took up where it left off, and the Slobs, arguably the best team in the state at the time, creamed the Durango Indians.

San Juan County was a veritable multicultural mélange, with nearly half of its population foreign-born, making life in the high country both more interesting and challenging. A majority of the new Americans came from the mountain regions of Italy and Austria, where the border between the two countries was somewhat fluid. There was a bar in Silverton for the Italians, one for the Austrians, and one for the French-born folks called, believe it or not, the Frog Saloon. In the boardinghouses, miners tended to congregate with their countrymen. The various elements in the melting pot didn't always mix well.

On a late-summer's night in 1904, an explosion echoed through Silverton's streets, waking up a good number of citizens, who soon found "the little frame cottage occupied by Peter Dalla with the north side almost blown out, the interior furnishings badly wrecked, and the lifeless body of Dalla deposited in the opposite side of the room from that where the explosion occurred."[30] This was no accident. Someone had murdered the young Dalla, and suspicion soon fell upon Barney Fiori (or Fori). "A feud of long standing between the Italian and Austrian elements in Silverton may have some bearing on the matter," noted the *Silverton Standard* shortly after the murder, "but to date no positive proof has been obtained." There was, indeed, such discord. Dalla was born Powel Patro Dallapiccola in Austria, while Fiori was Italian. Yet in this case it's likely that romance, not nationality, fueled the deadly quarrel. That May, Fiori had burst into Dalla's and Tona Todeschi's saloon with a Colt .44 revolver and ordered all hands up before shooting Dalla in the leg. Fiori, it turns out, had a hankering for Dalla's fiancée, Katie Satore. The law apparently didn't have enough evidence on Fiori to get him for the dynamite job, though. A year later, a newspaper article lauded him for shooting two 600-pound "silver-tip" bears northeast of Silverton.

Yet for all its drama and violence, the Dalla-Fiori affair was far from the ugliest incident of ethnic tension—make that ethnic *cleansing*—to occur in Silverton and its surroundings.

Even as Europeans flooded into the United States' East Coast, Asians, predominantly from China, were making their way to the West. Chinese immigrants joined the California Gold Rush, and many were hired in the 1860s to help build the transcontinental railroad. When the railroad was completed in 1869, the workers converged on the mining camps of the West, looking for jobs and entrepreneurial opportunity. In the mid-

1870s a handful joined the throngs of opportunity-seekers converging on Silverton.

For several years, the Chinese Americans were just another ingredient in the mountain cultural mix. While few seem to have worked the mines, Chinese-born citizens did locate and own the St. Paul Mine, near Red Mountain Pass north of Silverton, for a time. Silverton was home to a handful of Chinese laundries and several restaurants. Their neighbors tended to eye them with racism-tinged curiosity: "Last Sunday was the Chinese New Year and the Celestials celebrated the day in a becoming manner," noted the *San Juan Herald* in 1887. "For the past six weeks, Meng Lee, who keeps the washee shop next door to the St. Charles Restaurant has been fattening two domestic ducks and one old hen for the purpose of giving a blowout to his fellow Chinamen. . . . Besides the game mentioned above, the dinner consisted of several Chinese dishes which appeared to be quite palatable to them but we would want to have our own life insured were we to have partaken in the same."

Perhaps inevitably, curiosity eventually disintegrated into xenophobic derision throughout the region, despite the fact that there were never more than fifty or sixty China-born residents of Silverton or in other area towns at any given time. In 1880, the *Dolores News*, of Rico, Colorado, wrote: "The Mormons and Chinese should not be allowed to people Colorado." Soon the "Chinese Question," much like the "Ute Question," was on many a lip. In 1885, Silverton cops rounded up "a number of the almond eyed residents of Silverton, who were driving quite a trade in fine silk handkerchiefs, teas, spices, medicines, dried fish."[31] The case was dropped when the prosecutors failed to appear in court. Most heinously, in Rock Springs, Wyoming, that September, a mob of white union men massacred twenty-eight Chinese coal miners and beat fifteen others because they refused to join their coworkers in a strike for higher wages.

Ultimately, it would be organized labor dealing the final blow to Silverton's Chinese Americans, as well. In 1902, the Silverton Miners Union, the Cooks and Waiters Union, and the Federal Labor Union 112 turned on their fellow citizens. "Do you want the yellow man or the white man?" a union representative wrote. "The Chinese (opium) dens in this city have destroyed over 300 human beings. No white man can compete with their labor on account of their cheapness in living." Never mind that there is little evidence that opium dens even existed in Silverton, let alone killed off more than one-tenth of the population. The Chinese immigrants were largely self-employed, so could not take any jobs. "The *Miner* believes in 'America for Americans' and white men, and is therefore in sympathy with this movement. . . . It is a straight proposition: The Chinese must go, and with this concerted action (a boycott of their businesses) it will not be long until they are out of Silverton and without violence or injustice to anyone concerned."

Within a few weeks, the Chinese American population had gone. No one was killed or, so far as the newspapers let on, beaten. Yet the expulsion was a violent, hateful, unjust one all the same. The community of Silverton was the loser. The surrounding communities, particularly Durango, that tolerated and even embraced the exiles were the winners. As for the Silverton unions that drove the racist expulsion, in a few more decades they'd be on the other side of the stick.

THE GOLD KING COMPLEX FLOURISHED for the first five years of the twentieth century, and the investors raked in cash hand over fist. But like a gambler who hits the jackpot on his first pull of the jackpot arm and is unable to walk away with his winnings, they were never satisfied, and that would be their downfall. Cyrus Davis and company, encouraged by their success at Gladstone, believed that if they could make $1 million in profit off of one mine, they could make $5 million off of five mines. So in the early 1900s they bought up property throughout the San Juans: groups of claims in Bridal Veil and Marshall basins far above Telluride and, most notoriously, the Gold Prince in Animas Forks, a high-altitude mining camp north of Silverton.

Animas Forks had already boomed and busted hard by the time Davis started throwing money at it, building the massive Gold Prince Mill in 1904 and commencing full-blown development of the property. While local newspapers were quick to note every ore-strike, increase in production, or bonanza at the mines, they tended to pay less attention to the negatives. As a result, it can be difficult to trace the falling fortunes of the mining companies. In December of 1907, for example, several newspapers around the state reported that many Silverton mines, including the Gold Prince, had laid off their workforces on account of a massive metal market slump. Yet at the same time the local rag reported that the Gold Prince miners had struck a rich vein of ore and was thriving.

In hindsight it's clear that, layoffs and bonanzas aside, things weren't going well at the Gold Prince in 1907. Along with a series of unfortunate incidents that year and the next, the money-sucking Gold Prince would weigh heavily on the Gold King organization as a whole. The Gold Prince complex sent only about one hundred tons of concentrates to the Durango smelter each month that year, which is less than one-tenth of what a mine of that extent should have been producing. In May, the bunkhouse burnt down, nearly taking seventy-five men with it, apparently the result of arson.[32] Eleven months later, an eerily similar but scantly noticed event took place at the Gold King's Champion Mine in Durango. The manager there received a threatening letter, and days later the mine was bombed, killing one and severely injuring two others.

Meanwhile, over at the Gold King, management was dealing with an epidemic of high-grading, a sort of blue-collar embezzlement. While he works underground, or sorts ore, or in the mill, a miner or miller will occasionally slip a chunk of high-grade ore, usually a chunk with free gold visible in it, into his lunchbox or pocket to sell later on. It's an age-old practice, and mine managers have come up with various preventatives— Gold King superintendent Kinney reportedly put miners of different nationalities together so they'd rat one another out. High-graders managed to find more ingenuous ways around these measures. A February 1908 search of the Gold King bunkhouse yielded 150 pounds of rich ore worth thousands of dollars leading to the arrest of thirty-three miners.

Several months later a crippling blow was dealt to the whole enterprise, from which it would never really recover.

By that time, the American Tunnel #1, now known as Level #7, was the main entry point into the underground maze of the Gold King Mine.[33] It was closer to the mill down at Gladstone than previous portals, but the ore still had to travel a mile or so via tram from the mine. In addition to the tram house, other infrastructure clung to the hillside here: a three-story boardinghouse in which most of the underground miners lived and ate, a carpenter shop, stables, and power house. In the chill of an early June night, 1908, a fire started in the upper level of the tram house. It rapidly spread through the wooden buildings, and soon the entire complex was in flames.

Everyone in the buildings was able to escape unharmed, but as the flames subsided the bedraggled survivors realized that three men were still trapped inside the mine. Word was sent down to the mill and the "Gold King Hotel" at Gladstone, as well as to Silverton. Dozens of rescuers made their way to the mine, and a team of six ventured underground into the smoke- and carbon-monoxide-filled caverns. Two of the miners were rescued; a third perished along with five of the rescuers.

The cause of the fire, which, in addition to the human toll, caused some $150,000 worth of damage, was never determined. It was probably electrical in origin, though there were unsubstantiated rumors that the owners had intentionally set the fire in order to collect insurance money. The rumors were further fueled by the quiet news, almost exactly a month after the fire, that a major Gold King Consolidated Mines Co. creditor, Durango hardware store owner, wagon-builder, and politician, Harry Jackson, had asked the court to put the company under receivership. "This is but the preliminary battle for control and liquidation of outstanding indebtedness of this great property, the struggle for supremacy being between Coloradans and the New England states ownership," noted Dave Day's *Durango Democrat*. "Our understanding is that the Gold King property made $150,000 last year, and all that the New Englanders did not utilize for salaries, was blown in on the Gold Prince."

The company's bankruptcy didn't kill the Gold King altogether, but its glory days were clearly over. Shortly after the fire, W.Z. Kinney, seemingly the mine's lucky charm, resigned. After that, every bit of news of a new ore discovery, a new operator, a renovated mill, or other step forward was soon met with setback and even disaster. In 1909, another fire ripped through the newly rebuilt Gold King complex. A couple of years later, an avalanche blew out a good portion of the first floor of the boardinghouse, killing a woman and her infant granddaughter. In an eerie twist, the infant's last name was Schnee, German for snow. Floods ripped through the Cement Creek canyon, wrecking rails and road, in 1909 and 1911.

In 1915 Otto Mears, the Russian Jewish "Pathfinder of the San Juans," took over operations of the mine to much fanfare, but Mears' propensity for finding passable routes through the mountains didn't extend to getting the ore out of the Gold King, and in 1918 the mine again changed hands. Most frustrating for those involved was that the mine still contained valuable ore, but efforts to recover it were always stymied, by snowslides, floods washing out the tracks to Silverton, bad management, or technical difficulties. Even as the Gold King flailed, other mines, including the Sunnyside, just over Bonita Peak from the Gold King, flourished.

The string of operators throughout the early 1900s all sought salvation in the new American Tunnel, which would get a leading role in the Gold King blowout saga a century later. This version burrowed into the earth at a slightly upward angle from the mill at Gladstone, about 860 feet below the Gold King Level #7 (the "old" American Tunnel). The idea was to dig directly beneath the Gold King workings, then link the mine and the tunnel with a vertical shaft. That would provide an underground path from the Gold King workings straight down to the mill, making those pesky, avalanche-battered structures at the Level #7 portal, along with the treacherous tram, obsolete. Miners spent years drilling and blasting away. By the time they finally quit, the tunnel was 6,233 feet deep, but it was a tunnel to nowhere. The American Tunnel and Gold King Mine never did actually meet, but a hydrological connection that would rear its ugly head nearly a century later had been made. The tunnel "deep drained" the groundwater running through Bonita Peak, thus leaving the once watery Gold King Level #7 adit almost totally dry. The tainted water that had been pouring out of the Gold King Mine had been rerouted through the mountain, and now poured from the American Tunnel, instead. Gold King ore would never flow through the American Tunnel, but its acid mine drainage would.

In 1922, the then-owners of the Gold King went belly up, and their assets were put up for auction in a sheriff's sale. Whoever ended up with the property pretty much mothballed it, producing ore for a few months in 1924 before shutting the whole operation down. One of the greatest mines of the San Juan Mountains, having produced more than seven hundred thousand tons of gold, silver, lead, and copper ore, valued at $8.4 million ($120 million in 2017 dollars), was dead, at least for the time being.

Hard Rain's Gonna Fall

A fellow who thinks the "river of lost souls" won't do to watch, has all the feathers out of his willow plume. She may look meek and sleepy-eyed but don't tickle her heels.

—*Durango Wage Earner*, October 12, 1911

M Y FATHER'S MOTHER'S FATHER SET OUT FROM OURAY, COLORADO, in late September 1911, looking for land. His name was John Malcolm Nelson. His parents brought him to Colorado from Smaland, Sweden, in 1870, when he was a year old. He grew up on the ranch his parents homesteaded in a mostly Swedish American community northeast of Boulder,[34] and eventually moved to the small mining town of Ouray, just over the mountains from Silverton. He ran a mercantile store there, and married Myra Eggleston, in Boulder in 1908. They had two kids while in Ouray, John and Amy, my grandmother, and later another girl, Ruby. Myra and Malcolm wanted to raise their family on a farm, not in a mining town, so Malcolm took the train up to Telluride, over to Rico, and down to Dolores. While in Montezuma County, he heard about some land for sale on the "Ute Strip"—a checkerboard of private and Indian land within the boundaries of the

Southern Ute Reservation. So he headed east and purchased half of what was originally a 160-acre homestead in the Animas River valley about twelve miles south of Durango, right across the river from the Hispanic village of La Posta.

The rain began late on the morning of October 4, as Malcolm was still working out the details of the sale. At first, it came down gently—what some refer to as a female rain—and gave no cause for alarm. The harvested fields in the lower reaches of the Animas watershed would drink up the moisture and hold it until the spring and when the clouds lifted, the peaks would be blanketed in white. Or at least, that's how a typical October rainstorm in the Four Corners country goes. This one was anything but typical, and it would be a while before my great-grandfather made it back to Ouray.

It already had been a wet year. Snows were big that winter, and rains abundant in July and August, with another round hitting in late September. The earth was saturated. And just when it could take no more, the moisture-laden clouds backed up against the San Juans and dropped their watery load. The storm's tropical origins warmed the air ahead of it, so that even on the peaks, the precipitation fell as water, not snow, so there was no delay to the runoff.

The soft rain turned hard on the night of October 4, dropping two inches of precipitation on Durango in twelve hours, nearly twice what the town normally gets during all of October. Another inch fell on October 5, putting the total for the storm up to 3.4 inches. That was a sprinkle compared to what was going on closer to the Animas River's headwaters. Weather watchers in Gladstone, home of the Gold King Mine, recorded eight inches of rain on October 5—it was a virtual high country hurricane.

Sheets of water ran down cliffs, trickles became torrents, gurgling streams jumped from their banks and pummeled everything in their path: railroad tracks and roads and bridges and barns and fields. In Durango, Junction Creek, which normally runs almost dry by late summer, tore out the Main Avenue bridge then the railroad bridge before adding its load to the Animas, which carried an estimated twenty-five thousand cubic feet per second (cfs) of water through Durango during the flood's peak. It's an almost incomprehensible volume. A big spring runoff through Durango will hit five thousand to six thousand cfs; typical levels in October are generally below five hundred cfs; and the Colorado River through the Grand Canyon rarely exceeds twenty thousand cfs.

The force contained within that water was baffling to behold. It broke free the railroad bridge near Durango's fish hatchery and carried it downstream, despite the fact that two full coal cars had been parked on the bridge to provide ballast. The river jumped its channel and headed onto 15th street, creating a five-foot-deep river that today would go right through a Burger King. Several homes, cattle, hay barns, and hay were carried away. An estimated one hundred tons of toxic slag, piled up outside the Durango smelter, collapsed into the river. On the opposite shore the Santa Rita neighborhood was inundated, and several of the small homes carried away. Below Durango, the roiling, muddy waters were more forgiving, but still took out railroad and wagon bridges.

By no means was the storm limited to the Animas watershed. Huge rains pounded the entire San Juan range and beyond, but were particularly hard on the vast San Juan River drainage. As it flowed through Pagosa Springs, sixty miles east of Durango, the upper San Juan River swept away more than twenty structures and destroyed the town water plant, hospital, and jail, and its power plant "was wiped out of existence, nothing left but the water wheel."[35]

In Farmington the raging monsters of the upper San Juan and the Animas joined forces, to disastrous effect. The Navajo Methodist Mission was located on a low bench south of the San Juan River just below its confluence with the Animas. Like everyone else in Farmington, the missionaries received plenty of warning of the impending flood, yet they were certain that they'd be safe, so they didn't immediately evacuate. Finally, at about midnight, the children were moved to higher ground. Superintendent J. N. Simmons and staff members Frank B. Tice and Walter Weston chose to stick around. It was a mistake.

At around four a.m. on October 6 the three men awoke to find the new three-story cement-block building surrounded by water. Weston was able to quickly escape on horseback (and may have snuck out earlier). Simmons made a run for the horses, too, climbing atop an outhouse, apparently in order to launch himself onto a horse. Tice decided to stick around, heading for the top floor of the structure.

Simmons' outhouse-to-horse leap failed, and he ended up in the water, clutching a piece of debris, which carried him rapidly downstream along the broad river, bobbing helplessly among dead animals, haystacks, and pieces of people's homes. He grabbed onto a floating tree, then jumped from that to a barrel, then to a still-rooted tree, in whose branches he sat until he realized that it, too, was about to be torn from the earth. He leapt for another piece of debris, which carried him downstream to an island where he was able to start a fire, cook up some apples that he had snagged as they floated by, and wait for the waters to subside.

Tice was less fortunate. As the waters rose he went from the second story to the third, finally climbing onto the roof with his dog. It seemed safe enough; the water stopped rising after it inundated the third story. Little did he know that the rushing current was eroding the cement building away. People far away on the opposite bank watched as the building dissolved and Tice was swallowed up by the current. They found his body twenty miles downstream. The dog's fate remains a mystery.

The destruction was far from over. At Shiprock, the huge steel bridge was destroyed and the Shiprock Indian School campus covered with water five feet deep. Seven adobe buildings were destroyed. The surge took out every bridge in San Juan County, Utah, where a miniature oil boom was on. In 2001, USGS scientists conducted a paleoflood hydrology investigation on the San Juan River below Bluff, Utah, and concluded— based on flood debris they found far above the river—that during the 1911 flood, 150,000 cubic feet of water shot past the little town of Mexican Hat every second.[36] That's about one hundred times the volume of water in the river during a typical March or April, a popular time to raft that section.

Even more mind boggling is to consider what happened when the San Juan joined the flood-engorged waters of the Colorado in Glen Canyon, under what is now Lake Powell. Every side canyon also roared with the violent power of water and gravity, adding its load of water, silt, and debris to the grandest river of the Southwest. As it rushed past the current site of Glen Canyon Dam and headed toward the Grand Canyon, the Colorado was running at an estimated 300,000 cubic feet per second, all of it constricted into the narrow granite gorge. It would have been quite the sight to see—from a safe distance.

Mercifully, the storm moved quickly, leaving a bright sun to illuminate the wreckage scattered across the region. Remarkably, only a handful of human lives were lost to the flood. Meanwhile, the flood scoured away much of the stuff—roads, houses, bridges, railroad tracks—that humans had littered the valleys with over the previous decades. With virtually every railroad bridge in the region washed out or damaged, Malcolm Nelson could not go back to Ouray the way he came. So he went all the way around the San Juans to the east. In December of that year, he and his family moved to the land along the Animas.

My maternal grandmother, Emily Mead, was two years old when the flood roared past her house in Hermosa, on the farm that had been her great-grandmother Julia's. Julia had passed it on to her son, Ervin, when she died in 1894, and Ervin passed it on to Lyman and his wife, Clara. Though it was a powerful woman, Julia Mead, who planted the family's roots here, bought and cultivated the first plot of land, and established herself as a member of the community, the land subsequently ended up in the hands of the men, as did the credit for what was grown there.

Ervin and then his son Lyman were known for the fruit they, most likely with the help of their wives, Emely and Clara, grew. Ervin won a number of prizes at the 1902 Colorado-New Mexico Fair for their apples, which benefitted from the warm wind that blows down the Hermosa Creek drainage; Ervin was famous for his strawberries. When roiling, mud-red Hermosa Creek jumped from the banks that fall, it ran through their fields. Still, up until her death ninety years later, my grandmother hankered for another flood like that one, for a wall of water to blast out of the gorge at Baker's Bridge, rise up out of its banks, spread slowly and gently out across the wide, flat, and once fertile bottomland, and scour the valley of the golf courses, the luxury tract homes, the trailer parks, and everything else that sprouted up where once stood open meadows, cottonwood groves, ponderosa pines, hayfields, and orchards. She did not want anyone hurt, she just wanted her promised land returned to her in the way she would always love and remember it.

Any such catharsis would be temporary, however. A week after the flood ripped through every drainage in the San Juan Mountains and beyond, the headlines did not sensationally recount the flood, nor did they warn against rebuilding in the path of the next flood. Rather, they touted the resilience of the local mining industry, and celebrated the fact that the mines kept on cranking despite all the damage. It was a telling display of exactly where the community's priorities lay. Never mind that a horrific flood had caused millions of dollars of damage downstream, that the train couldn't get to Durango, let alone Silverton, and that reconstruction would take months. *We're a mining town*, the headlines screamed, *and nothing's going to get in our way.*

The attitude was prevalent throughout the region. Even before the waters had subsided, community officials vowed to rebuild, often in the same places the floodwaters had rushed through. There was something almost Old-Testament-like about their behavior, as if they were being tested by a higher power. God rained fire, pestilence, and locusts down on his chosen ones and even ordered them to slay their children, all to test their faith, to confirm they believed. Here, the mountains, rivers, and clouds did the same, and the newcomers had a choice: surrender and go home, or shake their collective fist at the sky and continue their quest to subdue the earth. Adapting to the vagaries of the place by building outside of flood plains or avalanche paths was a form of surrender. Defiance and perseverance was the only acceptable way.[37]

Still, the most difficult and tragic test of all was on the horizon: a global war followed by a global disease, the horror of both magnified and amplified by technology and the industrial, increasingly mobile age.

The Blackest Week

JAMES EDWARD COLE WAS THIRTY-SIX YEARS OLD WHEN HE DIED. You might say he was in the prime of his life. He was born in Durango, but grew up in Silverton. After high school he started working under the tutelage of his father, William, at the family retail clothing store. He played on the Slattery's Slobs baseball team. He married Adelia Bausman, and in 1916 they had a son, James. They built a house just down Reese Street from the new, stately courthouse. As the nights grew cold and the days crisp in the Silverton autumn of 1918, Adelia's belly started to show the signs of a second child. James would never meet him. By late October 1918, James was dead, one of dozens who perished during the "Blackest Week Ever Known" in Silverton and the San Juan Mountains.

SOON AFTER EUROPE BECAME EMBROILED IN A GRUE-SOME WAR IN 1914, the impacts rippled into the Colorado high country. Demand for metals increased, as guns and mortars and tanks and planes rolled off the assembly lines. Metal prices shot up, giving the miners incentive to dig deeper in search of low-grade ore, and new technologies emerged for processing that ore. The county's mines together produced metal valued at more than $2.5 million ($47.2 million in 2017 dollars) in 1917, close to a record.

In 1917 the United States entered the war, again sending ripples into mining country. By the time the war was almost over, in the autumn of 1918, at least 150 of Silverton's young men, or around eight percent of the total population, were in the European trenches. Nearly half were immigrants or the children thereof, some fighting against brothers or cousins. The mass absence affected the community in obvious ways, and it also created a labor crunch at the mines. The American Mining Congress begged young men to resist the temptation to enlist and instead be "truly patriotic" and remain at their industrial posts, where they were sorely needed.

Even as the bodies of soldiers piled up on the battlefields of the first modern war, the planet was struck with something even more deadly, the so-called Spanish Influenza—perhaps the first modern pandemic. It might have originated, or at least gathered strength, in Midwestern pig farms before making a run through Fort Riley, a military camp in Kansas that housed nearly thirty thousand men, in March 1918. From there, this dastardly but rarely fatal first wave of the virus spread rapidly overseas along with soldiers and supplies. In October, a second wave swept the globe. Unlike other strains of flu, which typically break down the immune system leaving the bodies of the very young, the old, and the weak vulnerable to secondary infections like pneumonia, the Spanish Flu could fell a person all on its own. Because the virus turned the immune system against the body, it was harder on the young and healthy, people like James Cole, than it was on the old and frail. First comes a fever and the same aches and pains that come with other strains. Within days or even hours afterward, victims might become so dizzy as to collapse. The lungs fill with fluid, breathing becomes raspy, delirium and even psychotic episodes follow. Finally, victims cough up a bloody froth that ultimately asphyxiates them.

"While there have been one or two cases of this disease reported in our midst, there has not so far been any serious results," noted the October 18, 1918, edition of the *Miner*. By then the virus was wreaking havoc all over, and some prophylactic measures had been put in place in Silverton: postal workers fumigated incoming mail, and large public gatherings were banned. But the people of Silverton were not overly alarmed. Maybe they thought their isolation would protect them; perhaps that's what led nearly every local citizen to ignore the ban on gatherings and participate in a premature celebration of the war's end on October 17. Just a day or two later, the symptoms surfaced: the ache of the back, the scratch in the throat, a fever's hot flash.

Within days, many of the people who had celebrated that night would be dead.

For the next two weeks or so, Silverton became a living nightmare. At least one member of nearly every household in town was struck. Miners collapsed on the job, mothers at the dinner table. The hospital filled to capacity and then some, so Town Hall became a de facto clinic and then morgue, with the dead stacked next to the dying. The coffins ran out and the undertaker died. The burly Swedish miner who tirelessly dug the graves ended up digging his own. On October 25, the *Silverton Standard* heralded the "Worst Week Ever Known in History." They had to issue a correction of sorts a week later, with a headline that read: "Past Week has been Blackest Ever Known . . ." So many died so quickly that a few went to their graves without being identified except as "Mexican from Sunnyside" or "Austrian from Iowa mine."

Herman Dalla, an already fatherless six-year-old, lost his mom and two brothers. In another family a toddler, a teenager, and their forty-year-old mother died. One little girl was orphaned. Temperatures sunk below zero, making the earth at the cemetery nearly impenetrable. There was no way to dig one grave for every corpse, so long, shallow trenches were gouged into the earth, the bodies tossed in by the dozens. Some of the dead were later recovered by the families, but an untold number remain in the mass grave, unidentified.

All in all, the Spanish Flu claimed at least 150 San Juan County residents, maybe more. The town and county had the state's highest per capita fatality rate from the Spanish Flu, and might have had the nation's except for an indigenous village in Alaska that lost eighty-five percent of its population.[38] Plenty of people got the flu in Durango and the surrounding areas—everyone in my maternal grandmother's family was stricken except for her father, Lyman—but the fatality rate was relatively low. Gunnison quarantined itself early on, enforced with armed guards, and escaped almost unscathed. Maybe Silverton's elevation exacerbated the effects, or perhaps it was isolation, or the dry, cold air.

Again, the community's reaction to the disaster once the worst had passed was eerily sanguine, even cheery. It was looked back on as a sort of bump in the road that delayed a few things, but that had no real lasting consequences. The news in the weeks following focused on the end of the war, the fact that business was quickly getting back to normal, the mines were gearing up again. The Caledonia Mine had imposed quarantine during the flu, not allowing any miners to leave or any to come in from the outside. That they didn't lose any miners to the flu was less remarkable to the local newspaper than the fact that their ore production hadn't faltered during the mass misery. The miners that weren't in Europe or dead from the flu were soon back at work. The community had been tested again. Perhaps they passed this trial, perhaps they didn't.

Slime Wars II

Where once you and I,—boys together—roamed the hills and streams, fishing and hunting—absorbing the character building atmosphere of the Great University of the Outdoors—our boys and girls will find bleak hills in which to roam, fishless streams, gameless open places, void of forests, and will find no Great University of Nature to attend, no character building atmosphere to absorb, it will be gone—gone beyond redemption.

—Izaak Walton League membership advertisement, 1927

I N 1903, MONTANAN HUGH MAGONE HAULED the Colorado Smelting and Mining Company,[39] along with other mining interests, into court. Magone owned a farm in the Deer Lodge Valley, downstream from Butte, Montana, arguably the mining capital of the West.[40] Magone—who served as a surrogate for a large group of neighboring farmers—claimed that the mining company's tailings, dumped into Silver Bow Creek, had clogged his irrigation ditches and washed onto his fields, hurting yields and killing some crops altogether. Magone's private property rights had thus been negated, and he asked the court not only for damages, but also for an injunction that would halt the dumping of tailings.

The case, which dragged on for years, represented an escalation in the Westwide Slime Wars, as downstreamers increasingly turned to the courts for some sort of relief.

The mining companies' defense attorneys readily acknowledged that their clients had polluted the river, and that it may have harmed Magone and others. But, they said, the mines, mills, and smelters had no choice: "There is no place in Montana where concentrating and smelting can be carried on with less damage than along the course of Silver Bow Creek in Butte; further, that one-third of the population of the state is directly dependent on the operations of the mines, and two thirds of the population would be materially affected by their closing down."[41]

It was the same argument fielded in courts from Idaho to Utah to California at the time. The mining industry was at the headwaters of the region's economic watershed. If miners make more money, the theory went, so will the merchants, the farmers, and the tax coffers downstream. Therefore, farmers that try to stifle miners' ability to make money are actually hurting themselves and the rest of the economy. Despite its flaws—the regional economic system is not just a linear, downward-flowing river, it's a cyclical ecosystem in which all parts are connected—the industry's argument held sway among the local business community, state lawmakers, and, it turns out, in the courts.

The Montana court partially ruled in Magone's favor by awarding damages to the farmer to compensate him for his wrecked fields. The amount, however, was a pittance—just $1,700, spread between a host of defendants. Meanwhile, the judge denied the injunction, first because the mining companies had senior water rights to Magone and his fellow farmers, which the judge apparently interpreted as a right not only to use those same waters, but also pollute them. Secondly, he cited the economic argument, essentially ruling that property rights are also determined on a sort of seniority basis, only in this case the senior rights go to those who are able to reap the most profit out of the exploitation of that property. Upstream eclipses downstream, profit trumps food, the rich eat the poor, and today the Berkeley Pit at Butte, a growing, toxic lake that poisons any bird tempted by its waters, is the end result.

World War I pumped new energy into the Silverton-area mines in the teens, and a wave of consolidation and corporatization brought new capital to the endeavors. In Silverton, the Stoibers had years earlier sold their Silver Lake properties to American Smelting and Refining Co., part of the Guggenheim mining empire that Magone had challenged in Montana. The family-owned Sunnyside Mine was purchased by U.S. Smelting, Refining, Milling, and Mining Co., a Boston-based conglomerate that owned mines and smelters throughout the West, including the massive mines at Bingham Canyon, Utah, and a smelter in Midvale.

This was supplemented with increased mechanization and the development of froth-flotation milling, which replaces the old mechanical means of separating out metals from the crushed ore with chemical ones. Smelters didn't do well with ore that had a high zinc content, and previous milling methods were not able to remove the zinc from ore. That meant that a lot of ore had to be left behind, regardless of what other metals were present. With the new flotation technique, and with smelters in Salida and Pueblo offering a decent price for zinc concentrates, high-zinc-content mines like the Sunnyside got a new lease on life.

Removing the zinc-filled ore from the mines left less of the toxic metal available to be taken up by acid mine drainage—a good thing for water quality. But the new process required pulverizing the ore to a much finer grain, meaning the tailings left over were less like sand and more like dust, and would stay suspended in water for much longer and further downstream. The tailings that didn't get washed down the river got whipped about in the wind, easily inhaled by passersby. The greater efficiencies in mining techniques led to more extensive mine workings and more rock being moved. That led to more and more tailings (the lower the ore grade, the more tailings are produced per ton of ore), and turned mines, some with up to ten miles of shafts, drifts, adits, and tunnels, into veritable acid mine drainage factories. Remarkably, despite all these technological breakthroughs, the mine and mill owners still couldn't manage to build simple containment systems for their waste, and even larger quantities of slimes ended up in the rivers, poisoning the water for miles and miles downstream.

That drew more folks into the fight against the industry. In 1913, people in the once-socialist-utopian colony of Nucla, downstream on the San Miguel River from Telluride, joined the list of towns that were fed up with the sullying of the water. "The pollution of these streams by mine operators has not only ruined all good fishing but has contaminated the water so that it is not fit for drinking purposes and is causing great expense to the ditch companies to operate their canals," read a statement from town leaders. "The scenery along the San Miguel River is unsurpassed . . . was at one time one of the very best trout fishing streams in the state. If this were true today there would be thousands of tourists visiting this section every year . . ."

The declaration mostly echoed what others on the Roaring Fork, Clear Creek, Animas, Gunnison, and Arkansas rivers had been saying for decades. Yet Nucla, perhaps unwittingly, had introduced the seed of what could become a new tactic for the downstreamers. They not only mentioned damage done to the farms and drinking water, but also to two other potential economic engines that were not tied directly to mining: recreation (sport-fishing) and tourism.

War overseas put the Colorado-wide tailings fight on hold, but once Europe was again at peace, strife kicked back in at home. In 1919, the Clear Creek farmers and the City of Golden again went to state lawmakers asking for legislation that would force mining companies to build settling systems for their tailings, so as to mitigate the problems experienced by irrigators downstream. While they were able to get legislation introduced, it was strongly opposed by the mining lobby, and never went anywhere. Leadville *Herald Democrat* editor Henry C. Butler summed up the fate of the bill—and the entire anti-tailings movement—in 1921: "Stream pollution by the pumping of water charged with sulphuric acid or by zinc tailings has come up for discussion in the legislature, and fishermen have complained that the fishing has been seriously affected on this account. As industry comes ahead of angling the streams had to rely on the work of Mother Nature in clearing up the pollution caused by waste from mine or mill."

Lawsuits kept piling up. In Butte, complainants went after not only the tailings and acid mine drainage, but also smelter smokestack emissions. On Colorado's Arkansas River sportsmen were finally getting more involved, and joined a farmers' lawsuit against the Colorado Zinc & Lead Co. in Leadville. The Izaak Walton League, a conservation-minded group of out-

RIVER OF LOST SOULS

doorsmen, hunters, and anglers, was formed and soon grew
to national prominence. By the late 1920s, several chapters
were active in Colorado. The League mostly steered clear of
the mine pollution issue, but it empowered a new coalition to
speak out on various issues, and pushed the Colorado legislature to affirm that streams and rivers were public, ensuring
access to fishing and boating.

In 1925 Charles Chase came to the Silverton Caldera in
search of a prospect for a group of Kansas City investors. Chase,
the son of a mining engineer, was educated as a metallurgist.
But by then he was better known for his skills as a mine manager, in the mold of Willis Z. Kinney of Gold King fame or
the Stoibers of Silver Lake, the kind of person who could meld
geology, engineering, and business to turn a profit from mountains of rock. Chase had spent most of his career in Telluride
as general manager of the Liberty Bell Mine, which brought its
owners more than $3 million in profit, or $40 million in today's
dollars, before ceasing operations in 1921. In the mountains
surrounding Arrastra Gulch, a few miles outside of Silverton,
Chase saw potential, and the Kansas City investors financed
his bid to buy and consolidate a handful of mines, including
the Shenandoah, the Dives, the Northstar, the Terrible, and
the Mayflower. The new Shenandoah-Dives complex was soon
cranking away, sending as much as one hundred tons of ore per
day to the Iowa Mill, and then to the Mayflower Mill,[42] built in
1929, near the Animas River. Originally, Chase hoped to contain the tailings from his new mill, in spite of his belief that
the minerals in the tailings actually helped crops. But when his
initial containment system failed, he gave up.

The Durango-area farmers, meanwhile, stepped up their
game. George Vest Day, the son of the anti-mine-pollution cru-

sader and newspaper owner Dave Day, had a farm along the Animas River about four miles north of the New Mexico state line. When he first bought the property in 1914, the tailings weren't too bad. But fifteen years later, ". . . We see much of it, and can truthfully say that in low water time our stock refuses to drink the water, so filled with slime is it. Within the last few years, what few fish (suckers) are left are having a hard time to survive." It was bad enough that Animas Valley farmer Henry T. Ambold sued the Sunnyside Milling and Mining Company, a subsidiary of U.S. Smelting, Refining, Milling, and Mining Co. Ambold and his fellow plaintiffs raised legal fees by holding big community dances, and pressed the judge to issue an injunction that would stop the mine from dumping the tailings.

Sunnyside's managers must have felt more vulnerable to the complaints than in the past, because they hired Albert P. Root, a well-known assayer, to study the water quality in Durango in order to bolster the mine's case. It didn't work out so well: Root's observations, that the river ran gray and turbid day in and day out, year-round, even during low flows, provided ammunition for the plaintiffs, rather than a defense.[43] Nevertheless, in 1932 Federal District Court Judge J. Foster Symes denied the injunction, though he did rule that Ambold was entitled to some damages, an echo of the decision in Magone's Montana case.

The farmers had lost yet again. This time, however, economic forces intervened where activism was unable and the courts unwilling. The Great Depression dealt a swift and brutal blow to metal prices, with the exception of gold. The Sunnyside, like most other base-metal-reliant mines, suspended operations in 1930, and stayed dark for most of the decade, reopening briefly in 1937. Only Chase's Shenandoah-Dives Mine, along with a handful of other smaller operations, kept churning out ore during the early 1930s, in part thanks to a deal Chase struck with his 240 employees to lower their wages until the hard times were through.

Pending cases against the mills continued to crawl their way through the courts, and in 1935 the downstreamers scored a substantial victory. The Colorado Supreme Court went four-to-three in favor of Jefferson County farmers on Clear Creek, ruling that tailings from mines and mills could not be dumped into running streams. The decision didn't result in immediate changes on the ground, but it did lay the foundation on which farmers, sportsmen, and other downstreamers could build their cases against the mining industry. And it gave the enforcers of the weak stream-protection laws additional leverage if they chose to wield it.

Chase promised to stop dumping tailings from the Mayflower Mill within thirty days of the decision, and by 1936 he had devised a reasonably effective system for containing the waste. Chase's impoundment system wasn't high tech by any means, just sand-walled settling ponds, something that any mining company could have built easily in the 1880s or 1890s. But it was cheap and relatively effective, which makes the industry-wide delay in implementing such systems more maddening. Other, smaller mines in the Animas River watershed continued to flout the court ruling through the early 1950s. And the tailings ponds put in place by Chase occasionally failed, most notably in 1947, 1964, and 1975, dumping thousands of tons of slime into the water once again.

Between 1870 and 1936, the mines and mills dumped an estimated eight million to nine million metric tons of tailings into the streams of the upper Animas watershed, according to a USGS report written by Bill Jones, a longtime Silverton mining man and historian. Much of it was carried downstream more than one hundred miles, altering the water chemistry and killing or hurting fish and insects and plants along the way. As it slid toward the San Juan and then Colorado River and then the sea, the slime settled out into the riverbed, particularly in the slow-moving parts, such as in the Animas Valley. Some of it remains today, mixed in with all those lost souls.

Strike

I dreamed I saw Joe Hill last night, alive as you and me,
Says I, But Joe you're ten years dead,
I never died, said he, I never died, said he.
The copper bosses killed you Joe,
They shot you Joe, says I.
Takes more than that to kill a man, says Joe, I didn't die.
And standing there as big as life and smiling with his eyes,
Says Joe, What they can never kill went on to organize.
From San Diego up to Maine in every mine and mill
Where working men defend their rights
It's there you'll find Joe Hill.

—Alfred Hayes

SOFT ORANGE LIGHT LICKED INTO THE COOL JULY NIGHT, illuminating the rusty steel grid of the tram tower and the quivering leaves of aspens and the faces of the standing men, staring into the bonfire, talking about nothing at all. The mood was festive, infused with a touch of nervousness, but the men were not partying, they were on duty, vigilantly listening for the telltale whir of cable against wheel, of the tram kicking into operation. Their job: make sure no workers went up to the Shenandoah-Dives Mine, and that no ore came back down to the mill. The 1939 Silverton strike was on.

Joe Todeschi was there that night, lean and young and wiry, with a hooked, crooked nose like some Roman welterweight fighter. Just twenty-four years old, he'd already worked enough for a man twice his age, milling ore, placing and spiking ties on the Silverton and Northern Railroad, drilling rocks to make way for the highway up at the Champion Cliffs. A year earlier, he'd gotten a job at the only real mine still running, the Shenandoah-Dives, working under Italian stone mason Carlo Palone to build a massive "slide-splitter"—a stone and concrete monolith placed above tram towers and other infrastructure to protect them from avalanches.[44]

This was Todeschi's first labor action, and so far it was a pretty good deal. To keep morale strong, the union threw picnics and parties and doled out enough money to the strikers to keep their families fed. Within weeks, however, things would go bad, real bad.

PRESIDENT FRANKLIN D. ROOSEVELT'S NEW DEAL PUMPED SOME LIFE BACK INTO MINING COUNTRY in the form of federal incentives and subsidies. But for the corporations running the mines it was a mixed bag. New regulations, particularly regarding labor, were also part of the deal.

Beginning in 1936, the Silverton Miners Union Local #26 (an affiliate of the Congress of Industrial Organizations, or CIO) began making demands on Chase and the Shenandoah-Dives for safer conditions, higher wages, and more union-friendly hiring practices. Although not all of the union demands were met, the union and the company were able to come to agreements and contracts were signed in 1936, 1937, and June of

1938. As the summer of 1938 dragged on, however, tensions between the workers and the Shenandoah-Dives began to build.

In the beginning, the *Silverton Standard* was with the union. "Wages are none too high in San Juan County, and while higher as a rule than in some of the past years of the industry, are paid to men doing more work and making greater output than in any time in the history of mining." Indeed, during 1938 San Juan County produced metals valued at $2,437,952, a sixteen percent increase over the previous year.

In November of that year, Congress passed the Wage-Hour Law, requiring that overtime wages be paid to a worker once he exceeds forty-four hours of work in a week. Since miners worked as many as sixty hours a week, the new law would cost mine owners dearly. Chase, like many managers, found a way around the new law. He paid the required overtime, but not until he had reduced hourly wages for all of his employees. The miners continued to work sixty hours a week with paychecks that remained about the same as before the law was passed.

The union was not impressed. The following spring, local union leaders passed a resolution that read, in part: "Those opposed to our Democratic form of government are the ones who live in hopes of forcing upon the American People the Fascist and Nazi forms of government which are un-American as they are opposed to unions, freedom of speech, press, and assembly." Immediately following the posting of this decree, the union went to the National Labor Relations Board and accused Chase of unfair labor practices, setting the foundations for a strike. Negotiations dragged on for months before finally collapsing in July 1939, when the union voted 175–48 in favor of striking.

Chase argued that the mine was unable to afford to pay the overtime required by the Wage-Hours Law and he appealed to the union and the community to work together in the spirit of cooperation that had carried them through the crisis of 1932. The union responded by agreeing to compromise on its overtime demands but not on seniority and closed-shop demands. With community support still behind the union, no agreement was reached.

In the meantime, following standard strike practice, A. S. Embree, a representative of the CIO, was called in by the union to help organize the strike and keep it running smoothly. Embree, a veteran of many union actions throughout the West's mining country and protégée of labor hero William "Big Bill" Haywood, arrived in high spirits. Silverton was well known as a pro-union town, and the Local #26 had been a stalwart of the community for decades. The newspaper had come out in favor of the strike, as had many town businesses. Victory seemed assured.

Even then, however, inklings of discontent sat beneath the surface. Gerald Swanson, who was a child during the strike, and whose ancestors, like Todeschi's, immigrated from the Trentino region of Italy, remembers other kids calling him "Swanson scab" because his father, a butcher, opposed the strike. A handful of other merchants also questioned the wisdom of battling against the only big mine left, as did some of the Shenandoah-Dives' foremen and shift bosses. The company also had the sympathy of the businesspeople of Durango, a town known for its anti-labor attitude.

By the middle of August, when the union voted to continue the strike, the relatively friendly relations between the company and the union began to bitter. Chase unleashed a vicious campaign to turn public opinion against the union. "The present situation started," said Chase in an August 22 speech, "when an avowed communist came into the mining camp and preached class hatred and other principles of communism."

The company printed out anti-union propaganda leaflets and circulated them throughout the town. A few days later, the San Juan County Board of Commissioners cast doubt on the legality of the strike, and asked in a resolution whether "workers are being illegally restrained from working?" Public opinion was changing rapidly. Idleness and resentment bubbled into tension. And on the evening of August 28, just six weeks after the strike began, the conflict reached an ugly climax.

It was a warm evening, at least for Silverton, the kind where you linger out on the porch in shirtsleeves with a cold beer in your hand, watching the last light illuminate Kendall Mountain, and think about all the trouble you could get into if you were just a little younger. A big crowd gathered inside the Miners Union Hall, a brick building on Silverton's main drag that would later become the Miner's Tavern, for a regular meeting and update on the strike. The tension was palpable. The miners hadn't worked in six weeks. They were antsy, anxious, pent up.

Rumors had been spreading that a group of insurgents—with the company's backing—would try to build support for a vote that night to end the strike. Unable to stay away, Chase, wearing his trademark round spectacles, fedora, and light-colored suit, drove around town slowly, passing the Union Hall on occasion to see if the plan was reaching fruition. The meeting remained fairly calm, however; the insurgency either got cold feet or couldn't muster the votes they needed. Yet outside the Hall, a crowd had begun to gather. Frank "Corky" Scheer, a compact but pugnacious miner, ardently anti-union, was there, as was mine foreman William Hughes, and other Shenandoah-Dives middle management.

At about eight p.m., as dusk took hold, the meeting ended and the union men came streaming out, eager to escape the stifling heat that two hundred people packed into a room in August can generate, and to get home or to the bar to blow off some steam. But like a river backing up behind an ice dam, the crowd slowed and eddied up as it encountered the growing pack outside. Faces scrunched and flushed with anger. A shout. Spittle. A fist thrown. "Several of the union members were attacked by the mob," a witness testified in a National Labor Relations Board hearing months later. "Frank Scheer initiated the hostilities by kicking Embree . . . eight to ten others then closed in on Embree. When John Hancock tried to come to Embree's assistance, he in turn was set upon. Scheer caught Hancock as he was running toward the union hall and threw him in the gutter. Meanwhile, Bert Ady was beaten by Claude Deering. Aaron Harper was also beaten."

After the union leaders had been roughed up, the sheriff and chief of police, clearly in the pocket of the company, ambled into the fray and escorted Embree and others out of town, ". . . for their own safety." The Ouray newspaper reported gleefully that when they were brought through Ouray, the men's clothes were torn, they were bruised, and their faces showed the "nail marks of irate miners' wives."

What was left of the crowd then convened their own meeting, dissolved the local union, and created a new one, the San Juan Federation of Mine, Mill, and Smelter Workers—a sham organization—with Scheer at the helm. It would later be revealed that Scheer had been hired by the company to break the strike, and that he had planned the union coup weeks in advance, even going so far as using Shenandoah-Dives money to get cards printed for the bogus Federation in blatant disregard of labor laws. In the coming days, the new "union" ended the strike and signed a contract with Shenandoah-Dives.

Those who remained loyal to the Local #26 were threatened, harassed, and discriminated against. "The town was split in two," recalled Todeschi when I interviewed him in 1996 (he died in 2011). "Either you were for or you were against the company union." Todeschi and his stepfather refused to join the strike-breakers, making life difficult for years to come.

Clyde Cerniway was a teenager in 1939. His father, Frank, was a Shenandoah-Dives employee and union member who went on strike, and like Todeschi refused to join the new, sham union. In a 1996 interview, Cerniway remembered the day, shortly after the strike was busted, that a car full of men pulled up to his Snowden Street house. "Three of the men in the car had artillery," said Cerniway, "and two were law enforcement people." The men ordered the family to leave town. While his family defied the order, many others caved in to the threats and left, never to return.

"The strike was broken by a mob of Company officials and business men of town," reads a 1941 letter from the Silverton Ladies Auxiliary to the International Union of Mine, Mill, and Smelter Workers. "Several CIO members and their families were driven from town and lives were threatened. We have very little relief as the whole town and county setup are against us. All CIO members are blacklisted throughout the state and many other states."

The demise of the Local #26 was far less bloody than the labor-related clashes that had broken out in Trinidad and Telluride a few decades earlier. Yet it was no less significant. Chase and his hired goons had managed to channel the anger and resentment of a few working-class men and turn it with chilling effect against their own allies. It was made to look like a populist revolt against elitist, socialist outsiders. In fact, it was suppression of the people by the moneyed elite—the Kansas City Shenandoah-Dives Syndicate—who were unwilling to give up a little bit of profit to make workers' lives a bit more bearable. Think Silverton, 1902 (when the Chinese were run out of town); Germany, 1932; or the United States, 2016.

The union that had watched the local workingman's back, and served as an unwavering pillar of the community since the 1880s, had itself been stabbed in the back on that August night. Organized labor in Silverton was dead. But it was more than that. This was a piece of something far larger, a tectonic global tilt toward modernity, sparked by world war, by scientists on a New Mexico mesa, by a flash of blinding light and tens of thousands dead in an instant halfway across the world. It would crash into the American West after the war, a giant wave of people, machines, prosperity, and destruction, leaving no ranch, no forest, no town untouched.

PART II

Fossils

Moving Mountain

CARBON MOUNTAIN, JUST SOUTH OF DURANGO, MOVED. MORE THAN THAT, IT *ERUPTED* — "The whole hill is quaking, grunting, groaning," wrote a reporter for the *Durango News* on a December morning in 1932. "Boulders, large and small and hundreds of tons of earth continue toppling from the crest of (Carbon) Mountain. Every few minutes a great cluster of boulders would break loose. Clouds of dust marked their pathway as they shot out into space, landing in the valley to the north."

The next morning hundreds of Durango folks headed south of town to the once unremarkable hill, located where the Animas River slices through the Hogback Monocline, to witness the geologic temper tantrum. Others flocked in from out of town, then out of state, and even from abroad. *Popular Mechanics* magazine sent someone to report back on "this huge mass of rock and earth, apparently loosened by some mysterious, subterranean disturbance . . . unlike any other such earth movement known to scientists who have visited it." A young man set up a hot dog stand near the mountain's base to capitalize on all the gawkers, and Carbon Mountain got a new, albeit unofficial moniker: Moving Mountain.

Eventually the mountain's jitters—possibly the result of subterranean coal fires encountering pockets of methane—eased. But not before reminding the people of the region that they were sitting atop a veritable bonanza—or bomb—of volatile substances that were becoming more and more valued by our fossil-fueled, industrial civilization.

IF, FOR THE OLDER SOCIETIES THAT MOVED ACROSS THIS LAND, GEOGRAPHY WAS DETERMINANT; if Place with a capital P dictated who these people were and how they lived, then for our modern extractive society, geology is destiny. The San Juan Basin, a ten-thousand-square-mile swath of mesas, valleys, and badlands, stretching from the edge of Durango down to Gallup, from Cuba, New Mexico, to around Shiprock, was once the edge of a vast, shallow, inland sea. At times the sea covered the area, its salty waters teeming with creatures big and small. Later, the shoreline receded, and a marshy, fecund swamp through which dinosaurs crashed emerged. It was a hot and sultry place, rife with flora and fauna.

That life is still here. The trees, the sharks, the dinosaurs, the birds, the weird-looking fish. They've been transformed by time, heat, and pressure into hydrocarbons, into vast underground storehouses of coal, methane, oil; fossil fuels, black gold, prehistoric sunshine. Drill or dig deeply enough almost anywhere in the basin and you'll eventually encounter hydrocarbons of one sort or another. Along parts of the Hogback Monocline, however, one need not dig at all. Think of it this way: if the basin were a big bowl, and you placed a multi-layered piece of carpet over that bowl, and piled dirt and rock on top of the carpet, the middle of the carpet would sink into the bowl while the edges would angle upward. The carpet represents layers of hydrocarbon-rich sandstone, shale, and coal. In the center of the basin, these strata are deeply buried. The upward-angling edge of the carpet, and the layers it represents, is the Hogback Monocline. Coal outcrops are often visible along the monocline, and methane and even oil sometimes ooze from it, particularly where rivers slice through it.

In the early 1920s, a herd of oilmen from Standard Oil, Standard Oil of Indiana, and Midwest Refining were hankering to drill for oil near where the San Juan River cuts through the Hogback formation.[45] There was one big obstacle in their way, though. The oil was on Diné land, and because of the Diné's ad hoc form of government at the time, it was tough to get permission to drill. Lucky for the oil companies, they had a friend in Washington, D.C., by the name of Albert Bacon Fall, President Warren G. Harding's Secretary of the Interior. Fall would become best known for his role in the Teapot Dome Scandal, but he had a far longer-lasting influence over the Navajo Nation's form of governance, and the development of its natural resources.

FALL WAS BORN INTO A POOR HOUSEHOLD IN KENTUCKY IN 1861, and by the time he was eleven was already working in the cotton mills. He soon headed west, first to Oklahoma, then to Texas, and finally, in 1885, to Kingston, New Mexico, east of Silver City, where he tried his hand at prospecting and, after failing at that, took up work as a ranch hand. In Kingston, Fall met another prospector, Edward L. Doheny, and the two became friends. It would be a fateful meeting. Doheny would go on to drill the first successful oil well in the Los Angeles basin, becoming a millionaire tycoon in the process and serving as inspiration for Upton Sinclair's novel *Oil!*, which in turn was the basis for the 2007 film *There Will Be Blood*.

In the 1890s, Fall entered New Mexico territorial politics, serving as a territorial representative and as attorney general. During a break from politics he practiced law and defended various notorious gunfighters, including the alleged killers of one of his former political rivals. In 1912, he was elected as one of the brand new state's first senators, and continued to serve until 1921, when Harding appointed him Secretary of the Interior. Together, Harding, a friend of corporations, and Fall, a consummate, cigar-smoking Westerner, were ready to squash the conservation ethic that President Theodore Roosevelt and Forest Service Chief Gifford Pinchot had brought to the nation's capital two decades earlier.

Fall was from the Manifest Destiny school of land use, and saw the West as a big grab bag of oil, gas, coal, timber, and minerals. He generally supported keeping most public land in public hands, but he believed that the resources of those lands should be available, without regulatory hindrance, to developers. His ideology extended to the Naval Oil Reserves, which he managed to open up to general leasing, and to Indian reservations, which fall under the auspices of the Interior Department. "All natural resources should be made as easy of access as possible to the present generation," he once said. "Man cannot exhaust the resources of nature and never will."

The oil companies looking to drill the Navajo Nation were not getting that easy access, however. Prior to the Euro-American invasion of Diné lands, the Navajo tribe was divided up into political units of a dozen or more families, each governed by their own *naataanii*, or headmen. That system collapsed during the brutality of the 1860s, when U.S. soldiers oppressed and abused the Diné, forcing them to march to southeastern

New Mexico, where they were incarcerated for four years. After they returned, a system of governance somewhat similar to the old one re-emerged, with headmen leading six "agencies" across the reservation.

The coveted Hogback oil was within the San Juan Agency based in Shiprock. The companies repeatedly begged the agency leaders to let them drill. The agency repeatedly refused until finally, late in 1921, the agency's headmen gave in on the condition that Midwest Refining hire Diné workers and pay higher-than-average wages. Midwest soon hit a gusher that produced three hundred barrels per day of some of the highest-grade oil in the United States at the time. Everyone wanted a piece of the action.

Fall saw that the Diné's decentralized system could hamper his efforts to develop the West. So he worked various channels in Washington, D.C., to grease the skids for his friends in the oil business. Then he went to work on the tribe itself. To sign off on leases on tribal lands, he created a Navajo Business Council, made up of three of his own appointees: Chee Dodge, Charlie Mitchell, and Daagha'chii Bikiss. All three were Diné with strong links to the white business community, Fall, or both. He ordered that any royalties from drilling on Diné land go to the entire tribe, not just the agency from which it came.

Bureau of Indian Affairs Commissioner Charles H. Burke saw that the Business Council was iffy from a democratic point of view, given that the members weren't elected. So he and Fall set out to plan a centralized, representative-style Navajo tribal council, with delegates from each agency. They assigned New Mexican politician Herbert Hagerman to be the special commissioner to "negotiate with the Indians." Then they laid their plan on the Diné.

These tricks didn't go unnoticed. Up in Durango, Colorado, the gadfly *Democrat* newspaper (edited by Dave Day's son Ron) saw the moves for what they were. A lengthy story on the matter in February 1923 was headlined, "Navajo Indians Almost on War Path As Result Of New Ruling." This "2nd Teapot Dome" for Fall was not only a giveaway to Standard Oil and Midwest, but also tinkered with the Diné's traditional system of government:

To understand just what had taken place it is necessary to explain that the Navajos have governed themselves ever since the treaty of peace with the whites was signed in 1868 as a pure democracy. . . . Oil leases were voted by the councils on such terms as the councils determined and no one, not even the secretary of the interior himself, had the power to alter those terms. . . . Today on the blackboard at the Shiprock agency was posted a departmental order doing entirely away with the old order of things and substituting a representative government for the democracy.

Though many Diné weren't happy about it, voters (only men at that point) elected twenty-four delegates, and in July 1923 the first tribal council was seated. The delegates chose Chee Dodge as Chairman, and promptly gave Hagerman all oil and gas leasing negotiating power. So much for tribal sovereignty.

Fall resigned later that year after it was revealed that his old buddy, oil tycoon Ed Doheny, had given Fall a one-hundred-thousand-dollar interest-free loan, and that fellow tycoon Harry Sinclair had bought into Fall's ranch. Shortly thereafter, Fall had issued leases to the two men to drill for oil in Naval Reserves in Elk Hill, California, and Teapot Dome, Wyoming, respectively. Fall was eventually tried and sentenced to nine months for accepting bribes.[46] Doheny managed to avoid being convicted of making the same bribe, and to top it off foreclosed upon Fall's ranch.

Fall's role in the Diné situation was never similarly scrutinized, though its impacts were probably greater. Fall had managed to open the Navajo Nation's door to the oilmen, their white commissioner handing out leases left and right, on his, not the Diné's, terms. The reservation town of Shiprock was in the middle of all of it, but reaped few of the benefits—the oil and gas companies tended to put their local headquarters in the predominantly white towns of Farmington or Aztec. Royalties from leasing were managed, or rather mismanaged, by the feds, and only a fraction made it back to the tribe, even less to the agencies in which drilling took place.

IT WAS LIKE THE GOLD RUSH ALL OVER AGAIN. Wildcatters descended on the region looking to drill outside investors' pocketbooks more than anything. Apocryphal stories abound of drilling rights changing hands in backroom card games, of shady deals with the Diné, of slapdash and rickety drill rigs falling apart in the Tocito Dome or Rattlesnake fields, of workers having to flee the drill site because the wind changed direction, which could lead to an explosion. To stimulate oil or gas flow in new wells, drillers tossed dynamite or nitroglycerine down the bores, a crude and potentially deadly precursor to the hydraulic fracturing that would one day revolutionize the industry.

When it came to the environment, the oil and gas fields were mostly lawless. Mine-related pollution is at least somewhat visible. You see the acid mine drainage eat away at a shovel and coat a stream bed with ferricrete. The tailings mucking up the water can't be missed. With the exception of oil spills, however, drilling's effects take place deep underground and may not manifest themselves for years or decades. Accidental spills were routine. "Produced water," the ancient, deep groundwater that accompanies oil and gas when it emerges from the well, and which is always brackish and often contaminated with hydrocarbons, heavy metals, and is even radioactive, was dumped by the thousands of gallons onto the earth or into washes. Drillers going after oil would simply vent the accompanying natural gas—which is mostly made up of the potent greenhouse gas methane—directly into the air.

Yet no one seemed to care. In the early 1920s an Oklahoma oilman came to Colorado to express concerns about oil migrating through the well bore to other subterranean layers and contaminating them. He wasn't concerned about groundwater that might one day emerge as a spring, or about poisoning people's wells, his worry was that the oil would contaminate the natural-gas-laden sands, thus rendering both the oil and gas unrecoverable.

In the early 1920s near the town of Aztec, one of the first natural gas wells drilled in the region was so pressurized that it shot huge tools one hundred feet into the air, thus sparking the natural gas rush that would ultimately define the region. The gas was piped into Aztec, then Farmington. A new pipeline carried gas to Albuquerque and another to Durango, where the coal power plant on the Animas River was converted to natural gas power in the 1930s. Still, demand couldn't keep up with new supply. So in 1951 El Paso Natural Gas opened up a new, large-capacity pipeline from the San Juan Basin to the border of California to tap into the burgeoning markets of postwar Los Angeles and San Diego. The effect on the local communities echoed that brought by the railroad's arrival in Silverton seven decades earlier.

In 1950 there were 245 producing oil and gas wells in the Basin. Five years later 1,600 wells siphoned hydrocarbons from their ancient subterranean lairs. Tens of thousands of apple, apricot, pear, and peach trees, their bounty once shipped by the trainload to Chicago and New York, were replaced by well pads, processing plants, gathering systems, and the "aluminum ghetto" trailer parks in which the workers, newcomers almost all of them, lived. San Juan County's population jumped from eighteen thousand in 1950 to fifty-three thousand in 1960, and the humble agricultural town of Farmington blew past industrial Durango to become the region's economic hub and population center. Transient labor flooded in from the oil and gas fields of Texas and Oklahoma—roughneck nomads, following the drill rigs like the Utes once followed the seasonal migrations of the deer and the elk.

When one fossil fuel commodity slumped, another would be there to keep a true bust at bay. Four Corners Power Plant was constructed in phases between 1963 and 1970; construction of the San Juan Generating Station, a mere eight miles away, began in 1973. Each burned more than a thousand tons of coal per day to generate electricity sent hundreds of miles over federally subsidized high-voltage transmission lines to Phoenix, Albuquerque, Las Vegas, and Los Angeles. Explosions shot gray earth into the sky. Draglines towered like skyscrapers over the spare, scrub-dotted land, shovels the size of houses exhuming the fossilized swamp. Ancient trees and soil and flora, millions of years in the making, were converted in moments to heat, smoke, earth-warming carbon dioxide, acid-rain-forming sulfur dioxide, mercury, arsenic, ash, all pouring from the looming smokestacks by the metric ton, day after day after day. The inky black plume issuing from the Four Corners Power Plant was one of the only man-made objects visible to the astronauts on the Apollo space flights.

Downstream on the San Juan, pumpjacks in the Aneth Oil Field on the Utah portion of the Navajo Nation did their slow grind, sucking millions of barrels of crude from the earth beginning in the late 1950s. The early wells and infrastructure were shoddy, and tainted produced water was dumped wherever seemed convenient at the time. It wasn't long before springs used by the Diné for generations became brackish and undrinkable, even for the sheep. In 1972, a pipeline leading out of the Aneth Field burst, spilling nearly three hundred thousand gallons of crude, which ran down a wash and into the San Juan River. The oil slick floated two hundred miles downriver, past Diné communities, Bluff and Mexican Hat, Utah, and beyond, a petrochemical precursor to the Gold King spill. Petroleum killed countless fish and coated rocks, birds, and beavers on the way. The fledgling Environmental Protection Agency led the multi-agency cleanup effort on the San Juan branch of Lake Powell, one of its first big actions.

The social fabric, shaped by ranching and farming, was torn asunder. Some might say the region was infected with Gillette Syndrome; others would call it mass culture shock. The newcomers overwhelmed the existing population, culture, and lifestyle, particularly that of the indigenous people. The Four Corners Power Plant and the adjacent mine displaced dozens of Diné families from their homes and their traditional grazing lands, and hundreds more were pulled from an agrarian economy into a wage-based, industrial one nearly overnight.

At the height of the 1950s natural gas boom, the federal

government lifted the ban on selling alcohol to Native Americans, even as the Navajo Nation continued its policy of prohibition. It was a boon for the booze industry in reservation border towns like Farmington and Gallup, New Mexico. The bars and liquor joints that followed the roughnecks now had a vast and thirsty new market to exploit—the poor, the disenfranchised, the hopeless, and those looking to drown two centuries of sorrows in a bottle of California Delight or Tokay. Business boomed.

The oil and gas workers and others partook in the mass drinking binge, as well, but they could drag themselves back to their Farmington homes or trailers during their benders. Not so the alcohol pilgrims from deep on the reservation. A subpopulation, the publicly inebriated, emerged on the streets and alleys and in parking lots and borrow ditches, primed for further victimization. A whole new economic sector grew up in reservation border towns to fuel and profit off of the sickness, including pawnshops, blood-for-cash places, and bustling bottle- and can-recycling centers.

Cops hauled thousands of people each year to the drunk tank, which was little more than a cage where people could sleep it off before being released to get drunk again. Cirrhosis killed many, but hundreds of others each year died more quickly—killed when they passed out and froze to death on long winter nights, or staggered out in front of traffic. One stretch of highway near the Turquoise Bar, strategically located on the edge of the reservation next to the Hogback Monocline, was so deadly for pedestrians that it was referred to as "Slaughter Alley."

White high school kids roamed "Navajo skid row" in Farmington in search of victims to assault and rob of what little money or other belongings they had on them. While not overtly condoned, the white police officers and community members tended to pass this racist violence off as a relatively harmless hobby, or they'd blame the victims. As a local assistant county district attorney put it in the early 1970s, there was an attitude "that is conducive to treating Navajos and intoxicated persons not like people but like things."[47] Then, in April 1974, as the energy crisis sent another boom rippling through the region, a group of teens took their pastime to a gruesome new level. The bodies of three Diné men were found on Farmington's fringe. They had been severely beaten, tortured, and burned. Three local white kids were arrested and convicted of the crimes. Yet because they were juveniles—and presumably because the victims were Native Americans—the murderers were sentenced only to a few years at New Mexico Boys School.

The white community was shocked, the Diné community outraged. No one was surprised. The killings were not isolated or random. "We didn't see the murders as the act of three crazy kids," Diné community organizer John Redhouse told an interviewer in 1974. "We saw it as part of a whole racist picture." The killers had been part of the wave of outsiders crashing into the region for the jobs in the gas patch. As such, they were merely cogs in a violent, colonial machine that had been set in motion decades earlier, its sole purpose to displace indigenous people from their homelands to make way for the mining firms, the oil companies, and even the farmers to exploit the resources of that land for profit.

The Farmington murders fueled the Native American movement that had risen up to resist the machine. Tribal leaders took to the streets and the courts to exert their sovereignty as human beings and as nations, and the tribes took control of the oil, coal, and uranium within their lands. Nevertheless, the machine of resource colonization continues to churn away even today.

"This can't be the United States"

TO DRIVE WEST OUT OF FARMINGTON IS TO TRAVEL THROUGH THE BORDERLAND, where the northeastern edge of the Navajo Nation melds with the non-Indian world. It's a cultural and economic mishmash. Here's a sex store next to a plumbing supply shop across the highway from a sprawling automobile burial ground not far from a Mennonite church. Justalaundry, Zia Liquors, Family Dollar, and numerous little booths or shacks where Diné sell kneel down bread or tamales or piñon nuts to passersby. And the "quick cash" joints that have sprouted like weeds in Gallup, Farmington, and other reservation border towns, preying on the poor, the desperate, and the "unbanked" with their thousand-percent interest loans. It's just an update of the exploitative pawn shops of yore. "It's a border town, and tribes around it constitute economic colonies," John Redhouse, who grew up in Farmington, told me, adding that things haven't improved that much since the 1970s.

Trailers perched on cinder blocks, tires on a roof. An old man in a recliner, sipping a tumbler of warm whiskey, selling his junk. Down in the lush Jewett Valley a sign pointing to an old metal building reads: "RABBITS GOATS CHICKS AVON AT DOUBLEWIDE." Just up the road, the Original Sweetmeat Inc., aka "Mutton Lover's Heaven," a slaughterhouse and butcher shop, sits alongside the highway and the Shumway Arroyo.

A few miles north looms the San Juan Generating Station, built in 1973 in the arroyo. Eight miles away, on the Navajo side of the river, sits the older, larger Four Corners Power Plant.

The Original Sweetmeats is owned and run by Raymond "Squeak" Hunt, a tall, gruff man prone to muttering inscrutable aphorisms, who deals mostly with mutton, or sheep (as opposed to lamb), and sells to a mostly Diné clientele. "You may think I'm one hard, mean son-of-a-bitch," Hunt told me when I first met him in 2002, as he unloaded a trailer full of sheep, bound for slaughter. "But it hurts me every time I kill one of these animals."

I wasn't there for the sheep, though. I was visiting because Hunt is surely the most stubborn—if unlikely—thorn in the corporate side of Public Service Company of New Mexico, the operators of San Juan Generating Station and the supplier of electricity to the entire state. That doesn't make him unique; hundreds of activists have agitated against the air pollution from the two coal plants' smokestacks over the decades. But Hunt was one of the most ferocious fighters against a rarely noticed form of pollution spilling out of the plants: the slag, ash, and dust left over from burning coal, otherwise known as coal combustion waste.

Hunt has lived here, along the banks of the Shumway Arroyo, for much of his life. Prior to 1973 the upper reaches of the Shumway contained water only after rains. Once the arroyo reaches the San Juan River Valley near Hunt's place, however, irrigation return and groundwater resulted in the arroyo's transformation to a perennial stream. The stream was a source for both domestic and livestock water for early settlers of the Jewett Valley, including Hunt's family.

When construction began on the large, mine-mouth, coal-burning power plant a few miles upstream alongside the arroyo, the arroyo changed. Coal power plants require vast amounts of water to function, and when SJGS went on-line in 1973, the plant dumped its wastewater and just about everything else into the Shumway. From that time on, the previously dry arroyo became a perennial stream from the plant to the river. Downstream users in Waterflow, in the meantime, continued to drink out of wells fed by the arroyo's flows and their livestock kept drinking straight out of the stream.

Like the slightly larger Four Corners Power Plant, which was constructed a decade earlier, San Juan Generating Station's smokestacks were subject to virtually no regulation. During its first decades of operation, Four Corners became notorious for the black plume of smoke—hundreds of tons of sulfur dioxide and fly ash each day—that it sent into the region's previously crystal clear skies. One account says that one plant produced more smog than New York City. With the addition of SJGS, the air quality in the region deteriorated, vistas were cut short by smog, and the one thing that remained visible from far away were the plumes emitted by the stacks.

It did not take long for citizen groups from around the region to protest the deterioration in the quality of their air. General citizen pressure and lawsuits forced the 1977 Clean Air Act to include a policy preventing the degradation of air quality. In 1978, San Juan Generating Station installed controls to reduce smokestack emissions and Four Corners followed in 1980. Air pollution from the plants was significantly reduced.

Other pollution was not.

When coal is burned the carbon reacts with oxygen to form carbon dioxide. But coal is a lot more than just carbon. It's got sulfur in it, which becomes sulfur dioxide during combustion, the main cause of acid rain. It contains a host of other elements, most notably arsenic, mercury, and selenium, some of which waft from the stack as smoke and particulates. Most end up as solid waste of one form or another. Each year, power plants in the United States collectively kick out enough of this stuff to fill a train of coal cars stretching from Manhattan to Los Angeles and back three times. It's stored in lagoons next to power plants, buried in old coal mines, and sometimes piled up in the open. It is the largest waste stream of most power plants, and a study by the Environmental Protection Agency found that people exposed to it had a much higher than average risk of getting cancer.

"Anybody who knows anything about coal ash chemistry knows that when you burn coal, what you have leftover is dramatically different from what you had originally," Jeff Stant, a geologist with the Clean Air Task Force, told me back in 2002. Coal ash can contain seventeen metals. Some, like mercury or arsenic, are already toxic, others become more so during combustion.

Because every pound of pollution kept out of the air ends up in the solid waste stream, the pollution control methods in the stacks only made the problem on the ground worse. The solid waste consists of fine and dusty fly ash; a gravelly, gray material called bottom ash; and the relatively benign glassy clinkers or boiler slag. The stack scrubbers that pull sulfur dioxide and nitrogen oxide out of the smoke create perhaps the most malignant material, called scrubber sludge. All of that was typically piled up near the plant, where it could blow into the air, or get washed into an arroyo, or leach into the ground. In San Juan Generating Station's case, the stuff was dumped right into or near Shumway Arroyo—an echo of the hardrock mining tailings that had been similarly dumped for decades one hundred miles upstream.

In the early 1980s, people who lived along the Shumway Arroyo and drank from wells began getting sick. Hunt suffered from muscle spasms, lost sixty pounds, and had a cornucopia of other problems. "I looked like a POW after World War II," he said. His wife and kids got sick; his neighbors, too.

Though Hunt's illness was never definitively traced to a specific cause, he and other activists are pretty sure some of the stuff in coal combustion waste made it into his water. Around the time Hunt got sick, researchers found extraordinarily high levels of selenium—which tends to be highly concentrated in coal combustion waste—in the Shumway Arroyo. His symptoms match those of selenium poisoning. His illness may have also come from ingesting too much lead, cadmium, arsenic, mercury, or sulfates, all of which are commonly concentrated in coal combustion waste.

Whatever the poison, it soon became clear that the water was tainted. Those who were sick sued the Public Service Company of New Mexico, which operates the plant; the company never admitted fault, but ultimately settled with the affected families. It also tightened up its waste disposal, becoming one of the first power plants in the nation to go to a zero discharge permit, which means it can't release any water onto the land. After a lot of legal wrangling, Hunt settled, too.

Hunt, however, remains convinced that the power plant continues to sully the water in the arroyo. He says that water leaks from retention ponds, coal-washing, and dust-control spraying, and even if it's clean, it picks up and remobilizes contaminants in the sediments of the arroyo, left by the dumping in the 1970s and '80s. During the late 1990s and early 2000s, 1,400 of Hunt's sheep, all of which had drunk from the Shumway Arroyo, got sick and died or had to be killed. Hunt blamed Public Service Company of New Mexico, or PNM, the state's biggest electricity provider. The utility said negligence on Hunt's part killed the sheep, with the help of minerals occurring naturally in the arroyo and the water. The utility and Hunt have been at loggerheads for years in very public ways. On their way home from work every day, the power plant's employees have no choice but to see a giant billboard erected by Hunt on his property, bashing both PNM and New Mexico's environmental regulators. A smaller sign above the big billboard reads: "WAKE UP you bunch of NUTS we ALL live DOWNSTREAM."

Hunt's fight isn't limited to his own situation, though. He's also worked to shine a light on the coal combustion waste issue in general. Despite the magnitude of the waste stream, and its potentially deleterious effects on human and environmental health, coal combustion waste disposal is regulated much like normal landfills are. The EPA has for decades worked on new rules, implementing some, letting others fall by the wayside.

"I hope you have a cast-iron stomach," said Hunt as we walked over to the little stand by the road where a Diné couple was selling, along with jewelry, bowls of extremely hot chili and kneel down bread. The lamb sandwiches inside looked good at first, but after a tour of the slaughterhouse and witnessing a sheep get stunned, decapitated, and dressed, I opted for the chili. We sat in a shady spot next to the parking lot and watched a steady stream of customers go into the butcher shop and haul out racks of lamb and mutton, chops, and something a Diné man called *b'chee*, little strips of meat or fat wrapped up in sheep intestines that Hunt's wife prepared.

After eating, as the afternoon clouds moved in along with a stiff breeze, we climbed into Hunt's truck and he drove us to the south side of the river, toward Four Corners Power Plant. We followed a dirt road skirting Morgan Lake, in the shadow of the soot-stained smokestacks of the plant. Each year about nine billion gallons of water are brought up from the San Juan River to form this reservoir, then it's circulated through the plant to cool the massive generators and for other purposes. The hot water is discharged back into the reservoir, so Lake Morgan is warm and steamy, even in winter, making it a popular, if surreal, windsurfing and fishing spot.

When early provisions of the 1970 Clean Air Act first were being implemented in the early 1970s, the smokestacks looming over Lake Morgan kicked out more than four thousand pounds of mercury each year, along with thousands of pounds of selenium and copper and hundreds more pounds of lead, arsenic, and cadmium, not to mention sulfur dioxide, nitrogen oxide, and other pollutants. Thanks to federal air pollution regulations, and to activists who push the government to enforce those rules, emissions have decreased considerably over the years. Now, with only two of five units still in operation, the plant puts out about 150 pounds of mercury and 520 pounds of selenium each year, along with varying quantities of other toxic metals. Most of these pollutants are then deposited in the surrounding water, on the land, and on homes. For years, rain and snow falling on Mesa Verde National Park—its backside visible from the shores of Morgan Lake—have contained some of the highest levels of mercury in the nation, and elevated levels have even been found on Molas Pass, just south of Silverton. The mercury is then taken up by bacteria in lakes and rivers, which convert it to highly toxic methylmercury, which then enters the food chain. Mercury messes with fishes' brains, and even at relatively low concentrations can impair bird and fish reproduction and health. It's not so good for people, either.

We continued out into the desert toward the Chaco River and the Hogback, and as we came over a rise an incongruous scene unfolded before us: a flat-topped, uniformly shaped mesa, its dusty soil gray and smooth, with eerie-looking deep-orange water pools on its surface. Nothing was growing there. I wondered if maybe it was this that I needed a strong stomach for, not the chili.

We were looking at the Four Corners Power Plant's dump, made up of ash impoundment piles, decant water, and evaporation ponds, containing some forty years' worth of accumulated coal combustion waste—tens of millions of tons of it—from three of the plant's five generators. At the time, Four Corners was burning about 8.5 million tons of coal each year, some 3.3 million tons of which were leftover as coal combustion waste, dumped both here and back into the nearby mine. A trio of unlined sludge-disposal ponds sat less than five hundred yards from the Chaco River, which empties into the San Juan River a few miles away. Two miles upstream is the Hogback Outlier, a Chacoan-era pueblo. A crescent-shaped structure known as a herradura—a piece of AWUF associated with Chacoan roads—sits atop the Hogback nearby.

Darker clouds headed our way and the wind kicked up, whipping the fine, gray ash and dust off the top of the piles and into the air, reducing visibility to thirty feet or so. When the dust cleared we saw a sign stuck into the base of one of the piles. It read: "No Trash Dumping. Walk in Beauty."

For people who worry about coal combustion waste and the way it's regulated, this place is Exhibit A. "My first thought when I saw this," Lisa Evans, an attorney for Earthjustice, told me, "was, this can't be the United States."

Like the Shumway Arroyo which runs past Hunt's home, the Chaco River downstream from this complex of ponds and piles has contained extremely high levels of selenium, as does the groundwater beneath the ponds. When ingested, selenium can adversely affect reproduction in fish, birds, and mammals. Fish along this stretch of the San Juan River often contain elevated levels of mercury, lead, selenium, and copper. In 1992 a U.S. Fish and Wildlife biologist surveyed fish downstream on the San Juan River from the Four Corners Power Plant to Mexican Hat and found that a majority of them had lesions, damaged livers, deformities, or other signs of disease. While the culprit appeared to be bacteria, the particular strains need the fish to be otherwise impaired, by contaminants, for example, in order to invade.

When I returned to Hunt's place in 2007, he gave me the same tour. Nothing had changed, but the spokesman for the plant's operator, Arizona Public Service, assured me that they were no longer dumping their coal ash in the piles Hunt and I toured, and that the company planned to clean up the nasty piles and ponds and replace them with lined impoundments. Since then, the piles have been covered, and the old ponds removed. Dumping continues here, but under more controlled conditions. Ash is also dumped back into the nearby coal mine, which has been owned by a Navajo Nation-owned company since the end of 2013. This alleviates some of the problems associated with dumping, but doesn't solve all of them, critics say. Chemicals can still leach into groundwater (though it's less likely here, where it's so arid), and unless the ash is covered, it can still blow around in the air, settling on nearby homes.

Arizona Public Service, which is owned by Pinnacle West Capital Corporation, sells electricity to nearly 1.2 million people across Arizona. The corporation raked in over $400 million in profit in 2015. At the same time, it lobbied hard to change state rules on net metering, which determine how much the utility must compensate homeowners for electricity generated by rooftop solar panels. They've managed to chip away at the incentives, thus discouraging people from installing their own panels and generating a bit of their own electricity.

As we drove back around the plant, seemingly to provoke the security guards, Hunt treated me to another rhetorical geode. "It's just like asking Patty Hearst's mother what happened . . . all you get is a bunch of excuses," he said. "These are some nasty sons-a-bitches. It's all about profit. They don't care about anything or anyone, they just care about their profits." As crude as the delivery might have been, it was hard to refute the concept.

When we arrived back at Original Sweetmeats, the after-work rush was on. We hung back by the truck and watched. It was late afternoon. The cottonwoods cast long shadows on the ground. "If I'm lucky, one day I'll die of a heart attack," Hunt said.

After a pause, he perked up to tell me about the petroglyphs that are pecked into the sandstone cliff band that runs up and down the San Juan for miles. I looked out at the valley, sliced up by the four-lane highway and the big transmission towers, and wondered why the Pueblo people would leave such a place, and I tried to imagine what the first Diné people, coming from the North, out of the cold mountains and across the parched high desert, thought when they came upon the silty river and the trees and the willows on its banks. It must have felt like home.

Up on the desert on either side of the valley, the plants chugged on, each burning twenty thousand tons of coal per day. They've brought jobs and industry to a once-impoverished and undeveloped place and keep the people in faraway cities cool in the unforgiving summer heat. They each send millions of dollars of property taxes and royalties to various governments. They also spew out thousands of tons of toxic waste each year. Power is not free.

An old pickup truck pulled into the parking lot, several cages holding roosters in the back. A large man tumbled out, wearing safety glasses and a dirty jumpsuit, his face spattered with some kind of black soot: a power plant employee, selling his chickens after work.

"Five dollars for the little ones," he told a man and wife who were inspecting the birds. Then he turned to Hunt and me and told us about how he can no longer smell anything after years at the plant, and about how his friend who lived nearby had to clean his television screen daily to wipe away the buildup of fly ash.

"I won't make it to sixty, I can guarantee that," he said, matter-of-factly. His wife sat in the cab of the pickup, smiling and quiet.

The haze seemed to be getting thicker in the west, the sun taking on an orange glow. Under my breath, to no one in particular, I said, "Looks like it will be a nice sunset tonight."

Hot Spot

Less than a year later, a half-mile long by fifty to seventy-five foot wide swath of previously healthy piñon and juniper trees, sagebrush and saltbrush stood dead as a stark testimony to recent environmental changes.

—*Coalbed Methane Development in the Northern San Juan Basin of Colorado,* 1999

THE RANCHER'S NAME HAS BEEN LOST IN THE FOG OF TIME, but we know that he lived near the little hamlet of Cedar Hill in the Animas River Valley just south of the Colorado-New Mexico state line. Cedar Hill is green—even lush—thanks to the river and irrigation from it, a stark contrast to the red and purple hills and beige cliffs on either side of the valley. It is a pastoral place, with huge cottonwoods shading small homes. It's also considered the birthplace of coal-bed methane drilling—an unconventional form of natural gas development that started here in the 1970s, and then boomed a decade later.

In the late 1980s, the rancher dug a new water well on his property. As folks around here sometimes do, he used his rifle to shoot a hole in the well casing, and thus develop it. The well exploded. Just as Jed Clampett of the Beverly Hillbillies struck oil by shooting a bullet into the Texas ground, so did our rancher find methane by shooting into his water well.

Similarly odd phenomena were occurring all around Cedar Hill at the time: swaths of alfalfa killed in previously healthy fields; well houses exploding; methane bubbles emerging from the river; water faucets that lit on fire. It was as though the earth was rebelling against all that poking and prodding it had endured.

WHEN IT COMES TO ENERGY POLICY, PRESIDENT JIMMY CARTER IS OFTEN REMEMBERED for turning down the thermostat and installing solar panels on the White House roof. Often forgotten is the fact that he was a pusher of energy development of all kinds, as long as it occurred on American soil, and that the Intermountain West paid the highest price for his quixotic quest for energy independence. Even as Carter donned a cardigan instead of turning up the heat, he called for a whopping increase by two-thirds of coal mining and consumption. Even as he pushed for more efficiency, he encouraged more oil and gas drilling—in 1980, sixty-two thousand wells were drilled in the United States, mostly in Texas and the West. And by getting a $25 billion synfuels subsidy program through Congress at the end of his term, he sparked a destructive oil shale boom in Western Colorado that busted catastrophically a couple years later, when Congress and the Reagan administration rescinded the subsidies.

The drilling and digging frenzy that resulted from Carter's policies and two energy crises helped to firmly establish the San Juan Basin as a national energy colony, just as the San Juan Mountains had long been a mineral colony. Farmington was a farming town no more. Oil and gas companies set up shop, and the once-transient workforce began putting down roots along-side all their pipelines.

At about the same time, Indian Country was rising up to take control over their energy resources, now coveted like never before. The Navajo Nation's centralized government, cynically formed to create an entity to sign off on oil and gas leases, was one of the leaders of this fight—Albert Fall's efforts had unwittingly given the tribe far more power to stand up to industry. In 1982, in an effort to improve oversight, Congress created the Minerals Management Service and passed the Indian Mineral Development Act, which gave tribes the power to negotiate mineral leases. That same year, the U.S. Supreme Court made a favorable ruling in a case involving the Jicarilla Apache tribe, saying that tribes could levy a severance tax on oil and gas produced on their lands.

Rather than stymie development, this movement in some cases encouraged it, as the tribes tried to bolster their sparse economies with coal mining and oil and gas drilling. The Southern Ute tribe, whose reservation straddles the lower Animas River, is perhaps the most successful at gaining energy sovereignty, eventually leveraging its resources into a multi-billion-dollar energy and real estate empire.

A FEW YEARS AGO, I WENT DOWN to the Bureau of Land Management's Farmington Field Office to speak with some officials there about oil and gas development. After giving a few curt, bureaucratese answers to my questions, Maureen Joe, then the assistant field manager, asked her colleague, "Should we show him the scare map?" Joe, a small woman with shiny black hair, seemed to delight in the prospect of frightening a reporter. Dave Mankiewicz, another assistant field manager—

the curmudgeonly cop to Joe's cheerful one—handed me the map, showing every well ever drilled in the San Juan Basin, with little red dots for gas, black ones for oil.

It *was* scary. The northern and central sections of the Basin are almost solid red; in the south and west, dense swarms of black dots string out along the oil-bearing formations like an ant colony on a sugar spill. Dark pinpricks surround Chaco Culture National Historical Park. Huerfano Mountain, or *Dzil Na'oodilii*—a sort of Garden of Eden in Diné cosmology—is embroidered with red and black. The modern BLM office we sat in, with its upscale stone-and-glass facade, located on a fine piece of real estate in the upper-class part of town, has three wells within a quarter mile, and a pumpjack grinds away right next to a golf course green down the road.

To find a stretch of land anywhere in the core of the Basin that hasn't been drilled or isn't covered by roads, tanks, pipes, or some other hydrocarbon-related infrastructure is nearly impossible—the infrastructure is the landscape. Other gas patches in the West are similarly riddled with the detritus of the industry, but none to this extent, thanks to geology and this BLM office's penchant for cozying up to oil and gas companies and advocacy groups. It's not just pipelines and tanks, either. The U.S. Atomic Energy Commission detonated a twenty-nine-kiloton nuclear device (twice the power of the bomb dropped on Hiroshima) underground northeast of Farmington in order to stimulate natural gas production, making it the granddaddy of all fracking jobs, and altering the subterranean world in un-known ways. "We've got so much pipeline in the ground, it's like rebar," said Mankiewicz. "If you had an earthquake, the ground wouldn't even shake."

The industry is similarly entangled with the community's

streetscapes, culture, and economy. A drive around the Aztec-Farmington-Bloomfield triangle is a bit like a cruise through a giant open-air oil-and-gas mall, with roadside businesses peddling goods and services for every link of the hydrocarbon production chain: Elite Swabbing Service, Compressco, Weatherford Fishing Tools, and Permian Power Tong. Halliburton's yard, brimming with giant trucks and byzantine equipment, is sandwiched between a Great Harvest Bread Company and a Walgreens on Farmington's main drag. In 2006 a spill of acidic fracking fluid in the Halliburton yard sickened residents of a trailer park nearby, and forced the yard's evacuation.

This melding of community identity and the industry is in part due to the State of New Mexico's relatively progressive fiscal policy in this regard, setting up a severance tax, a school tax, and a conservation tax, all on hydrocarbon production. A 2014 New Mexico Tax Research Institute analysis found that at least one-third of the state's general fund comes from the mélange of taxes and royalties paid by the industry. Donations from local energy companies to schools, libraries, and cultural events are layered on top of that. By the late 1970s, Farmington and Aztec had come to resemble an updated version of Silverton and Telluride, circa 1902, only this time the oil and gas industry, rather than hardrock mining, had a stranglehold on the communities.

This has effectively put these local, county, and state governments into the oil and gas business. The upside is that those communities get to share in the profits. One downside is that everyone, from the tool-pusher to the symphony-goer, is dependent on an extremely volatile global market. The other is that when industry and community amalgamate, it paralyzes dissent, because an attack on industry becomes, by extension, an attack on schools, local governments, and, really, the people who live here—even if the dissenters are just trying to get the companies to act a little more responsibly. We saw this play out in the slime wars of the hardrock mining days, and it continues today, as concerned citizens try to get the oil and gas industry to rein in methane leaks, reveal what goes into fracking fluids, and better manage wastewater.

Though the oil and gas and mining industries were beneficiaries of federal largesse and Carter's energy policies, they still believed themselves to be victims of an overreaching federal government implementing and enforcing new laws like the Clean Water Act, the Wilderness Act, and the Federal Land Policy and Management Act. So when Ronald Reagan was elected president in 1980 and brought on James Watt—cut from the same cloth as Albert B. Fall—as Interior Secretary, some of the shackles on industry were removed. It didn't quite work out as well as they'd hoped, however. Reagan rolled back regulations, but also freed up trade, leading to a wave of outsourcing. Manufacturing went to China, copper mining to Chile. Natural gas was deregulated, and OPEC flooded the global market with oil. Oil and gas prices crashed and the drill rigs were taken down and salvaged for scrap metal. The oil- and gas-patch economies collapsed, the people of Farmington, Aztec, and the other energy towns got angry at their helplessness in the face of the global market. Rather than lash out at the free marketeers that had enabled the pain, they became even more conservative and nationalistic.

Here in the San Juan Basin, though, the slump wouldn't last, again thanks to the feds tinkering with markets, this time to make drilling for coalbed methane—an unconventional type of natural gas—economically feasible.

Most of the drilling in the region had thus far targeted subterranean reservoirs of oil and gas within sandstone formations. Left untapped was the methane—the key component of natural gas—that was stored up in the coal beds that lay under much of the basin. Coalbed methane had long been considered only a nuisance, building up in coal mines and exploding or asphyxiating miners. Extracting it for commercial use was too expensive.

So the federal government, wanting to bleed the earth for every BTU it could, stepped in to help out. In 1974, Congress and President Gerald Ford created the Energy Research and Development Administration, which conducted and funded research into "unconventional" energy sources, such as coalbed methane, coal gasification, oil shale, and drilling in oil- and natural-gas-bearing shale formations. That research led to better coalbed methane drilling techniques and technology. In 1980, Congress passed the Crude Oil Windfall Profit Tax Act, which offered tax credits for oil and gas produced from newly drilled, unconventional wells. The innovations and credits together made coalbed methane development profitable. The credit was set to expire in 1992, so drillers went crazy to get their wells completed under the deadline.

Between 1988 and 1992 some three thousand coalbed methane wells were drilled in the San Juan Basin, mostly in the northern half of the Animas River watershed. Piñon, juniper, and sage were scraped away for the spiderweb of roads and pads that the wells required. Orange sodium lights dimmed the stars, the incessant hum of compressor plants blotted out even the coyotes' wail.

Coalbed methane wells were not only targeting a different formation than before, but they also operated on different principles. The methane is bonded, or adsorbed, to the coal by water pressure. In order to get at the methane, the water pressure must first be relieved by pumping between one thousand and twenty thousand gallons of water from the coalbed's aquifer per day from each well. Once freed, the methane follows the path of least resistance to the surface where it's gathered up and piped to market.

By the late 1990s, the San Juan Basin's wells were collectively the nation's top coalbed methane producer. They were also pulling up gargantuan quantities of water. Produced water varies in chemical composition from place to place—it can be more brackish than sea water, and contain mercury, arsenic, and other naturally occurring heavy metals as well as volatile organic compounds such as benzene, toluene, and xylene (monocyclic aromatic hydrocarbons) and naphthalene, anthracene, and benzopyrene (polycyclic aromatic hydrocarbons). When the New Mexico Oil Conservation Division tested coalbed methane water from the San Juan Basin in 1989, they found that it contained very high levels of sodium bicarbonate, i.e. baking soda, along with elevated concentrations of barium and radium-226 and -228. Produced water also contains chemicals shot into the well during hydraulic fracturing, which can include everything from walnut shells, to dish soap, to carboxymethyl hydroxypropyl, guar gum, zirconium-based crosslinker, and persulfate breaker.

The coalbed methane wells in the San Juan Basin together produce at least two billion gallons of wastewater each year. After it's pumped from the well, the water is usually put into storage tanks at the well site. The water is regularly transferred to trucks, and then taken to a disposal facility, which explains why dirt- and mud-encrusted water trucks are ubiquitous on the back roads of every gas patch in the West, even during times when the drill rigs are idle.[48] In the early days, the produced water was dumped right back into an arroyo or stream. Now it is put into lined evaporation ponds, which can be death traps for water-seeking birds, or it is injected thousands of feet deep into disposal wells. Each year, enough water to fill three thousand Olympic-sized swimming pools is sucked from one geologic formation, put in tanks, moved in trucks, and put back in ponds, before getting shot back into a deeper formation at extremely high pressures. What could go wrong?

In the 1980s, that question was partially answered near Cedar Hill as water taps were set aflame, well houses blew up, and dead zones emerged in farmers' alfalfa fields. The mystery was quickly solved. Methane liberated by dewatering the coalbed was mostly going into the gas wells, as intended. Some of it was getting away, too, and that stray methane found its way to inadequately cased oil and gas wells that had long ago been drilled into deeper formations. The methane migrated upward through the old well into the drinking water aquifer. The beauty of this scenario is that there was a clear culprit—the crappy old well—and a solution—plugging the old well—that didn't require curtailing coalbed methane production.

Things weren't so clear cut in other parts of the San Juan Basin, however. In 1993, a resident of a small subdivision east of Durango discovered that methane was emanating from his shallow drinking water well, which had served his home for ten years without a problem. Methane was found in another resident's well, and had built up to explosive levels near the foundation of yet another house. Nearby, methane bubbles were observed in the Pine River near where it slices through the Hogback Monocline.

Amoco, which later merged with BP, had drilled eleven

coalbed methane wells within a two-mile radius of the subdivision over the previous six years. But they were found to be adequately sealed, and this time there were no older wells through which the methane could migrate into the aquifer. Some other geologic enigma was occurring. The state's regulator, the Colorado Oil and Gas Commission, formed an investigative team made up of a wide array of local and state officials and scientists to unravel the mystery. Meanwhile, Amoco launched its own effort to come up with a cause.

What followed could be a case study in the way a corporate polluter manages to elbow its way into unbiased science in order to deflect blame from the polluter. The independent investigative team concluded that the Amoco wells had dewatered the coal seam, thus liberating the gas, which then migrated to water wells and the surface through the coal outcrop along the Hogback Monocline. In other words, the wells were indirectly causing the methane leakage, but this time the pathway to the water well was the coal seam itself, rather than another well. It was a fuzzier case than in Cedar Hill, but still seemed to put the onus squarely on Amoco's shoulders.

Amoco responded by throwing out a variety of other possible explanations for the methane leakage: the subdivision's water wells had sucked up enough water to liberate the methane in the coal seam; a dip in precipitation amounts had dried out the coal seam, freeing up the gas; an increase in precipitation had flooded the coal seam, displacing the methane; the seeps were there all along, there just weren't enough people around to notice; and so on.

Amoco's consultants didn't have to prove any of their alternative hypotheses. That wasn't the point. They only needed to inject a particle of doubt into the most logical explanation for what was going on. It's a version of the climate change denier's trope: "If the earth is warming up, why's it so cold?" "If humans are causing climate change, then how did the climate change dramatically back in the age of the dinosaurs?" Industry researchers dug up myriad anecdotes—some quite entertaining—to show that methane sometimes seeped from the earth prior to any oil and gas development. One man told a tale of a campfire ember igniting the Pine River when he was a kid, others of lighting seeps on fire during the holidays. And then there was this one: "A married man who enjoyed his liquor would return home after a night out on the town only to find that his wife had locked him out. . . . He would light methane flowing from a vent pipe attached to the main casing of a water well to produce heat to keep warm."[49] The Moving Mountain incident of the 1930s was presented as the most dramatic evidence that the earth was belching, shifting, groaning, and flatulating long before oil and gas development became widespread.

A Bureau of Land Management report concisely summed up the situation several years later: "The Pine River Investigative Team Report proposed straightforward cause and effect relationships, but industry-funded independent consultants filed a counter report proposing alternative theories based upon other assumptions, which confounded the issues." They set out to sow doubt, and sow doubt they did.

Over the next few years, however, it became clear that whatever was going wrong underneath the San Juan Basin wasn't limited to the Pine River subdivision. An abandoned gas well near Bayfield, drilled in 1951, periodically expelled a stream of water, gas, and highly poisonous hydrogen sulfide some two hundred feet into the air. Locals dubbed it Old Faithful. A freshwater spring in the Animas Valley just upstream from Durango went through dramatic changes. The flow increased, the water heated up to more than 130 degrees Fahrenheit, and sodium and sulfate concentrations skyrocketed. Old trees near the spring died, and the homeowner could no longer use the water for domestic purposes. Vegetation was similarly killed at the base of Moving Mountain, where the Animas River cuts through the Hogback Monocline, and the rotten egg odor of hydrogen sulfide wafted up from near the river's edge.

The problems weren't limited to wells, basements, and the air, either. In 1992, federal, state, and Southern Ute Indian Tribe biologists surveyed the Animas River fish populations from just below Durango to the New Mexico state line. As the surveyors moved downstream for the first several miles, all seemed in order. But as they approached the area known as Bondad, just upstream from a natural gas well, they started noticing something alarming. Many of the bluehead, flannelmouth, and hybrid suckers they caught had tumors, lesions, ulcers, and open sores on their bodies. It was some sort of mass outbreak. A fish pathologist examined the diseased suckers. His diagnosis: furunculosis, a bacterial infection often precipitated by poor water quality. Shortly thereafter, another set of fish, also with outward signs of disease, were captured and sampled in the Bondad area. Most of them showed evidence of exposure to polycyclic aromatic hydrocarbons, which are associated with fossil fuel combustion and oil and gas production.

In 1995 a geologist working for the Southern Ute Indian Tribe was walking along the portion of the Hogback Monocline southwest of Durango when he noticed methane gas venting from the earth with such force that it lifted grains of sand several inches into the air. Within months, according to a comprehensive BLM report, "a half-mile long by fifty to seventy-five foot wide swath of previously healthy piñon and juniper trees, sagebrush and saltbrush stood dead as a stark testimony to recent environmental changes. All together, locations along the Fruitland outcrop north of the New Mexico State line account for more than eight miles of stressed/dead vegetation." Hydrogen sulfide levels spiked to hazardous levels nearby, forcing the closure of a road.

Methane is not poisonous. Inhaling it won't kill you or make you sick unless the gas is so concentrated that it displaces oxygen; displacement is what kills vegetation in high-methane soil. Once methane reaches concentrations above five percent, it can combust and explode, which was the primary concern in the San Juan Basin in the 1990s. Without accepting blame, Amoco quietly bought up the contaminated properties near its wells and bulldozed the houses. Meanwhile, they agreed to work with the Colorado Oil & Gas Conservation Commission, or COGCC, to fund further studies. The Southern Ute Indian Tribe, which oversees its own energy empire, figured out a way to capture and market some of the gas from a "natural" seep; and the COGCC built a miniature power plant on another one, using captured methane to generate electricity to power six homes.

Each year a Durango environmental firm heads out and walks the Colorado, non-reservation portion of the Hogback Monocline measuring methane flux, or emissions, from the geologic seeps. Each year they file reports to state regulators. And each year, the reports are filed away with little notice. If anything, the problem has only worsened over time; the most recent report showed that some forty-five thousand metric tons of methane leaked from the monitored section of the coal outcrop, putting it on par with a large, underground coal mine.

Yet with no more homes getting contaminated, the massive methane leakage problem largely faded from the public consciousness.[50]

Until 2014.

That's when a team of scientists published a report about satellite imagery captured years earlier that showed a big blob of methane hovering over the San Juan Basin. They christened it the Four Corners Methane Hot Spot. By then, methane had gained notoriety as a major pollutant of the greenhouse gas kind, so the hot spot's discovery prompted concern among climate scientists and fear of more regulations in the oil and gas industry. Methane has eighty-six times more global warming potential than carbon dioxide over a twenty-year span, and up to thirty times more over a century. That means that for every hundred tons of carbon dioxide kept out of the atmosphere, it only takes three or four tons of methane leaking from a pipeline or other infrastructure to offset the gain. Methane leakage has become a tender Achilles' heel for natural gas, which continues to be widely touted as a cleaner choice than coal for generating electricity.

The obvious suspect behind the hot spot was the vast oil and natural gas industry infrastructure, which is woven into the landscape here, and burps and leaks methane and other hydrocarbons from valves, pipes, compressors, and newly fractured wells. Nearly every step of the natural gas extraction, transmission, processing, storage, and distribution process has potential for methane leakage. By its own reckoning, ConocoPhillips' San Juan Basin facilities collectively add up to the largest single methane emitter in the nation. Still, when the state or federal governments try to implement even the most common-sense rules aimed at reducing methane leakage—and thus curbing the loss of natural gas and revenue—the industry fights back just as the mine owners did when they were asked to contain their mill tailings. Industry boosters claim that stopping leaks is too expensive, and would kill jobs. Yet ConocoPhillips managed voluntarily to cut methane emissions in half between 2013 and 2014, while still netting a profit of $6.8 billion.

After the initial hot spot report was published, industry spokespeople launched an all-out obfuscation offensive. The hot spot was not caused by wells, pipelines, or the like, they said, but by the natural, geologic seeps that had been well documented over the years. Sow doubt. Present "alternative facts." Divert attention.

After the report was published, teams of scientists descended on the San Juan Basin to ground-truth the observations made from space, and to try to get a better idea of whence the methane was coming.

In April 2015 I accompanied a couple of the researchers on their quest. I rendezvoused with Gabrielle Petron, an atmospheric scientist with the National Oceanic and Atmospheric Administration and the Cooperative Institute for Research in Environmental Sciences at the University of Colorado, Boulder, at a well-known "natural" methane seep south of Durango. Petron wore jeans and hiking boots, a black jacket, and sunglasses, all given flair by the saffron-orange scarf wrapped loosely around her neck and shoulders. Petron initially studied mathematics in France, but eventually switched her focus to the atmosphere because of "the beauty of the air and the abstractness of it." Speaking with a slight French accent, she showed me around the van, with its dash-mounted real-time methane monitor and a fishing-pole-like air sampler sticking out of the top.

Back before the industrial age, the earth's background methane level was about 750 parts per billion. Beginning around 1850, that number began climbing and now the ambient level is approximately 1,800 parts per billion, or 1.8 parts per million. In the van, Petron pointed to the monitor: the methane line hovered around 5,000 parts per billion, or about three times the background level. Later, we checked out an even more prolific seep, where the levels shot up to a whopping 60 parts per million. Methane is, indeed, leaking from the earth, and probably has been for thousands of years. Perhaps the Pueblo people of Sacred Ridge even witnessed smoke from underground coal fires, or a methane seep gone aflame, 1,200 years ago.

Yet this case is far from closed. The hot spot scientists found that methane was leaking in significant volumes from various pieces of oil and gas infrastructure, and from an underground coal mine. Some of the leaks have already been fixed, others could be repaired, with a little prodding from regulators. The coal mine methane could be captured and piped to market or used to generate electricity, as has been done at some of the bigger geologic seeps, but this is unlikely to happen without a regulatory nudge from the state or federal government.

Meanwhile, the geologic seeps aren't so natural after all. Ample evidence links the coalbed methane drilling boom with the significant exacerbation of the methane and hydrogen sulfide leakage from the Hogback Monocline. The Pine River study showed causality in that limited area. A study released in 2000 showed a conclusive link in another part of the Basin. That Animas Valley spring that suddenly became a mineral-infused hot spring? That was caused by injecting produced water into a well nine miles distant. When the operators of the well shifted to injecting the water into a different geologic formation, the spring cooled off again; no one knows if some other spring, somewhere else, was transformed by the switch.

These are the effects we've noticed because they intrude on our day-to-day lives, or they're so dramatic as to be impossible to ignore. Yet surely other changes are occurring all the time as a result of our drilling and fracking and sucking and spewing, it's just that we don't notice or we attribute them to some other more visible cause. We've been messing with the system on a large scale. Logic tells us that the system will react, but doesn't tell us precisely how.

Yes, the surge of methane oozing from the earth is natural, in the same sense that acid mine drainage is natural, or hundreds of earthquakes in Oklahoma, triggered by oil and gas wastewater injection wells, are natural. Nature is acting, only it is doing so under the influence of humanity. It is the manifestation of the Anthropocene.

AS PETRON'S METHANE MYSTERY TOUR CONTINUED, we veered off the main road behind the high school of the little town of Bayfield, Colorado, and pulled off to the side of the street. The passenger-side door swung open and Petron motioned for me to look at the monitor again. Again, methane levels were elevated. This time the source was sitting out in plain view. Inside a chain-link-fenced enclosure next to the school's tennis court, the pipes, valves, and other equipment of a BP America natural gas well jutted from the ground. Everything was painted gold and purple, the school colors, with "Wolverine Pride" emblazoned on a metal box. This well was contributing to the methane hot spot and therefore also to climate change.

Petron let me flip the little switch that snatched an air sample from the breeze for later analysis. It would tell her precisely what isotopes of methane are here, and, just as importantly, what other compounds may be seeping out of the well alongside them. Methane's not going to hurt anyone in the short term unless it builds up enough to explode, but benzene, another pollutant emitted by oil and gas wells, has both short- and long-term health effects and is a known carcinogen—certainly not something you want your high-schoolers inhaling every day.

"Your air is being impacted," Petron said bluntly, after we had taken the sample. "You live on the edge of the gas field." Hell, I thought, we live right in the middle of a sacrifice zone, and our air, our water, our health, it's all being affected.

Radiate as Directed

I N 1955, A THIRTY-THREE-YEAR-OLD DOCTOR NAMED GEORGE MOORE ARRIVED IN DURANGO, his family in tow, to take the helm of the San Juan Basin Health Department, which had been created in 1949 to administer public health in four counties of southwestern Colorado. Moore served in the military during World War II, did his medical internship in Denver in the late 1940s, and then went to work in Kathmandu, Nepal, for the U.S. Public Health Service. None of that prepared the young doctor for what he encountered upon arriving in Durango: a leaderless organization in disarray, tasked with overseeing a region that was not only an environmental sacrifice zone, but a human health one, as well.

In Rico, a mining town on the upper Dolores River, Diné miners at a recently reopened lead and zinc mine were plagued with tuberculosis. Mesa Verde National Park didn't have a sanitary source of drinking water. The doctor wasn't even allowed access to the Ute Mountain Ute reservation to assess the situation there. On Southern Ute land closer to Durango, Moore encountered a full-blown public health crisis, with high rates of obesity, alcoholism, pneumonia, tuberculosis, and infant mortality. And the oil and gas boom that was in full swing had brought sexually transmitted diseases to the reservation, as well.

And then, plopped down on the edge of relatively affluent Durango, there was what Moore described as "an enormous mount of radioactive tailings on the bank of the Animas River. The Vanadium Corporation of America was processing uranium and dumping the waste material, still radioactive, into the river for disposal." Even as Durangoans worried about the mine tailings coming down from the high country, they had a potentially more dangerous problem right in their own backyard.

THE DURANGO SMELTER, WHICH HAD ENABLED THE GROWTH AND SUCCESS OF THE MINING INDUSTRY in the San Juan Mountains, shut down in 1930, another victim of the Great Depression. In 1942, shortly after the United States joined World War II, the government came to the rescue. The Reconstruction Finance Corporation, a federal agency created to stimulate the economy following the Depression, purchased the shuttered smelter. The RFC then leased the site to the United States Vanadium Corporation, which converted the facility into a mill, purportedly to extract vanadium—which is used in steel alloys—from uranium ore. The real target was the uranium. Throughout the war, USVC secretly processed it for use in the Manhattan Project and the atomic bombs that would be dropped on Hiroshima and Nagasaki. After the war ended, the mill shut down. But when the Cold War and the arms race beckoned, the newly formed Atomic Energy Commission bought the site as part of its region-wide, heavy subsidization of the nuclear industry that resulted in a frenzied boom on the Colorado Plateau. Prospectors with their Geiger counters combed canyons and mesas, looking for the next bonanza. To facilitate the craze, federal land agencies and counties webbed with roads some of the most remote land remaining in the lower forty-eight. Ranchers were pushed off ancestral grazing lands, and quiet little towns erupted into boisterous ones almost overnight. The AEC leased the Durango mill out to Vanadium Corporation of America, which in 1949 resumed milling of uranium ore and producing yellowcake.

Most of the ore for the mill came from the mines in the Uravan area in far western Colorado along the Dolores River.[51] Yet a portion of it came from a surprising place, the Graysill Mine in the San Juan Mountains near the headwaters of Hermosa Creek, which joins with the Animas River about eight miles north of Durango. It was one of two uranium mines in the upper Animas region; the other was a short-lived affair in Elk Park, near the Animas River below Silverton. Graysill yielded some 32,000 tons of uranium ore over two decades after World War II. The mining claim's current owner, Nevada-based Pacific Gold Corp., estimates that another 640,000 pounds of uranium oxide is still waiting there to be mined. Uranium mines are just as prone as others to produce acid mine drainage, provided that sulfides and water are available for reaction. The drainage from a uranium mine contains not only the usual metals and acidity, but also may be radioactive, upping the ante.

Like the metal mills up in Silverton, uranium mills produce tailings as a waste product. Vanadium Corporation piled its tailings out in the open. That alarmed Moore, so he sent members of his staff to take a closer look, particularly at the river below the mill. "The sanitarians brought back dead fish heavy with uranium ore," he later wrote. He also discovered that the mill had been giving tailings to area highway departments to use as road base. Alarmed, he notified his former colleagues at the Public Health Service. They came, took some samples, and did nothing.

Congress passed the Federal Water Pollution Control Act in 1956, and in 1957 the Atomic Energy Commission published its regulations for waste discharges. The Durango mill appeared to be in violation of both, and the New Mexico Department of Public Health, which had been keeping an eye on the stuff emanating across the state line via the river, asked the feds to investigate. In 1958, the U.S. Public Health Service sent a team of researchers, led by Ernest C. Tsivoglou, of Cleveland, to take a look at the Durango uranium mill and the river downstream. What they found was unnerving.

Each day, the mill churned through about 500 tons of ore. The chunks of pale yellow rock were first crushed, then pulverized into a sandy powder. This was then mixed with a chemical soup that included about 65,000 pounds per day of sulfuric acid along with similar quantities of salt and soda ash, 325 pounds of tributyl phosphate—something you don't want to touch, inhale, or ingest—and 370 gallons of kerosene. One ton of ore yielded around six pounds of uranium, with the remainder ending up as waste. The Durango mill kicked out some 997,000 pounds of tailings per day, containing leftover uranium, along with lead, polonium, bismuth, thorium, radium, arsenic, and other material that occurred naturally in the ore. The leaching chemicals were also part of the mix.

Norman Norvelle was in the seventh grade in Farmington, New Mexico, in 1958. His family had moved to the region not long before, and his father was a big fan of the mountains, so nearly every weekend they all drove up the Animas River, past the livestock sale barn and sawmill in what is now the big-box sprawl of south Durango, and then past the uranium mill. Norvelle, a tall man with a friendly demeanor, would later go on to work as a scientist with the New Mexico Health Department. Now retired, he's still keenly interested in pollution issues. He described the scene to me: "The [mill] had several large ponds next to the river that were usually full and a deep green. Many times when we drove by the ponds, the dirt walls and dikes retaining the acid process wastewater would be breached. The ponds would be empty and on the river shore you could see where the contents went into the river."

What the young Norvelle did not see, but the scientists did, was a separate liquid waste stream—actually, two of them—that flowed directly into the river at a rate of about 340 gallons per minute, or nearly a half-a-million gallons per day. Included in this particular broth were at least fifteen tons per day of spent ore solids, leftover acid leaching chemicals, and an iron-aluminum sludge that was a byproduct of extraction.

At the time, the Animas River below the mill was the primary drinking water source for Aztec, population four thousand, and Farmington, population twenty-two thousand.[52] At least two thousand rural downstreamers regularly consumed raw river water. Diverted Animas River water irrigated some twenty-six thousand acres of crops, and thousands of head of livestock drank from the stream. Below the confluence with the San Juan River, thousands more people, most of whom were Diné, relied on the water for drinking, irrigating, and livestock. Eventually, the water—and whatever it was tainted with—would reach the Colorado River and Lake Mead (Glen Canyon Dam did not begin impounding water until 1963). Of all the nasty ingredients, radium-226—a radioactive "daughter" of uranium, with a half life of 1,600 years—was of most concern to the researchers.

Radium, discovered by Marie Curie in carnotite ore mined in Western Colorado, was once seen as a sort of miracle substance. Paint it on watch numbers or even clothing and they'd glow in the dark. It purportedly could cure cancer, impotence, and give those who used it an "all-around healthy glow," and during the early 1900s it was put in medicine, cosmetics, sometimes even food. Male users of the Radiendocrinator were instructed to wear the "adaptor like any 'athletic strap.' This puts the instrument under the scrotum as it should be. Wear at night. Radiate as directed." Radium's glow dimmed, however, when the women who painted radium onto watches started dying, and the inventor of the Radiendocrinator was stricken with bladder cancer. Radium is highly radioactive and a "boneseeker," meaning that when it's ingested it makes its way to the skeleton, where it decays into other radioactive daughter elements, including radon, and bombards the surrounding tissue with alpha, beta, and gamma radiation. According to the Toxic Substances and Diseases Registry, exposure leads to "anemia, cataracts, fractured teeth, cancer (especially bone cancer), and death."

In order to get a grasp on just how much radiation people were being exposed to, Tsivoglou and company set up a water sampling station one mile upstream from the mill as a control,[53] and several more for another seventy-five miles or so downstream. They sampled locally produced milk and crops that were irrigated with river water, and surveyed aquatic life above and below the mill.

Their findings were shocking. The Animas River below Durango was polluted with chemical and radioactive materials. Water, mud, and algae samples from Station 2, two miles below the mill, were one hundred to five hundred times more radioactive than the control samples taken above the mill. Another twenty miles downstream, near the state line, farmers were drinking and irrigating with water that was twelve to twenty-five times as radioactive as the Animas above the mill, and double the "maximum permissible concentration," or MPC, as determined at the time by the Public Health Service.

Water that young Norm Norvelle drank from the taps in his Farmington home had ten times the radioactivity of Durango's tap water. Cabbage, lettuce, sweet corn, apples, and other crops from downstream farms were similarly high in radioactivity. Folks who lived near the state line, drank from the river, and ate local food were taking in at least 250 percent of the maximum permissible concentration of radiation. This was added to the strontium-90, another bone-seeker, that wafted in high concentrations over most of the Interior West as a result of the extensive nuclear bomb testing at the Nevada Test Site during the same time period.

In addition to the radioactive materials, the river had high levels of zinc, arsenic, aluminum, lead, and other toxic metals, both from upstream metal-mining tailings and the uranium mill. The river was virtually devoid of "bottom fauna," such as aquatic bugs and algae, and fish, for nearly thirty miles downstream from the mill. Jack Scott was in fourth grade at Aztec's Lydia Rippey Elementary School in 1959, and vividly remembers the slow-moving disaster. If you thought the electric orange color of the Animas post-Gold King spill was alarming, he told me, you should have seen it back then: "The river was a pea green color during low flow near the state line. The river was mostly dead except for a few suckers."

Clearly the Vanadium Corporation was violating the laws and regulations. But since the same laws were virtually toothless, there was little the feds could do except ask them to stop. Shortly after the results were revealed to the general public, Vanadium Corporation officials vowed to build a treatment facility that would substantially reduce the poisoning of the Animas River. "I am happy to report that the first Federal enforcement action to control contamination of interstate waterways by radioactive wastes has now reached a successful conclusion through voluntary agreement," noted a press release on the subject from the Secretary of Health, Education, and Welfare. It went on to say that the "situation was brought under control before the population of the area had ingested sufficient amounts of this radioactive material to cause detectable health damage."

The declaration, while calming, is dubious. By that time, downstreamers had been drinking tainted water for at least a decade, if not more, and no one had done a systematic investigation of the effects on human health. There was no way of knowing what damage had been done. In 1959, the Public Health Service launched a study to much fanfare, collecting baby teeth from school kids in Farmington and Aztec. Jack Scott remembers the researchers coming to his school and asking kids to bring teeth that had fallen out to school, rather than turning them over to the Tooth Fairy. In return, they'd get a lapel pin that read: "I gave a tooth for research!"

And yet, there's no record of the study ever being completed, nor was any other epidemiological study ever done on the downstream residents, who for nearly two decades had consumed radioactive and otherwise poisonous food. No one knows what kind of havoc the radium and other pollutants wreaked on downstreamers' health.

It's no wonder then that, a half century later, after the Gold King spill, governmental assurances that the Animas River had returned to "pre-spill conditions" were eyed with suspicion. What did that mean, anyway? And what had the spill deposited in the riverbed that might one day be churned up again without warning?

The Vanadium Corporation tried to fix its pollution problem, but failed. Fearing more public outcry, and grappling with a drop in uranium prices, the company gave up and in 1963 shuttered the Durango mill, transferring its operations to Shiprock, New Mexico, where it took over the Kerr-McGee uranium mill that had been constructed in 1954 on the banks of the San Juan River.

It's hard to see the move as anything but a blatant act of environmental injustice. The mill was on the Navajo Nation, and nearly everyone for hundreds of miles downstream was Diné. There was no Dr. George Moore to sound the alarm. Government scientists did not show up to get to the bottom of the pollution problem.[54] In 1960, when Kerr-McGee was operating the mill, one of the evaporation ponds broke, sending at least 250,000 gallons of highly acidic raffinate, containing high levels of radium and thorium, into the river. None of the relevant officials were notified and individual users continued to drink the water, put it on their crops, and give it to their sheep and cattle. It wasn't until five days later, after hundreds of dead fish had washed up on the river's shores for sixty miles downstream, that the public was alerted to the disaster. In its new, less visible location, Vanadium Corporation continued the old and negligent practices, systematically dumping slurry and waste into unlined evaporation ponds in the open.

WHEN VANADIUM CORPORATION LEFT DURANGO, it left a big, festering mess. Two huge piles of tailings, with some old smelter slag thrown in for good measure, totaling about 1.6 million tons, lay piled up at the mill site, perilously close to the Animas River. There was no lining below the piles to prevent leaching into the groundwater, and no cap on the piles to prevent tailings from running off into the water. Wind picked up the fine, thorium-, radium-, lead-, and radon-infused dust and blew it over the river onto town; the closest neighborhood to the pile was poorer and predominantly Hispanic. At some point, a rudimentary sprinkler system was installed to keep the dust down, but it often broke, and the surge of water would wash more tailings into the river. Kids played in the tailings, reveling in the sandy beach-like texture; one local old-timer told *High Country News* that it was "the biggest, best sandpile in the world." For a long time folks would go over to the mill and fill up a truck with the stuff to put in their garden to break up the clay-like soil, or use it in the foundation on their house, or under the concrete on their sidewalk.

The piles still stood there in September 1970, when the remnants of a tropical storm off the Pacific dumped its load of moisture onto the San Juans and sent torrents running down the river, swelling the Animas River up to almost eight thousand cubic feet per second, about one-third the size of the 1911 flood. The rushing waters didn't quite reach the bottom of the uranium tailings piles, but it reminded residents that the potential for such a catastrophic event existed.

I was born in a Durango hospital just days after the floodwaters subsided, and while I was still an infant, my mom, dad, older brother, and I moved from a little trailer on my grandparents' farm into a house in town a couple of blocks from the river and about one mile north of the old uranium mill and its tailings piles. It was a quiet neighborhood, with several other kids around our age, and as we grew up we made for a motley little crew.

The river, running through Durango like a scoliotic spine, was our playground. We spent hours there, wading, swimming, fishing, and chasing minnows. We'd dislodge old cottonwoods that had drifted down from the valley, drag them into the current, and grip them with our skinny legs, making it maybe twenty yards before the half-submerged log spun, bucking us into the icy waters. My brother, a trout-whisperer of sorts, reeled in a half-dozen fish daily, feeding the family all summer long. When we got older we stripped off our clothes on warm summer nights and plummeted from the footbridge behind the high school into deep, calm, and icy waters. We mostly had the river to ourselves. There was little to no commercial rafting. Fly fishing had yet to catch on as a trendy sport. Even tubers were few and far between. High school and college kids left town and headed to Navajo Reservoir to party by the water. I wasn't cool enough to be in that crowd, but then, I didn't need a far-off reservoir. I had the river.

In the background the tailings piles loomed. I don't remember ever playing on them—they must have been fenced off by then—but we did occasionally traverse the rocky banks of the river just below, where rattlesnakes posed a more immediate danger than radon or thorium. Occasionally, after a big winter storm, one or two people would sneak up at night and ski the smooth, steep surface of the piles by the orange glow of the streetlights, leaving daring, curvaceous signatures in the snow. When I was eight years old, fifteen years after the Durango mill stopped operating, a scientist examined river bottom sediment downstream from the old mill site. One sample registered 800 picocuries-per-gram (pCi/g) of radium-226, which is 160 times the EPA's limit for drinking water, and at least as radioactive as a typical uranium mill's wastewater. Perhaps this stash of radium has since been flushed downstream, or maybe it's just buried, silently awaiting the next big flood to stir it back up again.

In the late 1970s a local doctor named Scott McCaffrey noticed what seemed like an unusually high number of lung cancer cases in town. When state health department researchers took a closer look, they found that McCaffrey's statistics were off, but did notice anomalies on the south side of town, where folks were being dosed with elevated levels of radon-222, which can cause lung cancer. They cautioned against alarm, saying the sample size was too small to be conclusive. A more systematic epidemiological study was never performed.

My father was on the Durango City Council at the time, and he and his colleagues were pushing hard to nudge the city out of its fading industrial, extractive past and into what today we might call a New West amenities economy, one that banked on quality of life, cottage industry, tourism. He thought the town should value the river not because it is a conveniently located dump, but for its intrinsic, ecosystem, and recreational values. I still remember when he brought home plans for the riverfront through town—parks and walking paths and restaurants with patios overlooking the water—and how exciting it seemed at the time. Sometime during his term, someone put a big yellow placard atop the piles, warning of their radioactive dangers. I remember my dad being upset about it, though I'm not entirely sure why. I suppose he felt it was alarmist, and that such scaremongering might hamper their effort to replace the old with the new. No one would want to come live in a radioactive town and play in a radioactive river.

In 1986, the Department of Energy finally came in to spend $500 million in taxpayer dollars to clean up the mess that it had originally financed with taxpayer dollars. I was in high school then, and vividly remember going out onto the roof of the school to watch the tall, brick chimney that had been left over from the original smelter crumple into a cloud of dust. The chimney had served as a sort of monument to a hundred years of industry that had built our community, and its fall was mourned even then. Over the next five years it and all the tailings and detritus from mill and smelter were scraped away and buried up in Ridges Basin. Especially hot spots around town where tailings had been used for construction were also cleaned up, but a lot of tailings were left behind, and still lurk underneath streets and sidewalks. The site of the once sprawling industrial complex is now a dog park. The place where the radioactive water once poured into the river is the biggest rapid in town, and a favorite of rafters and kayakers alike.

Mills all over the West were cleaned up at around the same time. Uravan, Colorado, was so contaminated that the entire town was demolished and hauled away. Trains loaded with tailings from the Atlas Mill on the banks of the Colorado River near Moab head northward several dozen miles to get buried. At Shiprock, the waste was impounded on site in a giant tomb-like repository. Yet no matter how many millions of tons of tailings are removed, the toxic legacy endures, somewhere, somehow. Studies done in Shiprock have found elevated levels of birth defects, kidney disease, cancers, and other health problems that continue to persist. Radioactive, heavy-metal-laden water continues to seep into Many Devils Wash, adjacent to where the Shiprock mill operated, and then into the San Juan River, flummoxing scientists. Groundwater beneath the

Durango dog park still swims with high levels of uranium, lead, and other contaminants. We can only guess what lurks deep in the silt of the Animas riverbed.

If my father were still alive, I suspect he'd be surprised and even a little baffled about how quickly the people of Durango managed to forget. How soon after it was gone they'd push not just the tailings and the old mill, but all of the region's industrial and often-toxic past into the dark corners of their minds, convincing themselves that it was all safe now, all cleaned up, that it made sense to drop a million or more on a house in south Durango, where for decades sulfur-dioxide-tinged train smoke, lead-loaded smelter smoke, and radon-tinged dust had settled out of the sky. He had hoped that historic preservation and remembering would not only attract people to the region, but also would help us learn from all of our mistakes. Instead we got mass amnesia as a form of economic development.

There are those, however, who will never forget. The surviving mill workers whose friends died painful deaths won't forget. Those who lived downwind or downstream from the mill whose grandmother, father, aunt, or friend died of cancer or kidney failure will always wonder if it was the tailings, the Nevada nuclear tests, not enough sunscreen, or just terrible luck that killed their loved ones.

My dad died of lung cancer. Most likely it was caused by smoking too many damned cigarettes, but I will never forget the way, on spring days when the wind really kicked up, the yellow and gray dust lifted off the tailings piles and fluttered so lightly through the bright blue sky.

PART III

We're All
Downstreamers

Black Decade

PASSENGERS STEPPING OFF THE OLD STEAM TRAIN IN SILVERTON during the 1950s or '60s would have been greeted by a gaudy, chaotic scene, part Western movie set, part third-world Medina. A truck kicks up dust on Blair Street, a loudspeaker affixed to the top blaring out advertisements. A giant cowboy cutout juts up from the facade of the Bent Elbow bar and restaurant where a white-hatted guy shoots a black-hatted guy off the balcony, the latter's dying words a list of the lunch specials at the Bent. Effie Andreatta's dog runs by, its fur painted—yes, painted—with an advertisement for the San Juan Cafe. And then a scuffle—this one real—as a merchant punches his competitor in the head.

This was Silverton sans mining. The Shenandoah-Dives Mine, the last big operator in the Silverton Caldera, hung on through World War II. But after the war the global market was thrown open, causing metal prices to plummet. In 1953, the Shenandoah-Dives was shuttered for good. The local economy, which was fueled almost entirely by that single mine, sputtered and gasped, ushering in what Silvertonians would come to call the "Black Decade."

The town clung to life, however, thanks in part to a

Hollywood-fueled, global fascination with the Wild West of American mythology. At the time, the historic remnants of the Old West, and thus the natural backdrops for movies about it, were being erased by post-War population and energy booms. Silverton was insulated, however, by its own hard luck; while other towns were getting mid-century architectural makeovers, Silverton's decades-old streetscapes were falling into disrepair. Meanwhile, the Durango-to-Silverton stretch of railroad, on the brink of being abandoned, was a perfect symbol of those days of yore. It starred alongside the likes of Clark Gable and Barbara Stanwyck in films such as *A Ticket to Tomahawk* and *Across the Wide Missouri*. It switched from hauling ore to carrying sightseers, and almost overnight Silverton morphed from mining town to a facsimile of a Hollywood version of a place that never existed.

Tourism wasn't new to Silverton. Sightseers had been riding the train to the mining town since the 1880s. Yet catering to the visitors had always been gravy atop the mining money that had built and sustained the community for eight decades. Now the townsfolk were reduced to peddling hamburgers or tchotchkes to a limited crowd of people that got off the train, spent a couple hours walking around, and then left again. It felt undignified and desperate to hawk a false "rinky-dink, rubber tomahawk" version of history, as lifelong Silvertonian and local historical society leader Bev Rich told me. And for what? The pay was lousy, the tourist season only a few months long, and the people's labor produced nothing.

Mining, on the other hand, provided the metals with which the nation's vast infrastructure was built, sustained the war efforts, and supplied the raw materials for the booming automobile factories. The industry in Silverton had built a strong middle class, providing enough financial security to encourage families to put down roots, start businesses, and work to improve the community. During World War II, when many of Silverton's young miners left to Europe or the Pacific, a lot of older Hispanic people came up from the San Luis Valley to take their places, adding to the multi-cultural tapestry that was Silverton. "It was a blue-collar town but an upper-class blue-collar town," Rich says. "It was a great place to grow up because everyone's dad worked in the mine and everyone was equal. Mining was the great equalizer. It was racially diverse and it was safe."

That, it seemed, had vanished, even as much of the rest of the nation was enjoying unprecedented prosperity. Silverton's population plummeted as miners and their families fled to the uranium mines and gas fields of the surrounding lowlands. Those who remained had little choice but to open businesses selling t-shirts, shot glasses, and hot dogs, desperately hanging on until the good times came back.

No one could have guessed that the same uranium boom that lured miners away from Silverton would indirectly save the town, too, but that's what happened. In 1959 Standard Uranium Corporation, which was founded a few years earlier by Moab's uranium magnate Charlie Steen, announced it was getting into the metals mining business and would revive the Sunnyside Mine that had lain dormant for two decades. The Sunnyside stood alongside the Gold King as one of the Caldera's grandest and oldest operations. The first claims were staked on the shores of Lake Emma back in 1873, over Bonita Peak from the Gold King, and the mine was soon making its owners rich.

Operating the Sunnyside had always been a challenge,

however, because the mine's entrance was above most of the workings. That meant that ore had to be hauled up out of the mine, against gravity, then shipped by tram back down to the mill at the company town of Eureka. Meanwhile, large volumes of groundwater poured into the mine and pooled there, so it had to be pumped upward out of the workings. All this added up to higher, unbearable costs, which led the owner, U.S. Smelting, Refining, Milling, and Mining Company, to shut the mine down in 1930. While it reopened briefly in 1937, the water issue and low metal prices shut it back down, seemingly for good this time, in 1938.

Standard Uranium had a solution. It would use some of the hefty profits it had reaped from its San Juan County, Utah, uranium mines to extend the existing American Tunnel from the old town site of Gladstone two miles underground to the Sunnyside's extensive workings under Lake Emma. The owners of the Gold King Mine had first driven the American Tunnel in the early 1900s as a safer, better way to access their workings in Bonita Peak, but the Gold King shut down before the tunnel was linked to it. Now, the American Tunnel would serve its intended function, only for the Sunnyside Mine, not the defunct Gold King. Ore could more easily be removed via the tunnel, then trucked to the old Shenandoah-Dives/Mayflower Mill just outside of Silverton. The tunnel would also serve as a giant drainpipe for the Sunnyside's acid mine drainage.

Standard Uranium changed its name to Standard Metals and in 1960 began the formidable job of widening and extending the American Tunnel. Along the existing six thousand feet of tunnel, water dripped and poured in from above via fissures and faults. And when the tunnelers got about nine thousand feet underground, they hit faults and fractures that gushed three thousand gallons of water per minute. The multi-million-gallon mine pool that had built up in the Sunnyside's workings in the absence of pumping was gradually draining through the fissures, vastly preferable to all the water coming out at once. The tunnel's drivers reached their target, the Washington vein, in January of 1961, as well as a mine pool with some eight hundred feet of hydraulic head. The water pressure was so great it destroyed 150 feet of drill string. Large-scale mining had returned to the Silverton Caldera.

The young tourism industry didn't skitter off and hide at the return of its older economic brother, however. Tourism continued to grow, though the locals accepted it grudgingly. Miners, working underground, looked out for one another. Tourism, on the other hand, was a crassly commercial, dog-eat-dog world that favored tchotchke shops over grocery stores or other businesses that catered to locals. Silverton was torn apart by these conflicting identities in a long-running, Dr. Jekyll-Mr. Hyde struggle.

Not long after the Sunnyside was revived, a young man named Allen Nossaman partnered with Durango schoolteacher Tommy Neal to buy the *Silverton Standard* newspaper from Ross Beaber, who had run it for many years. Nossaman—tall and lanky with a long beard and a balding pate, even in his twenties—was extremely bright and had recently graduated from the University of Colorado, Boulder. He was hardly the stereotypical country newspaper man. Yet he would run the *Standard* for a decade, go on to be the county judge, its archivist, and preeminent historian, deeply influencing Silverton and the region. Running a weekly newspaper isn't easy now. Back then it was orders of magnitude harder: Nossaman had to be a mechanic as well as a reporter, as the paper was produced on letterpress equipment, including a byzantine contraption known as a linotype, blocks of wood type and graphics, and the cantankerous beast of a press. Ross Beaber's son, Paul, a teenager at the time, helped Nossaman keep the equipment from going haywire.

Nossaman jumped into the ring swinging, immediately dispensing with the folksy tone that characterizes most small-town rags. He spoke truth to power in scathing but well-reasoned editorials. And when in 1963 he went off to National Guard basic training (one way to avoid the draft), he called in his old friends to run the operation, including my father, Ian Thompson, who interrupted his studies at CU to head down to Silverton. My mom, Janet Billings, who was an artist working as a school teacher, came to town not long after to work at the little school. None of them were exactly newcomers to the region. My mom grew up on her parents' farm in the Animas Valley with six siblings; Nossaman was born in Denver but grew up in Cedaredge, Colorado, where his parents ran the newspaper. My dad's father had a debilitating Parkinson's-like sickness, possibly from being gassed while fighting in World War I, so his mother was the sole breadwinner, teaching in various country schools around the Four Corners—Allison, Colorado; Peñasco, New Mexico; and Dolores, Colorado, where my dad graduated high school.

All of them fit the type—smart, creative, educated—that normally fled the Interior West for stimulation and careers on the coasts. Yet they bucked the trend and remained in the region. And over the next decade or so, Silverton became an unlikely destination of a sort of rural Western intelligentsia, drawn by the mountains, the wildness, the culture, the history, and perhaps most of all, the authenticity of the community.

Even as surrounding towns were becoming homogenized by cookie-cutter suburban development, mass franchising, and mobility, a sense of something called Place was flourishing in Silverton.

Nossaman and his cohorts were mostly unabashed environmentalists. After the passage of the 1964 Wilderness Act they fought relentlessly to get nearly a half-million acres of the San Juan Mountains preserved as the Weminuche Wilderness. And in early 1964 my dad wrote an editorial bashing the newly built Glen Canyon Dam and praising David Brower, the Sierra Club's executive director at the time and the dam's biggest foe. Although *Standard* co-owner Neal would work for Senator Wayne Aspinall, Colorado's staunchest supporter of plumbing the West, the *Standard*'s writers took an adversarial stance toward the gargantuan Animas-La Plata Project. A version of the project that included a reservoir on the Animas River just above Silverton, a variety of lower elevation reservoirs, and hundreds of miles of canals and pipelines, got congressional approval in 1968 thanks to Aspinall's efforts. The Vietnam War killed that particular iteration. After many more false starts, the controversial project would finally come to fruition, albeit in a diminished form, in the 1990s, thanks in large part to Durango attorney Sam Maynes, who came from an old Silverton family known for their work ethic and as Prohibition-era bootleggers.

In the Silverton identity conflict, however, the group sided with mining over tourism. In July 1963, Terry Marshall wrote a blistering treatise for the *Standard* on the surreal scene that unfolded every day at "train time":

You realize that Silverton, its hardrock mining fortunes dwindling, must rely more and more on the tourist. . . . But you wonder if the carnival atmosphere must prevail—the loudspeak-

ers, the cheap souvenirs, the cotton candy.... You wonder if there is not something else, something more authentic that will distinguish this small town with its vast mining history, its beautiful scenery, its narrow gauge railroad from the thousands of other small towns in the United States ...

It wasn't that tourism itself was evil, it's just that the brand of tourism that Silverton had come to rely on was inauthentic and inaccurate. Silverton had an inferiority complex, falsely believing that its intrinsic assets—its true history, the most spectacular mountain range in the lower forty-eight, its people—were not good enough to draw visitors. Instead, it needed to create some sort of artificial lure. Back then it was the Wild West theme show, these days it's opening town streets to all-terrain vehicles.

Silverton certainly had the terrain, the snow, and the skiing history to follow in the footprints of Aspen, a former mining town that was building skiing into its growth industry at the time. In the early '60s some locals cut a couple runs and installed a ragtag rope tow at the base of Kendall Mountain on the edge of town, and a proposal was floated to build a more substantial ski area on the north-facing slopes of Sultan Mountain. Thompson advocated hard for winter recreation, and for establishing Silverton and its surroundings as a high-altitude Olympic cross-country ski team training ground. That might have at least balanced out what was rapidly becoming a one-season economy.

The old businesses that catered to locals—the bakeries, the grocery stores, the insurance agencies, and the hardware stores—gave way to new ones whose sole *raison d'etre* was to get some of the dollars carried in by the thousand or so people who spilled off the train each day. Naturally, when the train stopped running for the winter, so did the businesses. The merchants boarded up the windows and headed south to wait until the train emerged from hibernation in May. More and more, Silverton was becoming a summer-only town, even with the mine running full bore.

"Today, downtown Silverton is all but dead as a year-round community center, and one has only to look at the names over the boarded-up doors and dark windows on a winter night to know that The Train is the instrument of death," George Sibley, a longtime western Colorado writer, wrote in the *Mountain Gazette* in 1975, referring not to the railroad itself but to the new economy it ushered in. "To run a four-month, Train oriented business and go south for the winter has become simply too lucrative—too natural, within the existing, rational system. Among the miners, still the core of what remains of the Silverton community, there is an attitude ranging from bare tolerance to outright disgust toward The Train."

When it came to the local mining industry, the *Standard*'s new guard took a more nuanced stance. When Standard Metals' mill leaked cyanide into the Animas River in the early 1960s, Nossaman held the company's feet to the fire. And the *Standard*'s editor did not try to gloss over the 1966 state health and wildlife departments' determination that a century of mining had rendered the Upper Animas watershed uninhabitable to fish. The situation was especially bad on the stretch of Animas River above Silverton, thanks to leaky tailings ponds at the Pride of the West Mill and Standard Metals' inadequate tailings pond containment system.

Still, Thompson was quick to distinguish between hardrock mining in the Silverton area and the dams, strip mines, and power plants that were industrializing other parts of the region at the time. Silverton-area mining was getting more mechanized, but remained mostly a person-to-rock relationship, with men and women going underground and chipping away at the ore with hand and power tools. It may have been destructive, but the people doing the mining were connected to the land, nonetheless. The same couldn't be said for the draglines gouging away at sacred landscapes, or for the power plants' sulfur-dioxide-tinged smoke blotting out the sun and turning rain into acid.

The stately architecture and distinctive culture of Silverton and its sister towns around the West—Butte, Bisbee, Telluride—sprang from a slower-paced style of mining, Ray Rasker, an economist and Executive Director of Headwaters Economics, told me once. "Mining today is at a much faster pace and a much larger scale. As a result, there is not a long-term investment in the communities, so you don't get the architecture and the culture and the sense of place."

In 1964 the Sunnyside Mill's tailings pond was breached, sending tons of slime into the river, sullying the waters down to Durango and beyond. People in Durango were livid; the old slime wars were rekindled. Thompson responded with an editorial that, if not quite defended the mine, definitely took Silverton's side over Durango. He bashed Durango's "self-righteous indignation," and pointed out that the bigger town should clean up its own messes—such as the uranium tailings pile on the river's banks—before casting stones upstream. "To the realist," he wrote, "the issue was between tourism and a basic industry. Silverton depends on the basic industry and Durango on the tourism. Silverton acted straightforwardly in defense of its economy and Durango borrowed a twentieth century ideal which it has shown no sign of living up to in order to hide its equally economic motivation. Morally, it would be easier to accept the Silverton defense."

Project Skywater

ATALL, SKINNY GUY BY THE NAME OF DON BACH-MAN arrived in Silverton in May 1971 to begin a long stint working, indirectly, for the federal government. "I stopped at the Grand Imperial to listen in on a busy town of 850 people supported by the employment of two large mines, the Sunnyside and the Idarado," wrote Bachman years later in the *Silverton Mountain Journal.* "I wasn't long on the bar stool before two fellows got up from a table and sandwiched me, right and left, with the admonition from the big one on the right of, 'We don't allow no fucking hippies in here' . . ."

Bachman wasn't even all that scruffy at the time, nor did the Crested Butte barkeep consider himself much of a hippy. He explained that he was an avalanche professional, in Silverton to partake in the most comprehensive study ever taken in the United States of snow and the destruction it brings when it slides down mountains. If anything, this made him look worse in the eyes of the miners. But just as they were about to toss Bachman out onto Greene Street, a state highway worker came to Bachman's aid. He survived the evening, went on to tip back many a beer with the miners who had accosted him, and would eventually repay his rescuer by helping develop a program to keep highway workers safe. He was in Silverton for the San Juan Avalanche Project, a sub-study of Project Skywater, a massive effort to control the weather in the West.

"BEFORE THE DAM," reads the brochure handed out to people who come to gawk at the enormity of Glen Canyon Dam, "the Colorado River was a sediment-laden river that fluctuated in flow according to the seasons." It was a living being, in other words, muddy, wild, tumultuous, and unpredictable, teeming with weird-looking razorback suckers and giant Colorado pikeminnows. Mostly, it was imbued with power. It took 9.6 million tons of concrete—a sterile and awe-inspiring plug 300 feet thick at its base, and 1,500 feet long at its crest—to harness and diminish that power.

The history of white settlement of the West is one of trying to wrest control over the natural world, particularly water, and redirecting it to fit our needs. After World War II, this effort climaxed with a paroxysm of dam- and tunnel- and canal-building on the Colorado River and its tributaries: the San Juan, the Gunnison, the Dolores, and the Green. It was the largest plumbing project the world had ever seen, and its centerpiece was certainly Glen Canyon Dam, behind which the waters of the Colorado started backing up in 1963.

Still, we weren't content. Our engineering marvels had succeeded in catching what little water the mountain snows offered, but they were impotent against an outright lack of snowfall. We could thumb our noses at the gods with our bigger-than-life dams and our pipelines, but we couldn't force the gods to deliver precipitation. "Yet with all our planning and building and looking ahead to try to outguess the future," Interior Secretary Stewart Udall said in a 1966 speech to Congress, "we find ourselves still at the mercy of the weather."

To get the upper hand, the Bureau of Reclamation decided to turn to shooting chemical nuclei into moisture-laden clouds, otherwise known as cloud seeding, to aid in the formation of rain and snow, thus increasing precipitation. Before implementing this untested technology across the West, however, the Bureau needed to experiment in a place without too many people to suffer from side effects. It chose one of the Colorado River watershed's largest natural reservoirs: the San Juan Mountain snowpack. It called the test phase, launched in the early 1970s, Project Skywater.

Silverton didn't need or want any more snow. With no agricultural land in the entire county, spring runoff was an irritant rather than an asset. San Juan County never got its hoped-for ski area, so there was no recreation economy that an extra helping of powder would benefit. Indeed, since its establishment a century earlier, the denizens of Silverton had waged an epic struggle against the snow. Snow blocked roads and railroads, it crushed roofs, it piled up so high that houses were built with second-story doors as snowbound escapes. When it finally melted, come March or April, the snow made an even bigger mess, turning the dirt streets to mush and pulling the cold underground and freezing the pipes solid. More than one hundred lives had been lost in the county to avalanches over the decades, from miners crushed in their cabins or boardinghouses, to a reverend and his two daughters swept away in 1963 by the notorious East Riverside slide on Highway 550, to a state plow driver killed by the same slide in 1970. The amount of money that had been spent to plow roads and to rebuild snowslide-pummeled infrastructure was incalculable.

So the Bureau of Reclamation decided to expand its experiment to take a comprehensive look at avalanches in the San Juan Mountains, too. The University of Colorado's Institute of Arctic and Alpine Research was chosen to lead the San Juan Avalanche Project from 1971 to 1976. Scientists and support staff were imported to run the show, including Dr. Ed LaChapelle, one of the world's preeminent snow scientists, who was accompanied by his wife Dolores, a pioneer of the environmental philosophy known as Deep Ecology, a groundbreaking powder skier, and the author of several books, including *Sacred Land, Sacred Sex: Rapture of the Deep* and *Deep Powder Snow.* Others, such as Bachman, Betsy Vesselego, Richard Armstrong, Tim Lane, and Jerry Roberts came to Silverton to work on the project, too. A select few are remembered not only for their contributions to the science, but also for their eccentricity, for pioneering many of the area's backcountry ski routes, and for being able to hold their own in a tavern full of rowdy miners.

If ever there was a time that Silverton lived up to the Wild West image that the Blair Street carnival barkers promoted, it would be the 1970s, not the 1880s. Miners, members of the burgeoning counterculture, folks fleeing the outside world, and snow scientists all converged here at a time when the planet seemed on the verge of a political and social meltdown—Vietnam, Watergate, Patty Hearst, hijackings. Rather than insulating Silverton from the collective insanity, the isolation only served to amplify it. It was a yeasty, intoxicated, rip-roaring, and sometimes violent time and place.

Two major mines were operating, the Sunnyside at the old town of Gladstone and the Idarado just north of Red Mountain Pass's summit, each employing hundreds of miners and support staff. A handful of smaller mines also produced ore. The wages were substantial, and every Friday miners would line up at the bank and cash their paychecks—many of them didn't have bank accounts—and blow a good portion of their earnings on parties, booze, and cocaine. I've heard stories of flocks of miners chartering a plane and flying to Las Vegas for the weekend, of nights that ended with revelers literally crawling home from one drinking hole or another at dawn. In August 1970 a mass brawl broke out at The Place, a "3.2 bar," where eighteen year olds could swill diluted beer. It spilled out into the street and a horde of humanity containing as many as 150 people oozed down the street for an entire block even as they punched, shoved, grappled, and scratched. "It was not exactly slow," said Bill Gardner, Silverton's town cop for three years in the 1970s, who had returned to work as town administrator just weeks prior to the Gold King spill. "You had domestic violence, bar fights . . . everything from lost dogs to attempted homicides."

Dynamite, easy to come by in a mining town, was often used in crimes, including in a robbery of Standard Metals. Someone bombed the old train depot in September 1975, the explosion's report echoing through town moments before the train passed by. Earlier that summer the train tracks were greased on the steepest incline between Durango and Silverton, as though someone had been watching too many of the Westerns filmed here, and in a separate incident someone rolled a boulder onto the tracks, nearly taking out a maintenance car and the person in it. The crimes were never pinned on anyone, and motives never discovered.

Down south, Durango experienced its own social upheaval. It was sandwiched between two extractive industry booms—oil and gas to the south and hardrock gold mining to the north—yet was left out of the frenzy. Durango's uranium mill had shut down in the 1960s, the smelter long before that. The sawmill and other industries faded, as did ranching and farming. Durango—with its made-for-myths moniker—embraced the Old-West-seeking tourists and refashioned itself accordingly, its residents happy to move beyond what was increasingly seen as a rape-and-pillage economy into a kinder, gentler, amenities one.

Yet in reality, Durango's economy was as tightly bound to mining and drilling as was Farmington's or Silverton's. It's just that, thanks again to the geology-is-destiny concept, the community was able to reap the benefits without having gas wells in school yards or hydraulic fracturing chemical depots next to strip malls. Lawyers and doctors who served the region and the oil and gas and mining companies had offices in Durango. In 1965, Purgatory ski area opened thirty miles north of Durango in the San Juan Mountains, instantly giving Durango a winter tourist economy to supplement the already healthy summer one. It was financed by oilfield cash: Purgatory's founder and owner for decades was Ray Duncan, an oilman who had set up shop in Durango with his father in 1958 before moving Duncan Oil to Denver.[55] Silverton folks traveled to Durango with mining-earned money to buy clothing or groceries and eat at the upscale restaurants that had popped up to cater to tourists. The tourists, in turn, were from Houston and New Mexico, flush with oil and gas boom dollars. Durango's nascent amenities economy was an extractive economy, once removed. It all added up to give the place a boomtown feel, tinged with boisterous ski bum culture.

LIKE SPLICES FROM A SCRATCHY HOME MOVIE, my memories of the time are lucid but limited to disjointed glimpses.

I don't know in which order they occurred, or whether I was four years old or eight.

After Nossaman, the young Silverton newspaper man, returned from basic training, my dad was out of a job at the *Standard*. He worked a stint at the Silver Wing Mine above Silverton, but he was no miner. So he and my mom headed back to Boulder, where my brother was born, and then back to Durango, where I was born and where my mom took up her weaving and other textile arts and my dad worked for the *Durango Herald*. We lived in an old house in Durango not far from the river. Our next door neighbor was an old Italian American coal miner named Frank. He took my brother fishing for giant catfish over in Navajo reservoir. He called me Penelope because of my floppy long hair and my squeaky voice.

We went to Silverton a lot back then, sometimes for several days in the winter when my dad would guest-edit the *Standard* for the owners so that they could escape to milder climes for a week or two. I remember one trip up there in particular. This clip of mental film starts on the north side of Coal Bank Pass between Durango and Silverton: *We are in our old white station wagon and I'm wearing that stupid fuzzy blue coat that I refused to take off, even when we went to Silverton where I'd surely get teased by the miners' kids, who were tough and scary. A big storm went through last night and we are in a traffic jam on the highway waiting for the big rotary plow to clear the avalanche debris from the West Lime Creek slide. It is a sunny day, the sky almost painfully blue, the new snow sparkly and deep.*

The plow cuts a one-lane-wide canyon through the snow, and the cars file through. We're near the end of the line as we head up Molas Pass and then back down the other side. We watch intently for the first view of Silverton far below. Then something

compels me to look up the slope next to the road and I see it, a
waterfall of snow bearing down on us. It pounds into the pave-
ment just feet behind us. I gasp and turn back to my mom and
my brother to see if they noticed. They did not. I say nothing. Life
is like that sometimes.

I don't know that I really understood the turmoil of the
times in which I was growing up, since I had nothing to com-
pare it to. But moments stick in my mind still, like when an
arsonist burned down almost an entire block of commercial
buildings on Main Avenue in Durango, killing a firefighter and
a police officer. My dad went down to take pictures of the fire
and my mom drove us up onto Cemetery Hill to watch the
drama unfold. A few years later, we were awoken in the night
by the sound of an explosion. The next morning we learned
that the owner of a motorcycle shop just across the river from
where we lived had been building bombs to blow the place up
so he could collect insurance when one of the bombs went off
prematurely. Cops swarmed the neighborhood; my friends and
I, fancying ourselves amateur sleuths, discovered droplets of
dried blood on the sidewalk and on the footbridge across the
river.

Sometimes the river ran yellow-gray from tailings spilled
upstream, not the color of Tang, but that of Grey Poupon.

I remember the soothing rhythmic sound of my mom's
loom, the staccato of my dad's typewriter; racing our bikes
around the block in the dark; playing hide-and-seek with all
the neighborhood kids on summer nights and the euphoric
feeling you get just as day slips into night and you're running
for base with all you've got and your feet leave the ground and
for a second you're flying, really flying.

Most of my memories from the 1970s, though, are of my

mom's parents' farm in the Animas Valley several miles north of Durango. Up until I was five or six, they lived in the old house, a rickety place with crooked floors and a thick, scratchy, hemp rope in place of a stair rail. Then they divided off a chunk of the forty acres and built a new house, which seemed luxurious at the time to me, but really was quite modest and small. They moved in there, kept a couple of acres, and sold the rest of the land. So even after they retired, they still lived on the Farm, and still lived a lot like farmers.

And sometimes, especially in the spring after the first cutting of hay, the smell and the light ignite a conflagration of images in my mind, of sensations of the Farm: *The way the tiny droplets of water condensed on the side of the metal ice cream container; it is the way the apples hung so heavy on the trees in autumn when we drove underneath in the old white pickup and shook the fruit off to be ground up then pressed in the old cider press; it is the feeling of comfort hiding between rows of corn, the red dirt warm underneath; the smell of her oatmeal cookies baking in the kitchen; the precise, cloying taste of the orange-flavored chocolate my grandpa bought me when we went to the sale barn to buy or sell livestock; it is in the flavor of fresh, home-made strawberry ice cream; it is in the smell of the Avon lotion that she used to put on my hands after I took a bath; it is in her hands, snapping peas; it is in the sound of an irrigation ditch, gurgling its way down to the fields; it is in the smell of hay.*

It is that stormy day when I am trying on a shirt that my grandmother bought me. It has pictures of cowboys and horses and just as I snap the last fake-pearl snap lightning flashes and thunder so loud it seems to have come from within my head. We used to play in that haybarn, climb up on the bales so itchy and wobbly and jump and dive and I think a cousin broke her leg up there once. Now a wisp of smoke issues from the roof. My dad and grandpa run down to save the tractor and the neighbor's boat from inside. It explodes in glorious red-orange flame.

It is a place where, in the evenings in summer, it gets real cool and it gets quiet, just a few cars drive by on the new highway, the frogs chirp, the mosquitos buzz, the red-winged blackbirds talk, and in the distance a dog barks. The ditch gurgles on by and my cousins are laughing and my aunts yell to us to get inside 'cause the mosquito man is coming with the fog of malathion. The apples are small and green still, but the raspberries are ripe.

And far down below the pasture, past the new highway, through the milkweed and asparagus and beyond the cottonwood trees, is the river. It is muttering quietly to itself. Its fish come up from the murky depths for the bugs, and swallows skim the still waters. And it runs slowly here, the river does, oh so slowly.

PROJECT SKYWATER NEVER PROGRESSED BEYOND THE PILOT PHASE. Small-scale attempts to tinker with the weather have continued, sporadically, in the San Juan Mountains, however. Each year the water conservation folks and the ski areas pitch in thousands of dollars for the effort. As the clouds build, private contractors aim their silver iodide generators at the sky and flip them on, hoping to coax reluctant snow to fall. The technology remains unproven, but for water managers it serves as a good placebo; they can say that at least they're trying to create more precipitation. Ski areas get a good PR boost just by saying that they're spending $20,000 on a mass cloud-seeding campaign.

The San Juan Avalanche Project may never get its own chapter in Silverton's rough and tumble history, but it probably should. One of the biggest such studies ever conducted, it informed San Juan County's creation and implementation of avalanche zoning regulations for backcountry development. It also provided the foundation for the U.S. Highway 550 Avalanche Reduction Project, which was finally implemented in 1992 after yet another plow driver was killed by the East Riverside Slide on Red Mountain Pass. Up until then, the state highway department didn't close the highway because of avalanche danger—the highway closed itself, as they liked to say, when snow and avalanches came down so fast and furious that the plows couldn't keep up. This non-policy got a fair number of people killed.

More importantly, though, the project and the people it brought to town subtly introduced a new concept here, even if it is one that has yet to be fully realized. There is life, an economy, and an identity for Silverton apart from mining and tourism, and it doesn't require selling out or wrecking the land on which they depend.

Lake Emma

MAYBE THE MINING ENGINEERS MADE A MIS-TAKE, or they chased the vein too recklessly, or they were blinded by greed. Certainly they were lucky. Had the timing been a little different, had the rock and ice and soil given way just hours later, it would have gone down as one of the deadliest mining disasters in the history of the West. But Lake Emma was drained on Sunday, June 4, 1978, and no one was working underground at the Sunnyside Mine at the time.

Prior to the disaster, the Sunnyside Mine, still operated by Standard Metals, prospered. Gold prices tend to increase during times of economic or political instability, and between 1969 and 1978 the price of gold went up fivefold. The Sunnyside was the state's leading gold producer, while also producing lead, zinc, and copper. It employed some two hundred people and churned through hundreds of tons of ore per day. Yet it had also had its share of problems.

When Standard Metals took over the Mayflower/Shenandoah-Dives Mill just upstream of Silverton it inherited Charles Chase's tailings disposal system, which consisted of sand walls containing the tailings and associated water. In June 1975, in one of many preludes to the Gold King Mine spill, heavy rains on top of ice buildup breached the sand wall, sending an estimated fifty thousand to one hundred thousand tons of tailings into the Animas River. As the slug of heavy-metal-laden mill slimes moved downstream the river became the color and consistency of "aluminum paint," according to a *Durango Herald* reporter at the time. Of thirty-one rainbow trout placed in a cage in the water in Durango, all but four died within twenty-four hours. Cyanide was found in the river at levels of three parts per million. Aztec and Farmington had to shut down their municipal water pumps.

Folks downstream, who had watched their river turn various shades of yellowish-gray countless times, demanded accountability. By then there was a statutory framework to provide that, though without sharp enforcement teeth, yet. Three years earlier Congress had passed significant amendments to the Federal Water Pollution Act, creating what's now known as the Clean Water Act. The law required all polluters to get permits for point-source discharges, like a wastewater drainpipe, for example, or a draining mine adit. Mining-specific rules were not finalized until 1978, however, so initially the law had little effect on Standard Metals' operations aside from requiring it to permit and monitor its discharges. About 1,600 gallons per minute of acid mine drainage—or nearly one Gold King Mine spill every thirty-six hours—was pouring out of the American Tunnel. It carried with it three hundred pounds of zinc each day, along with an assortment of other metals, all of which flowed directly into Cement Creek without any treatment.

Sunnyside's mine manager, Allen Bird, downplayed the tailings spill. He claimed that there was no fish kill—he sent employees down the river by boat to prove it—despite the fish cage results that showed otherwise. His protests echoed those of Charles Chase, who claimed that tailings were good fertilizer for farmers' crops. Ultimately, Standard Metals was slapped with a $40,000 fine, but got the amount reduced to $15,000. While hardly commensurate with the damage done, it did show that the state had made some pollution regulation headway from just a few decades earlier (an equally catastrophic spill by Chase's mill in 1947 had gone unpunished).

In early June of 1978, deep within the bowels of the Sunnyside Mine, miners worked their way upward along a high-grade gold vein. The mine's engineers knew they were driving toward the base of Lake Emma, a once-pristine high alpine gem at about 12,600 feet in elevation. There was no reason to be concerned, however, because the geologic maps showed that a thick layer of solid bedrock separated the mine workings from the lake's cold, shallow waters. In fact, while the lake itself was no more than fifteen feet deep, it rested atop a thick, V-shaped pile of silt, which itself sat atop a big crack that had probably been formed when an ancient glacier pulled a section of the vein out of the surrounding rock. Little did the geologists know that the only thing keeping the lake from draining into the mine was a plug of frozen mud and ice lodged in the crack.

On Friday, June 2, a couple of veteran miners noticed an inordinate amount of water pouring into the workings from the rocks above. They didn't like what they saw, and vowed not to return to work on Monday. They'd never get the chance, anyway. The warmth from the mine softened the ice plug, and sometime that Sunday afternoon, with the workers all off for the weekend, it gave way.

As many as one million tons of thick, black mud, combined with somewhere between five million to twenty-five million gallons of water—estimates vary wildly—poured into the mine, tearing out timbers, crushing equipment, filling tunnels up with mud. It surged through two miles of the American Tunnel before shooting out of the portal at Gladstone like a giant stream of projectile vomit. San Juan County Sheriff Virgil Mason watched a ten-foot-high wall of black water careen through the canyon towards Silverton. Once again, the Animas River was defiled for one hundred miles or more downstream. Fish were killed. A lake vanished. As would be the case with the Gold King blowout thirty-seven years later, the disaster was the result of a gross miscalculation. Some might call it negligence. The state deemed it an "act of God," so the company wasn't fined or otherwise punished for the damage done.

For Standard Metals, the disaster's timing couldn't have been worse. Gold prices shot up 120 percent to a new high in 1979. Yet instead of cashing in on it, the Sunnyside miners were working full-time to muck the mud and debris out of the mine. When Standard Metals tried to collect on its $9 million insurance policy its carrier refused to pay, partly dispelling rumors that the company had intentionally breached the lake in order to collect insurance. Finally, after a long and costly court battle, the company got just $5.5 million for its troubles.

By the time the mine reopened in 1979, the EPA had—after a three-year delay—issued a final rule on ore-mining point-source discharges under the Clean Water Act. That meant that Standard Metals would have to start cleaning the acid mine drainage pouring from the American Tunnel, or at least create the appearance of doing so. The treatment plant they installed was substandard, and allowed upwards of one hundred pounds of zinc per day to enter the watershed. The state department of health, which deals with permitting and enforcement under the Clean Water Act, appears to have turned a blind eye. Perhaps that's because there was virtually no public outcry regarding acid mine drainage, regardless of how harmful it may be to river ecosystems; the downstreamers primarily had raised a fuss over the far more visible tailings spills. Meanwhile, the state hadn't even bothered with setting water quality standards on the area's streams as required by the Clean Water Act because the Upper Animas River and its tributaries were considered to be polluted beyond repair, the waters long since sacrificed on the altar of economic progress and profit.

As had always held true in Silverton, the profits from the Sunnyside were being siphoned out of the San Juan Mountains to faraway executives and shareholders. Standard Metals was a publicly-traded corporation, incorporated in Delaware because of that state's corporate-friendly tax laws. Boris Gresov took the reins of the company in the mid-1960s, then branched it out, acquiring cosmetic companies, of all things. When gold prices ballooned again in 1980, Gresov made other acquisitions, including the National Smelting and Refining Company and National Smelting of New Jersey (which owned a lead-battery recycling center that would ultimately be designated a Superfund site). Some of the big shareholders weren't pleased, and the largest shareholder, the Oklahoma Publishing Company, launched a takeover bid, alleging that Gresov and his fellow board members had artificially inflated stock prices, spent assets wastefully, and otherwise acted fraudulently.

The takeover bid failed, but not without dealing a blow to the already beleaguered company. At the same time, the subsidiaries were all struggling. The hits combined to force Standard Metals into bankruptcy in 1984, ending yet another chapter in San Juan Mountain mining history.

The Fish Question

The Zuñis, like the Navahoes, will not, under any circum-
stances, eat fish or any other water animal. The reason is this:
Abiding in a desert land, where water is scarce, they regard it as
especially sacred; hence all things really or apparently belonging
to it, and in particular all creatures living in it, are sacred or
deified. But, in the case of the fishes, they eat water, chew it, and
are therefore, since they also breathe water and the currents or
breaths of water, especially tabooed. . . . the eating of fish seems to
the Zuñis no less than cannibalism, and is followed by the direst
consequences, chief among which is madness . . .

—Frank Cushing in a letter to Washington Matthews,
October 5, 1897

THE HIGH MOUNTAIN STREAMS WERE RUNNING
ICE-COLD AND CLEAR in July 1985 as Bill Simon shoul-
dered an awkwardly-weighted backpack just northeast of
Silverton. He wasn't toting gear for some alpine excursion. In
his pack he carried thousands of fingerling trout, to be released
into Minnie Creek, a small tributary of the Animas. The fish
were a question. The answer would change everything.

Bill Simon grew up on Colorado's Front Range in the 1940s
and '50s, where his dad, a machinist, tried his hand at farm-

ing. When that didn't work out, a young Bill took over, leased the farm, and turned a profit. He attended the University of California, Berkeley, on a ski scholarship in the 1960s. After earning his undergraduate degree, he went to work on getting his doctorate in evolutionary ecology on a NASA fellowship. He helped start the Environmental Studies College there, and was on the founding board of Earth Day.

The Vietnam War was raging, and the military started taking an interest in Simon and the work he was doing. That's when the young scientist, who had also been doing some community organizing with the anti-war effort, decided it was time to go. He took a "permanent leave of absence" from Berkeley and landed in Silverton, as do so many other refugees from the outside. Simon found work on salvage mining operations, going into closed and abandoned mines and recovering ore that had been left behind. Later, he did some large-scale welding, building cyanide mills for the Sunnyside and Pride of the West mines. He even worked a bit at the Gold King for Apache Energy, which had designs, never realized, on reopening the long-defunct mine. Oftentimes, after completing whatever work he was hired to do, Simon would also clean up some of the junk from the old mines, and even plant a few trees.

The Colorado Department of Public Health and Environment and the state Division of Wildlife (now Colorado Parks and Wildlife) had pronounced most of the Silverton Caldera's waters "dead," thanks to natural mineralization, acid mine drainage, and tailings spills. As Simon cruised around the backcountry for work and for fun, he began to doubt the state's assessment. Sure, Cement Creek was never going to support fish, and probably never has. But other stream segments appeared healthy, even if they were fishless at the time. Maybe they could support trout.

In 1984 Simon was elected to the San Juan County Board of County Commissioners. It provided him a platform from which he could test his theory using fish as his guinea pigs and the watershed's streams, beaver ponds, and lakes as his laboratory. With a group of miners, who were also anglers, he hiked into the backcountry carrying packs that held thousands of tiny brook and cutthroat trout, donated by the state Division of Wildlife, and poured them into the healthiest-looking streams and lakes.

Over the months to come, Simon and his fellow citizen stockers returned to their test streams and checked on the experiment's progress. To their surprise, the fish in some places were doing well, and a smattering of the brook trout, a hardy, though non-native species, grew to as much as two pounds. The Clean Water Act's listed objective is "to restore and maintain the chemical, physical, and biological integrity of the Nation's waters." Its goal was to eliminate the discharge of pollutants into navigable waters by 1985, and "wherever attainable, an interim goal of water quality which provides for the protection and propagation of fish, shellfish, and wildlife ... be achieved ..." Prior to Simon's experiment, the "wherever attainable" phrase did not pertain to the Upper Animas. Now it did.

MOST OF AMERICA'S ENVIRONMENTAL INITIATIVES were built upon the notion that these lands, waters and the air were pristine, wild, and void of human influence prior to the arrival of Euro-American invaders. This was a place of "chemical, physical, and biological integrity," where bears and wolves and beaver roamed free, and the streams teemed with fish; where bands of Ute people followed the deer and the elk into the mountains, took only what they needed, and left nary a trace. All was in harmony, until the colonizers, the miners, the loggers, and the hunters came and subdued the earth, poisoned the waters, and killed the fish. The job of the Clean Water Act, the Clean Air Act, and the Endangered Species Act, then, is to restore the Paradise that was lost.

Eden, however, was a lot messier than once imagined. Pristine is an illusion. Humans altered the landscape for millennia before the Euro-American invasion. Archaic hunters may have wiped out ancient megafauna. The Ancestral Pueblo people likely cut too many trees, killed too many rabbits, and tried to reap too much from the soil, forcing them to migrate. Evidence suggests that the Ute people torched forests to drive deer and elk into their arrows, and burned grasslands to increase forage for game. And long before that, without the help of humans, some streams issuing from the Silverton Caldera ran orange with iron and others milky-green with aluminum.

Simon's fish experiment showed that fish could live in some parts of the Caldera. Yet it left another unanswered: Did fish ply these icy waters prior to mining, and if so, which species? Only by answering it will we know whether the efforts to clean up the watershed amount to restoring something that was lost, or creating something new, an artificial world fashioned after our myth.

There is no baseline data in this regard. The journals of the early Spanish explorers offer clues to what the ecology along the paths they followed looked like, and some of their botanical descriptions are illuminating. Yet they rarely mention aquatic flora and fauna except when Silvestre Vélez de Escalante writes about the Timpanogos people near Utah Lake, whom he calls "fish-eaters." Archaeology is not helpful: there aren't fish bones in Animas River Valley ancestral Puebloan sites because the people who lived there did not consume fish as part of their regular diet, and doing so may have been taboo due to the sanctity of water.

The first white settlers give a few more clues. In 1872, George Howard, one of the early white settlers of Bakers Park, hiked from what would become Silverton, up Mineral Creek, over what is now Ophir Pass, to the San Miguel River drainage and Trout Lake (née Fish Lake née San Miguel Lake) with two friends. From log rafts, using bacon and grasshoppers as bait, they caught a total of 220 fish, which they packed back into Baker's Park and sold to other miners for $1.50 per dozen. This suggests that the lakes closer to Silverton, in the upper Animas watershed, were devoid of fish, or at least were less bountiful than the trout-rich lake to the west.

The 1874 Hayden expedition, which included among its ranks that chronicler of a disappearing Eden, Franklin Rhoda, spent a few words on the ichthyology of the region. "No fishes were collected, although numerous attempts were made," wrote Ernest Ingersoll, the trip's zoologist. "The majority of our time was spent where they seemed to be entirely absent, or so extremely scarce that, although all were interested in the capture of certain species, not a trout graced our table during the whole trip." Yet they, too, traveled to Trout Lake on a peak-bagging expedition, and noticed that it was teeming with trout. Apparently they made no attempt to catch the fish.

Ingersoll and Hayden didn't make any systematic study of fish; their faunal focus was on mollusks—mostly freshwater or terrestrial snails. Cunningham Gulch, a cold, clear brook that enters the Animas River a few miles upstream from Silverton, was particularly rich with various freshwater and terrestrial snail species, including *Pupilla blandi*, *Vertigo californica*, and *Zonites fulvus*, which Ingersoll found slithering along a snowbank at eleven thousand feet in elevation.

Rhoda described Mineral Creek at its junction with the Animas River just below the new town of Silverton as being "highly impregnated with iron, sulphur, and other ingredients. . . . Almost all the water in this country is as pure as any in Colorado, but this stream is so strongly impregnated with mineral ingredients as to be quite unfit for drinking." Oddly, neither Rhoda nor anyone else in his party similarly described Cement Creek, which today is considered the nastier of the two streams.

It was not until Rhoda got down to "Animas City," the abandoned settlement that the Baker party had founded near what is now Baker's Bridge, that he mentioned fish in the Animas. "Trout are found in the river here, but how abundantly I cannot say," he wrote. "They have never been caught as far up as Baker's Park (Silverton)—due, probably, to the falls between the two points." Rhoda was referring to the Rockwood Gorge, a narrow stretch of granite-walled canyon above Baker's Bridge through which the Animas River rushes. There are no waterfalls, per se, but the gorge is choked with boulders and rapids that challenge even the most intrepid kayakers, finishing off with a "sieve" of rocks and debris that will kill anyone who attempts to boat it. It was into this stretch of river that Robert Redford and Paul Newman's stuntmen jumped in the 1969 film *Butch Cassidy and the Sundance Kid*.

Rhoda may have been right about a dearth of fish around Silverton, but his explanation was likely wrong. Trout are able swimmers, and while they can't make it up high waterfalls, they should have been able to navigate the Rockwood rapids. Nevertheless, the theory would hold for a time. In March 1885, Colonel Francis Snowden set about to fill the upper Animas fish void. He got forty thousand hardy, non-native, red-speckled eastern brook trout from a hatchery in Denver, and dumped them into the Animas River above Silverton. "Heretofore no trout have ever been known in the Animas above the falls in the box cañon just above the town of Rockwood," wrote the editor of the *Dolores News*, sticking with the Rockwood theory. "Below that point, fine trout have always abounded and all that was needed in the upper Animas was a start."

Finally, four years later, ichthyologist David Starr Jordan made an exhaustive survey of the fish in nearly every river basin in Utah and Colorado. It's a fascinating account, in which he catalogs the diverse and sometimes odd array of fishes in the Colorado River Basin and its tributaries and also lays out some of the existential threats to the same fish.

Of the Animas River, Jordan wrote: "Above its cañon of 'Lost Souls' it is clear, shallow, and swift flowing through an open canon with a bottom of rocks. In its upper course it is said to be without fish, one of its principal tributaries, Mineral Creek, rising in Red Mountain and Uncompahgre Pass, being highly charged with salts of iron. In the deep and narrow 'Cañon de las Animas Perdidas' [presumably the canyon between Silverton and the Rockwood Gorge] are many very deep pools, said to be full of trout."

Since Jordan did not survey the canyon himself, he doesn't know what species lurked in the deep, jade-green pools. Therefore he couldn't say whether they were native Colorado River cutthroats that had been there all along, regardless of the "falls" at Rockwood, or brook trout that had been stocked upstream then got washed into the canyon. And that leaves the pre-mining fish picture of the Upper Animas River rather fuzzy.

The snapshot of the Animas River below Rockwood is far sharper. Jordan and his colleagues did run nets through portions of the lower Animas River in the Animas Valley, which he refers to as Hermosa Park, and above and below Durango. Along with plenty of trout, presumably native and non-native, he also found a cornucopia of indigenous fish suggesting that Eden was a bizarre place indeed. Among the finned characters he encountered were *Catastomus latipinnis*, *Pantosteus delphinus*, and *Agosia yarrowi,* two suckers and a minnow. They found *Cottus bairdi punctulatus*—mottled sculpin, miller's thumb, the blob—under nearly every rock. As kids, my brother and I used to catch these homely, bigheaded, prehistoric-looking things in the Animas River in Durango with our hands for no particular reason except because we could.

Xyrauchen cypho, or razorback suckers, skulked in the murky green waters. With their torpedo-like heads giving way to a prominent humped back, they look like a fishy eighteen-wheeler with an especially tall trailer. And then there were *Ptychocheilus lucius*, "which ascend the river in the spring, going back to deep water after spawning in the summer." This monster was commonly known as "white salmon." Nowadays it goes by Colorado pikeminnow. These things can live for up to fifty years and grow to be six feet long; the biggest pikeminnow ever caught weighed ninety pounds. Old newspapers tell of anglers regularly reeling in twenty and thirty pounders on the Gunnison River near Delta and the Colorado River near Grand Junction. The best bait was a whole mouse. Pikeminnow travel extreme distances at times. In 2014, tagged fish were caught in Lake Powell, 144 miles downstream from where they were stocked. Once, these giant, finned torpedoes migrated throughout all but the coldest waters of the Colorado River Basin. But Glen Canyon and other dams all but extirpated them in the lower Colorado River Basin, and only several thousand still survive in warmer, upper reaches of the basin. There are probably fewer than fifty wild pikeminnows swimming the silty waters of the San Juan and its tributaries these days. But they are no longer the titans that they once were, and rarely grow larger than three feet long.

Large-scale milling of ore was just getting going in the San Juans when Jordan came through, so he didn't witness the river in its gray and turbid, mill-slimed state. He did note that in the Platte River and Arkansas River basins of eastern Colorado, "placer-mining and stamp-mills have filled the waters of otherwise clear streams with yellow or red clay, rendering them almost uninhabitable for trout." But in the southern and western part of the state he saw an even bigger danger—irrigation. He wrote: "Below the mouth of the cañons dam after dam and ditch after ditch turn off the water. In summer the beds of even large rivers (as the Rio Grande) are left wholly dry . . . the beds of many considerable streams (Rio la Jara, Rio Alamosa) are filled with dry clay and dust. Great numbers of trout, in many cases thousands of them, pass into these irrigation ditches and are left to perish in the fields. The destruction of trout by this agency is far greater than that due to all others combined, and it is going on in almost every irrigation ditch in Colorado."

The ichthyologist, however, was not similarly concerned about what effect filling up the streams with non-native fish would have on the aquatic biodiversity. He was a big advocate of stocking, and urged wildlife commissioners to keep adding rainbow and brook trout to Colorado's coldwater streams and catfish to the slower, muddier, warmer rivers, like the San Juan and the Colorado.

Within a decade of Jordan's study, the streams of the Animas River watershed had been completely altered, not just by the mill tailings and acid mine drainage now sullying the waters, but also by an industrial-sized program of fish stocking. The Colorado fish and wildlife agency dumped not only thousands of brookies and rainbows into the Animas River, but also, in the late 1890s, largemouth black bass, of all things. Carp escaped from private ponds and colonized the river. In 1898, ten thousand trout were dumped into Molas Lake above Silverton, an event hailed as "the first batch of any fish dumped into the lake by the hand of man." A decade later, twenty-two thousand trout fry were dumped in South Mineral Creek, the "clean" tributary to the larger Mineral Creek. By the 1920s, the state fish and wildlife agency was stocking nearly every creek in the watershed; soon they'd be dumping fry into high alpine lakes with helicopters. As of today, some seventy non-native fish species have been introduced into the Colorado River Basin, and at least twenty of these still swim alongside the few remaining native suckers, chubs, and pikeminnows in the San Juan River and its tributaries, including the Animas River.

By the time Simon came around with his fish experiment, we could no longer distinguish between the natural world and the world we had imposed on Nature. We didn't know if our Eden ever had fish, or if our mines had come along and killed them. As for all these efforts to make amends, it is not at all clear whether we are clawing our way back to Paradise Lost, or are merely restoring something that never really was, rebuilding our own constructed facsimile of Eden.

Mine Down

O N MARCH 13, 1987, DONALD "DONNIE" GOODE
WALKED INTO THE DARKNESS like he had many
times before, and continued nearly a half mile underground through the Gold King Level #7 tunnel into Bonita
Peak. As he worked a jackleg drill, a 150-pound rock broke free
from the ceiling of the mine, striking Goode directly on the top
of the head. His two companions rushed Goode's broken body
back through the tunnel into the blinding light of day, then
loaded him into a Suburban and raced down the muddy road
to Gladstone, where an ambulance and paramedics met them.
It was too late. Goode died, becoming the last of a long list of
Gold King Mine casualties.

After seventy years of dormancy, the Gold King Mine had
awoken in 1984 when Gerber Minerals Corp., a subsidiary of
Denver-based Gerber Energy International Inc., acquired the
property. Two years later, Gerber—which changed its name to
Gold King Consolidated—applied for and received a mining
permit for the Gold King and started working it. Notably, it did
not apply for a point-source discharge permit under the Clean
Water Act because, according to its application materials, "No
drainage occurs from any of the portals—the district is deep-

drained by the American Tunnel located at Gladstone." This was true. Photos from the early 1900s show the Gold King's Level #7 tunnel discharging a substantial amount of acid mine drainage. But by 1920, the tunnel had gone almost completely dry because the American Tunnel, driven directly underneath the Gold King Mine, had hijacked the already altered hydrology within Bonita Peak, pulling all the groundwater downward.

This latter-day phase of the Gold King lasted for a few more years, and officially ended in 1992. During that time the mine produced a reported thirty-three thousand tons of ore, with a "smelter value" of about $3.3 million. In the wake of the 2015 Gold King spill, when the history of the mine was being bandied about, this phase, curiously, seems to have been forgotten.

IF THE WORKINGS OF AN UNDERGROUND MINE ARE A HARD-TO-NAVIGATE MAZE, the corporate ownership structure is an even more dizzying and byzantine labyrinth of LLCs, subsidiaries, back and forth leasing, operating agreements, and the like. When times are good, everyone wants a piece of the mine's action. When things get tricky, particularly when a mine gets caught up in a Superfund designation and the EPA starts searching for "potentially responsible parties" to help pay to clean up the mess, everyone wishes for a touch of amnesia.

In 1985, Standard Metals, still in bankruptcy, sold the Sunnyside Mine to Echo Bay Mines, a Canadian company with offices in a Denver suburb, for a reported $20 million. That seemed a good deal at the time. After all, while gold prices dropped after a 1980 peak, they remained relatively healthy up into the late 1980s—the Sunnyside could easily gross $20 mil-

acquisitions, some with Alta Gold, others on its own. In 1984 it bought a fifty percent stake in the Round Mountain Gold Mine in Nevada, an open pit behemoth where the cyanide heap-leach method for extracting gold from the ore was employed.[56]

By then the Sunnyside had cemented its status as the last big mine around. The Idarado, whose underground workings reached from Ouray County into San Miguel County, above Telluride, shut down for good in 1978. The mine's main portal near Red Mountain Pass, an area of high mining-density, was discharging acidic drainage into Red Mountain Creek, which then made its way to the Uncompahgre River, which joins the Gunnison River in Delta, Colorado. The huge tailings piles at the edge of Telluride were leaching into the San Miguel River and blowing heavy metals into the air over the mining-turned-ski town; the mine owner's own study found that seven percent of Telluride kids had blood lead levels more than twice the Centers for Disease Control level of concern, and that the town average was also above the level of concern. In 1983, the State of Colorado sued Newmont Mining, which owned the mine, under CERCLA, the Comprehensive Environmental Response, Compensation, and Liability Act of 1980, otherwise known as Superfund, thus sealing its metaphorical coffin.[57]

In 1988, the corporate mishmash behind the Sunnyside finally began complying with the Clean Water Act. It installed a new water treatment plant at the American Tunnel portal to treat the 1,500 to 2,200 gallons per minute of acid mine drainage. The discharge was mixed with about one ton of lime, or calcium oxide, per day, which raised the water's pH level. With the help of an added polymer, the metals precipitated out of the solution in a series of unlined ponds (the Clean Water Act contained no protections for groundwater). The lime and metal mixture then settled to the bottom of the ponds as sludge, also at a rate of one ton per day, which was then trucked to the giant tailings ponds above Silverton. For about $500,000 per year, the company was able to reduce zinc loading to about four pounds per day, yielding relatively clean water.

Ironically, the company then dumped this crystal clear water into Cement Creek, which had a pH of four and ran orange with iron and other metals thanks to natural sources and to leaking abandoned mines upstream. By the time Cement Creek reached Silverton, it was pretty nasty, with or without the treatment plant at the American Tunnel. Still, the treatment made a big difference in the watershed as a whole. The mine was a major contributor to overall heavy metal loads in the watershed, and any reduction in those loads had positive effects downstream on the Animas River, where even incremental reductions in metals were reflected in the health of the fish and other aquatic life populations.

Mining industry boosters inevitably list the rising cost of complying with environmental regulations as a primary factor in the industry's decline, but it's a dubious claim. Water treatment wasn't free, but it also made up only a fraction of the mine's overall operating costs. Other factors played a bigger role. In the early 1980s Chile modernized its mining industry, and took over a big chunk of the global copper market. And the operators of the big open pit mines in Nevada, Echo Bay included, utilized economies of scale to produce far more gold far more cheaply than could possibly be done in the underground mines of Silverton, where the ore reserves, after more than a century of extraction, dwindled. In 1988, gold prices began a long, downward slide, dealing the fatal blow.

On May 30, 1991, Echo Bay announced that it would close

down the Sunnyside Mine for good. Nearly 150 miners—nearly twenty percent of the entire county's population—lost their jobs overnight. Most left, heading to the gold mines in Nevada, the copper mines in Chile, or the coal mines in other parts of Colorado and in Wyoming's Powder River Basin. Houses were put up for sale for dirt cheap; in some cases you could get two for the price of one. The assessed value of the county's properties plummeted, meaning tax revenue did, too. Student numbers at the town's one school fell so fast that it surely would have shut down, except that busing kids to neighboring towns wasn't even remotely feasible. And Silverton's economy was left entirely to the mercy of the train-driven tourism industry.

Lost Soul, Found Soul

I ARRIVED IN SILVERTON IN SPRINGTIME, a twenty-five-year-old with an expensive undergraduate degree in philosophy, a shitload of student debt, the memories of a couple failed relationships, a 1973 Toyota Corona, and not a whole hell of a lot else.

After graduating from college in Santa Fe, a fellow Durangoan and I had tried to flee for the coast, as was expected of educated rural Westerners from the Interior like us. But just after we passed by Winslow, Arizona, our car made contact with a big rig's rear wheels, sending us hurtling end over end across the desert at sixty-five miles per hour and aborting our attempted pilgrimage.

We ended up back in Santa Fe instead, living on a friend's floor, reading his back issues of *Esquire* and *Playboy*, looking for employers that could appreciate our degrees, and methodically emptying our buddy's beautifully curated liquor collection. I finally got a job at a seed factory, and before long had moved up the corporate ladder from seed packer to germination technician. We worked in a seed warehouse that was kept so cold that computer monitors regularly exploded and we needed gloves, hats, and jackets always. My boss was originally from Bolivia, and was world-renowned for his knowledge of potatoes and quinoa. Every morning he came into the warehouse with a purposeful stride, looked me in the eyes, and yelled, "Hey, fucking guy, come at me like you have a knife!" I did as I was told. "No, not like that! Like this," he'd say, demonstrating. I'd obey. Then he'd pull some jiujitsu move on me, disarm me of my fake knife, and throw me to the ground. Only then could I go back to counting how many of the seeds, wrapped up in wet paper towels in plastic bags, had sprouted.

I rented a room in a big house from a guy who was probably ten years older than me and had done pretty well as a builder. He was clearly befuddled by my lack of ambition, my aimlessness. One winter's night he hosted a party at the house, and a bunch of folks who were older than me or maybe just had their shit together better than I did showed up. "So . . . what do *you* do?" an attractive, well-appointed woman who didn't seem to be attached to anyone asked. "I germinate seeds," I replied. She quickly left to "get another drink" and never came back. Maybe she thought it was some perverse pickup line, and maybe in Santa Fe, where people got rice taped all over their bodies to ease stress, it was. I needed something else to do, though I had no idea what that might be. Pardon the cliché, but I was a bit of a lost soul.

And then in February 1996, my mom called and told me about an ad she saw for a reporter at the *Silverton Standard & the Miner* newspaper. I didn't have to think about it at all. That night I typed up my application and neatly folded it and put it in an envelope for the mail carrier to pick up the next day. Self-confidence was hard to come by back then, but I knew right away that I would get the job. I didn't care that I'd have to work fifty or sixty hours a week, or that I'd have to attend meetings that reached deep into the night, or that it only paid $275 per week. I didn't care about living in a drafty shack in a dying mining town. What I did care about was that I'd have an answer for the what-do-you-do people at parties: "I'm a reporter. I'm a journalist. I'm a writer. . . . I'm a *Writer*. What about you?"

On a cold and dreary April day I pulled into Silverton. Greene Street, the main drag, was empty except for a couple of dirty cars parked here and there. Sheets of plywood covered most of the old commercial buildings' windows. There were glimmers of glamour—the Grand Imperial, the outsized courthouse, a gothic-style near-mansion on a side street with what I swear was a tree growing out of a second-story window. Yet I only saw the melancholic ghost of wealth gone by, a town whose better days had come and gone and who was now waiting for death—a city of long-departed, long-lost souls.

Mining had been gone for almost five years and nothing had come in to fill the void. Hordes of tourists still arrived by train from May to October, but just as the 1970s prognosticators had feared, the economy then went into hibernation for the next six months or more. Officially there were about 450 year-round residents at the time—about half the population of a decade earlier—but even that number seemed high. The school had maybe sixty kids, kindergarten through high school. Running even the most basic errand required driving over two mountain passes to Durango to the south, or the more treacherous Red Mountain Pass to Montrose to the north.

By that time, the backcountry skiing seeds planted by the avalanche project guys in the '70s had sprouted and flourished, and on the weekends dozens of Toyotas and Subarus packed into the parking lots on the passes. Few ever bothered coming to Silverton, but if they popped down for a meal their choices were sparse—a greasy burger and fries at the Silverton Drive-In and little else. There was, however, a coffee shop called the Avalanche. The demographers, I'm sure, put the Avalanche on their *Atlas of the New West* and counted it as a sign that Silverton was yuppifying. But there was no gentrification here, at least not yet. Sure, Jodi, the proprietor, slung a mean espresso and even cafe latte, but she did it in the converted half of the living room of a shotgun shack that had been dragged down from Eureka sixty years earlier when the Sunnyside went belly-up the first time. Being the only caffeine dispensary within a fifty-mile radius, it drew folks from across the demographic spectrum, most of whom had at least one piece of duct tape on their clothing. Effete coffee snobs from Santa Fe were only barely tolerated. Once, when I politely pointed out that her cookies were full of egg shells, Jodi charged me double.

I got a room at the Benson Hotel, down the block and across Greene Street from the *Standard* office, until I could find a real place. My room was small, the mustard-colored walls bare. It had a little sink in the corner, an old squeaky bed, thin walls through which I could hear my neighbor scream at Kramer, George, and Elaine as he watched *Seinfeld* reruns. It was run by a woman named Liz, who reputedly would spike your sheets with itching powder if you disobeyed the rules (No hot plates!). She routinely drove laps around Silverton's muddy, potholed streets, her collie-mix running behind excitedly. After a few weeks there, I rented a drafty and decrepit little shack that was literally sinking into the muddy earth, throwing every allegedly flat surface off kilter. It redeemed itself with the great big clawfoot bathtub and the dandelion-infested lawn.

THE NEWSPAPER OFFICE OCCUPIED THE SAME SPACE
THAT IT HAD SINCE THE 1920s, the same space where Ross
Beaber, Allen Nossaman, the Duthies, the Chapmans, and even
my dad had put out the paper. It was a long, wooden building
with creaky floors, office supplies and books up front, and
desks, a darkroom, old printing presses, light tables, and so on
in the back. It was a newspaper nostalgic's dream. The 120-year-
old "morgue," newspaper jargon for all the back issues of the
publication, moldered away in a long, musty closet, alongside old wood type and lead engravings of advertisements. It
smelled of old wood and dust, of photo-developing chemicals
and decaying paper. The light from the windows didn't reach
the office area, so it was always dark and always cold, even in
July.

My job was to attend all the school board, town board,
and county commissioner meetings and write about them,
along with the rare school sports event, plays at the community theatre, road closures, big storms, deaths, and biennial tax
assessments—that sort of thing.

When I wasn't busy with all of that, I walked up and down
Greene Street, stopped in at the courthouse to get the latest
gossip from Melody or Judy, at the town hall for news, the
Avalanche for motivation, or Tyrol Liquors to pick up a bottle
of wine and listen to Lorenzo, the proprietor, sing more than
speak with his joyful Dolomite accent. On one of my first days
in town, I saw a tall, almost gaunt man, the top of his head
bald and hatless, wearing round spectacles from another age,
his long beard blowing about in the cold wind, trudging up the
street. I followed him to the historical society's archive building
and trailed him inside. He looked at me with both suspicion
and annoyance until I introduced myself. Allen Nossaman, by

then the county judge and archivist, smiled and welcomed me with his booming voice.

In many ways, Silverton was like a high-altitude, hypoxic version of Norman Rockwell's Stockbridge, a community of quaint charm with raw and rough edges. The mayor was also the milkman, the coal furnace stoker, and the tree guy; one of his town board colleagues was the community cat lady. The library—in a Carnegie-funded old brick building—was both stereotypical and downright bizarre (also, very noisy) and was one of my favorite places to hang out.

But underneath the idyllic veneer was a simmering stew of dysfunction, fueled by economic malaise, isolation, and alcohol. There were two layers of local government—town and county—despite the fact that there was and is only one town in the county, and the combined population hasn't cracked six hundred since 1992. For a long time, the county and town fought with one another like a recently divorced couple over control and funding of shared services such as law enforcement, the ambulance, the fire department. One of the first meetings I attended ended with one of the ambulance managers punching the town administrator. I was shocked. No one else seemed fazed. Much later, when the town board took up numerous complaints about the aforementioned cat lady trustee, she was forced to sit in the audience aside its one other member, me. As the cat details emerged she turned to me and hissed: "If you write about this, you're done!" I didn't write about it.

A relatively wealthy attorney had moved to town a few years before I arrived, and he promptly bought up various properties, including a heliport outside of town and the trash service. He also served as the town attorney. As one might imagine, he provided fodder for all sorts of controversy. Meanwhile, the seeds of another internal town battle, between the public works director (who is in charge of plowing the streets and is therefore the most powerful guy in town) and the town administrator, were being sown. The battle would rage through multiple town administrations, finally reaching a climactic end in 2015, not long before the Gold King blowout.

One of the school board members would come to meetings while inebriated, going on belligerent tirades targeting the school's administration and its teachers and the curriculum. One local told me, matter-of-factly, that she voted for him because he wasn't afraid to speak his mind, would "tell it like it is," and shake things up a bit. I would watch him in action many, many times and take it from me, that is no way to elect an official, whether it's to the school board or the presidency.

My favorite type of story to write were profiles of seemingly regular folks, all of whom were extraordinary in their own ways, from Phil Dodd, a retired Atomic Energy Commission geologist who resembled Trotsky, to "Grandma" Alva Gallegos, to Dolores LaChapelle, to my friend Ann, a potter who came to Silverton because it reminded her of Cuba.

I was unknowingly part of a wave of young people—artists, writers, snow scientists, mountain lovers, and the like—that was spilling into Silverton. Some were there for work. Others, like the woman who I would eventually marry, were just passing through—or so they said. Still others sought something, though they weren't really sure what it was. Part of it, I think, was that we were seeking the very dysfunction that tangled up the political system. Engaging in crazy or antisocial behavior was not only tolerated, but sometimes embraced. No one in Silverton ever asked me, "So, what do you do?" Yet at least two people asked me, "What are you escaping from?"

DAY THREE IN SILVERTON. Day three of subsisting on coffee and a bagel for breakfast, coffee and a bagel and an egg-shell-chocolate-chip cookie for lunch, and a peanut butter and honey sandwich in my room for dinner. I needed to mix things up, which gave me only one option: the Silverton Drive-In.

The name was a bit misleading. There were no carhops at the Drive-In, nor even a drive-up window, for that matter. It was just a burger and bacon and eggs joint on the corner that doubled as the Greyhound stop and whatever that entailed. It was the only place in town that was pretty much always open, be it February or July. A film of dirty grease, built up over who knows how many decades, clung to the pale yellow walls. Catherine had owned and run the place for years. She must have been in her late sixties or early seventies, and had sharp features and the lined face and sweet but firm disposition that one might associate with someone who ran a ranch.

I ordered dinner and sat down. A man sat down across from me in my booth. He looked like he could have been eighty years old, but over time I'd learn not to try to guess ages in Silverton, as it was a losing game: life there tended to age folks far beyond their actual years. His name was Russ, and he sort of lived at the Drive-In. In between furtive sips off a bottle of Old Crow he'd push a mop around, or gather up dirty dishes. Mostly he just hung out, talking to whomever might listen, like me.

"These streets used to be full of men with boots," he said, motioning toward the empty street, the last sunlight of the day giving a warm glow that belied the actual conditions. When I got up to get my cheeseburger, oily fries, and coffee, I tried to catch Catherine's eye, thinking that maybe she'd eject this guy so I could eat in peace. No dice. I sat back down. He was still there, with the faint, sour smell of an alcoholic.

He launched into a monologue about his days working the mines in New Mexico, Utah, even Mexico, which included a few comments too bigoted and sexist to repeat here. Then he stood up—he was tall, and carried the ghost of a once-strapping, handsome man with him—and ambled over to the Coke machine. A bunch of rocks of various shapes and colors sat atop the machine, and he reached up and clumsily lifted a yellowish one about the size of a football, and cradled it awkwardly in his arms and carried it across the brightly lit restaurant to my table. He stood there for a moment and then slammed it onto the Formica next to my dinner. A fine dust rose upon impact, swam around in the beam of evening sun, and settled as a thin film atop my coffee. "That there," he said, "is uranium ore."

AS SOON AS I MOVED OUT OF THE BENSON AND INTO MY NEW SHACK, I headed to Durango for my first grocery and supply shopping mission. It was windy and cold that early May morning, and as I walked out to my car a dust devil, carrying with it face-stinging particles of gravel, ripped through a flurry of snowflakes. The aspens and narrowleaf cottonwoods had yet to emerge from winter dormancy. The south side of the mountains was brown and mucky, but the north-facing slopes were still covered with snow that held a patina of red dust, blown in from overgrazed and developed desert to the south and west. I felt pretty stupid when I stepped out of my car in the Durango City Market parking lot, dressed in a taped-up down jacket, jeans, and boots, only to see that everyone else was in tanktops and Tevas and that it was at least seventy-five degrees, sunny, the trees fully leafed out.

Inside the grocery store, I saw an old friend from high

Mine Pool

FTER WE PASSED THE LAST BARE LIGHTBULB
HANGING FROM THE WALL, the darkness overwhelmed. The visible universe was reduced to whatever was caught in my headlamp's dim pool: a swath of rock,
cold water dripping from the ceiling, the bright yellow slicker
of my guide. The cart carried us along rails at a jogger's pace
but it felt far faster, as if in a dream. I was certain that I could
feel the billions of tons above me—the innards of Bonita Peak
and its rock, dirt, water, history, lives lost—pressing down into
this void through which we passed. Straight above me, through
eight hundred feet or so of rock, were the workings of the Gold
King Mine.

It was early summer 1996. An older Sunnyside employee, a miner-turned-reclamation-worker, took me a mile and
change into the dank, cool world of the American Tunnel to
see Bulkhead #1, a boxcar-sized concrete plug built into the
mine. Soon the big wheel on it would be turned, shutting a
valve, forever sealing the American Tunnel and the Sunnyside
Mine's fate. We looked at it for a few moments in the light of
our headlamps. I tried to think of questions to ask, but the only
one I could come up with was, "How the hell did you work in

here day after day after day?" I stayed silent, instead. I took a picture, the flash an explosion of white. Then we headed back toward the light.

I hadn't asked to go into the mine. The manager had invited me, as the only member of the local press, to go see the bulkhead, so I went. I think we ran the photo, which was unremarkable, at best, along with a short caption. Little did I know that the bulkhead was one of the main components of a huge story that was just then unfolding in Silverton.

HAD THE SUNNYSIDE MINE SHUT DOWN IN 1921 or even 1961 rather than 1991, the company could have just packed up, sold off its mining claims, and walked away, most likely dodging any responsibility for the mess it had made. By the time Echo Bay was ready to leave, those days were long gone. Echo Bay's permit—secured by millions in financial bonds— required the company to tear down its surface infrastructure and restore the site to something resembling what had been there previously.

As for the mine itself, and the acid mine drainage, Echo Bay's Sunnyside Gold Corp. had a solution, as well: it would plug up the American Tunnel at the mine's property line with what amounted to a giant, concrete cork, or bulkhead. At the time, between 2 million and 3.1 million gallons of lightly acidic, metal-laden water poured out of the American Tunnel portal each day. A little less than half came from the Sunnyside Mine workings deep underground, the rest entered the American Tunnel in the last mile or so of the tunnel, which was still considered part of the Gold King complex. That's why Sunnyside Gold proposed installing the bulkhead deep underground rather than at the portal. A substantial amount of water would continue to pour out of the American Tunnel, but Echo Bay figured that it wasn't their problem since that water didn't originate in their mine.

The water would back up behind the plug into the mine's 150 miles of underground workings. Eventually, the old mine would be interred in an aqueous grave, more than one thousand feet deep, known as a mine pool. Hydrological modeling done by a Reno consulting group in 1993 predicted that, most likely, about seventy gallons of water per minute would migrate through the mountain via natural fractures and faults, finally emerging to the surface as springs anywhere from 160 to 4,300 years later.[58] Presumably, the water chemistry of the springs would resemble pre-mining conditions, though no one really knew what pre-mining conditions would have looked like.

The plan seemed to make sense. After all, the mine's permit was for the American Tunnel discharge. Stop the discharge from that point, and the permit is no longer valid.

Yet the state's regulators were working from a different premise: that it was not the point of discharge that was permitted, but the water itself, regardless of whether it emerged from the American Tunnel, from a neighboring mine, or from a natural spring a thousand years from now. Go ahead and plug the American Tunnel, regulators told Sunnyside, but you'll still be responsible for every spring that pops up as a result of the plugging. The regulators wanted Sunnyside Gold to keep the water treatment plant open, staff it with a few people, and keep treating the water forever. In retrospect it might have been cheaper and easier for them to do just that.

Sunnyside Gold, however, wanted out, so they sued. The company's lawyers argued that whatever the quality of the water that emerged as springs, Sunnyside Gold was not adding any pollutants to it, so therefore needed no discharge permit. Legally, they argued, the discharge would be like water coming out of a dam—it's running through, rather than from, the mine, meaning it should need no discharge permit. The state regulators, taking a far stronger tack than their nineteenth-century predecessors, refused to give any ground. They knew that when the water eventually emerged, it would be of lower quality than Sunnyside's treated discharges, and that would result in dirtier water downstream.

Finally, in the spring of 1996, politicians stepped in and pressured the state health department's Water Quality Control Division to back down and sign off on a consent decree with Sunnyside Gold. The terms were straightforward: Sunnyside Gold could shut down its water treatment plant and vamoose once it was able to do so without worsening water quality on the Animas River below Silverton. The benchmark would be zinc concentration at water sampling site A72, a little ways downstream from where Mineral Creek, Cement Creek, and the Animas River come together. The baseline was the average of water samples taken at A72 up to that point. Zinc was chosen both because it's harmful to fish, and because it signals the presence of other harmful metals.

The only way treatment could be shut down without a net deterioration in water quality would be to reduce metal loading from elsewhere in the basin. So the consent decree required Sunnyside to clean up errant tailings, plug abandoned mine adits, and do other work, mostly on long-abandoned properties with which Sunnyside Gold had never been involved, to compensate for the pollution that issued from the American Tunnel. Once Sunnyside Gold completed enough of these off-set projects to balance out the consequences of shutting down treatment, the company could get out of its permit, and leave.

The deal would allow the mining company to avoid the prospect of perpetual liability; it would keep water quality from getting worse, and might even improve it; Echo Bay would burnish its corporate image; and a private party would fork out tens of millions of dollars for cleaning up some nasty abandoned mine sites that would otherwise be on the taxpayers' tab. On paper, it seemed like a tidy, innovative, and even groundbreaking solution. It would turn out to be anything but.

EVEN AS THE SUNNYSIDE LEGAL DRAMA UNFOLDED, a quieter but no less significant water quality story was playing out in parallel. In 1989, inspired in part by Bill Simon's fish experiment, the Colorado Department of Health and Environment's Water Quality Division began an extensive, four-year-long water sampling project in the Upper Animas River Basin. As benign as that may sound today, it left many in Silverton frightened and even livid. At the time, the local mining economy was crumbling, and the mining industry blamed its decline, in part, on heightened environmental regulations. Testing would surely lead to water quality standards which would then lead to more rules and maybe even Superfund. And given the ubiquity of abandoned mines, a Superfund designation could not be limited to any one site—most of the basin would need to be included. That would scare off new mining investment, keeping the industry from making a comeback. On a less emotional level, people like Simon were concerned that the state wasn't accounting for the complexity of the geology and hydrology of the region, and would base its standards, and its approach to cleaning up the mess, on poor science.

The early days of the Upper Animas saga happened to be

playing out at a time when collaborative efforts were cropping up around the West as an alternative to heavy-handed, top-down environmental regulation. Given the local backlash in Silverton, the state opted to try the approach here and, with the help of Simon and Steve Fearn—who has been involved in numerous mining ventures in the San Juans—it created the Animas River Stakeholders Group in 1994. Simon was chosen to be the coordinator. "We figured we could empower the people in the community to do the job without top-down management," says Simon. "I'm not saying Silverton is that big on stewardship, but giving the power to the people develops stewardship for the resource, and that's particularly useful in this day and age."

A little bit of power is exactly what the people of Silverton craved at the time. They watched helplessly as mining dried up and blew away. They were similarly impotent when it came to tourism. But with the stakeholders approach, they were given at least a little bit of say over how mining's mess was handled. And by opposing Superfund, they believed, they were not fighting against clean water. Rather, they were exerting what little power they had over their own identity and culture and future.

The Stakeholders Group was set up not as a democracy, but as a consensus group, meaning no decisions could be made, or actions taken, without the full support of every member of the group. It can be a tedious process, the meetings downright soporific.

In the beginning the group's membership spanned the ideological spectrum. There were those who believed that the Animas River was once a pristine and healthy trout habitat that had been wrecked by mining, and the only salvation was in a massive cleanup effort. Others, particularly local old-timers and miners, felt that the rivers were already so mineralized from natural sources that mining's impacts had been relatively insignificant, and cleaning up the mines would be futile. Everyone else was scattered in between. Over time, the extreme ends, frustrated or perhaps bored by the slow-as-molasses process, dropped out, leaving those who either felt compelled by occupation to be there, or who simply reveled in the complexity of it all, to hash it out.

Among those early members were Larry Perino, reclamation manager at the Sunnyside Mine, representatives from the BLM and Forest Service, which manage most of the land in the watershed, and local elected officials. Peter Butler, director at the time of Friends of the Animas, who was just finishing up his doctorate in Natural Resource Policy, was active from early on, too, as was Bill Jones, a mining assayer and owner of the Old Hundred mine tour, and Todd Hennis, current owner of the Gold King. Agency representatives, such as Kay Zillich with the BLM, and Carol Russell and Sabrina Forest with the EPA, were also key players. It was this team that embarked on a massive science project with a simple, yet elusive goal: to understand what was happening in the mines, the rocks, and the water of the Silverton Caldera, and then to try to figure out how to fix it.

Working with a team of U.S. Geological Survey scientists and intent on identifying all the ingredients of the watershed's acid-drainage chowder, Simon and other stakeholders took thousands of water samples, studied draining mine portals and natural springs, counted bugs, and subjected fish to doses of metal and acid. Like the San Juan Avalanche Project had done two decades earlier, they turned the Upper Animas River Basin into an open-air laboratory of sorts, producing a comprehensive report on the hydrology, geology, chemistry, aquatic biology, and even mining history of the region.

They found that the concoction was considerably more complicated than just a couple of spewing mines. Nature, it turns out, is the biggest polluter in the watershed. Some springs, untouched by mining, were as acidic as lemon juice or Coca-Cola, inhabited only by extremophilic microbes. About ninety percent of the aluminum and eighty percent of the copper in the middle fork of Mineral Creek was from natural sources, a finding that jibed with Franklin Rhoda's 1874 observation of a stream "so strongly impregnated with mineral ingredients as to be quite unfit for drinking." Cement Creek's banks were rife with ferricrete that had been deposited thousands of years earlier; it had never been a fish stream, and never would be.

That didn't let mining off the hook, however. Of the nearly 5,400 mine shafts, adits, tunnels, and prospects in the upper Animas watershed, almost 400 were significant enough to have some impact on water quality. About 60 of those sites contributed eighty-five to ninety percent of the mining-related loading. Dozens of abandoned mine adits collectively oozed more than 436,000 pounds of aluminum, cadmium, copper, iron, and zinc into the watershed each year, with waste rock and tailings piles contributing another 80,000 pounds annually. At least one tailings pile had become an ad hoc playground for motorcyclists and ATV riders; another sat just outside Silverton, adjacent to the ski hill, its lead-tinged dust wafting into the air with every breeze. Neither the Sunnyside nor the Gold King were included among these sites because the Gold King was dry, all of Bonita Peak having been drained by the American Tunnel years earlier, and both were under permits. Since they weren't officially abandoned, they fell outside of the Stakeholders' purview.

The research did not provide a solid answer regarding the pre-mining fish situation in the upper reaches of the Animas River and its tributaries. Nor was it able to establish a definitive pre-mining water quality snapshot. But by quantifying the mining-related metal loading, it did provide more evidence that mining continued to hurt aquatic life for many miles downstream. In the stretch of river running above, through, and below Durango, for example, Jordan, the ichthyologist, had found a diverse and healthy fish population back in 1889. By the early 1980s, on the other hand, most of the native fish were gone. Non-native rainbow, brook, and brown trout—all of which are less sensitive to metals than native cutthroats—were plentiful in the Durango stretch of river, but they were unable to reproduce at sustainable levels; most of those populations at the time originated in hatcheries, and were replenished by stocking. During spring runoff zinc levels shot up to double the aquatic life standards all the way down to the New Mexico state line. Reduce those concentrations and fish just might be able to reproduce.

With funding from federal and state grants and mining companies, the Stakeholders organization did a handful of cleanup projects of its own, including removing or capping mine waste dumps, diverting runoff around dumps, and revegetating mining-impacted areas. They were able to acquire water rights to reverse a decades-old trans-basin diversion, thus adding clean water back into Mineral Creek to dilute the metal loading. They couldn't, however, mess with any of the draining adits, because to do so would require a water discharge permit under the Clean Water Act, and that would make the Stakeholders liable if anything went wrong.

Meanwhile, Sunnyside Gold was checking projects off of its offset list, scraping old mill tailings out of stream beds, reclaiming the former site of Lake Emma, and plugging draining mine adits. In 1996 the company closed the valve on the first of three bulkheads in the American Tunnel; within a few months, the mine pool held about one hundred million gallons of water. In theory, the mine pool would displace oxygen, thus stifling the acid mine drainage-forming chemical reaction. To further reduce acidity, Sunnyside Gold injected 625 tons of lime into the mine pool from above.

By 2001—a decade after the Sunnyside had shut down and five years after the first American Tunnel bulkhead had been sealed—the combined cleanup efforts seemed to be working. Metal concentrations had decreased significantly in Mineral Creek and further downstream on the Animas. Trout populations were getting healthier, and fish were reproducing where a decade earlier they could not. Between 1989 and 2000, the number of trout per mile in the Animas River below Durango tripled, and biologists even found a few trout in the Animas River just below Silverton, a stretch of water that had long been considered uninhabitable.

Fractures, Faults, and Leaks

A FUZZY BLANKET OF GRAY DROOPED OVER SILVERTON THAT AFTERNOON, a good six inches of slush underfoot. It was March 2001, the middle of Silverton's cruel season, when locals tromp around wearing dog-shit-encrusted Sorel boots, muddy snow pants, and chronic scowls. I was in Gladstone, six miles north of Silverton, paying Larry Perino a visit at Sunnyside Gold's corporate HQ, a big metal-walled building with exposed pipes wrapped in Christmas tinsel, brim-full ashtrays sitting on just about every flat surface.

Perino, a civil engineer is a taciturn man who doesn't talk a whole lot, particularly to the press. But he had reluctantly agreed to sit down with me and chat, perhaps because it seemed as though his job here was finally almost done, and he'd soon be moving on.

I had gone through some changes since arriving in Silverton five years prior. I had quit the *Standard* to open a little bakery with my girlfriend-now-wife Wendy, and then we moved to Durango to help start another bakery. We had a daughter, then returned to Silverton where, for reasons too complicated and still too fuzzy to explain, we started our own publication, the *Silverton Mountain Journal*, to compete with the *Standard*.

Silverton had evolved, too. On the slopes just downstream from Gladstone, a young snowboarder named Aaron Brill had installed a chairlift on a strip of patented mining claims to haul intrepid skiers up to the ridgetop, from which they could ski the ungroomed slopes of Silverton Mountain Ski Area. Despite the scrappy, small-scale nature of the area, it wasn't universally embraced. True backcountry skiers mourned the loss of exclusive powder, snow scientists predicted avalanche-related death and mayhem, and some old-timers feared that Silverton would become another Telluride or, God forbid, Aspen. As unlikely as that seemed, housing prices had increased tremendously over the previous few years, even if economic opportunities and population and amenities had not. The national housing boom, combined with some ski-area-related speculation, had made it over the mountains into the Silverton Caldera.

Sunnyside Gold and Perino, meanwhile, were ready to pack their bags and shimmy out of town. The company had completed its pollution offset projects and reclaimed most of its own property. The first bulkhead, located about a mile underground from Perino's desk, had done its job; the mine pool was 1,200 feet deep, exerted more than 400 psi on the bulkhead, and was thought to have reached equilibrium, meaning it wouldn't get any deeper. Now the company just needed to put two more bulkheads in the American Tunnel, to stanch the flow of water that was pouring into the first mile of the tunnel, presumably from the Gold King. Then it could leave, maybe. Despite all the improvements in water quality, the zinc levels at A72 had not decreased appreciably; the consent decree's terms, therefore, had not been met.

When I met with Perino that day, he was optimistic that Sunnyside and the state would come up with a compromise releasing the company from its permit. But he also seemed befuddled. After all, Echo Bay had officially spent more time cleaning up various messes here than they had spent mining. And they had forked out at least $10 million, much of it to deal with other companies' problems. What more could they do?

EVEN AS SUNNYSIDE WAS TRYING TO SKEDADDLE, others were looking to dive into the mining game in the San Juans.

Todd Hennis, of Golden, Colorado, operating as at least eight different companies, had been buying up mining claims left and right since the 1990s, in San Juan County and beyond, including the Mogul Mine in Upper Cement Creek. Hennis had worked for Goldman Financial Group on acquisitions, and his principal company, Salem Minerals, sells mining-related souvenirs, such as little bottles filled with gold flakes, to retailers. He was vague about his plans for the various parcels—he talked about building a campground, a parking lot, maybe even condos. But he also expressed an intent to start mining some of the claims, and marketed others as viable mining properties. Via Green Energy Metals, one of his businesses, Hennis peddled claims in the La Plata Mountains west of Durango based on their purported abundance of "critical and strategic metals America needs for the green economy."

Steve Fearn, a longtime Silvertonian, a founding member of the Animas River Stakeholders Group, and an engineer who once designed power plant turbines, was very clear about his intent: he wanted to bring mining back to the San Juans. He bought the Gold King in 2000 from then-owner CCTV/

Pitchfork "M" Corporation, and hoped to mine it and his Silver Wing Mine on the banks of the Animas River above Silverton. Fearn was also well on his way to refurbishing and reopening the Pride of the West Mill at Howardsville. Now in his seventies, Fearn was long ago bitten by the mining bug and over the past four decades he has been involved in a variety of San Juan mining ventures (and one in Indonesia). Some succeeded, some flopped.

Still, this particular effort by Fearn was unique. Fearn would use the mill to process the abandoned waste dumps that the Stakeholders were cleaning up, opening the door to federal or state funding for mined-land remediation. Then he'd have the only custom mill for hundreds of miles, which would encourage small-scale mining in the region.

It may seem oxymoronic, but in a heavily mined area, active mining can actually foster clean-up, at least theoretically. Any new mining is likely to occur in existing mines (more destructive open-pit mining is not considered feasible here) where drainage is already a problem. Re-opening such a mine would require a discharge permit, and a plan for treating the drainage, bringing in a responsible party—a company—where none currently existed. Citizen groups like the Stakeholders could then work under the mining company's permits to clean up draining mines, or to test new water treatment technologies. And when the company was ready to leave, it, rather than the taxpayers, would be on the hook for cleanup.

IT'S NOT CLEAR WHO KNEW WHAT OR WHEN. It's not clear what was going on or why. What is clear is that something strange was happening in the innards of Bonita Peak, and the strangeness was manifesting as leaky adits, first in the Mogul

Mine in the Cement Creek drainage upstream from the American Tunnel, and then at the Gold King Mine.

In 1996, the state division of minerals and geology conducted a routine inspection of the Gold King Mine's Level #7 portal. Though the mine was dormant, the mining permit acquired in the 1980s was still in place. The inspector observed just one to two gallons of discharge per minute. The mine was still effectively dry, as it had been since the American Tunnel was driven eighty years earlier. That same summer, Sunnyside Gold sealed shut the first bulkhead in the American Tunnel. In 1997, consultants working on an environmental protection plan at the Gold King found that the mine was no longer dry. Discharges had kicked up to between four and thirty gallons per minute of highly acidic—pH 2.25—water. Still, that wasn't much. The consultants determined that it was groundwater, perhaps resulting from excess snow and rain, and not mine pool water.

But the precipitation theory was debunked when a 1999 water analysis again found water with a very low pH and very high concentrations of metals coming from the Gold King. A year later, the findings were duplicated. Just after Steve Fearn took over the Gold King in 2000 the state inspector noted: "Though this year has been abnormally dry, the No. 7 level discharge appears to have increased significantly . . . from around 30 gpm to around 45 gpm."

Upstream on Cement Creek, the Mogul Mine, owned by Todd Hennis, was going through even more dramatic changes. Like the Gold King, the Mogul had been mostly dry in the 1990s; it probably was deep-drained by the American Tunnel decades earlier, as well. But in 2000, while doing routine sampling, a Sunnyside Gold employee noticed that Cement

Creek's zinc levels were increasing. When the company did an upstream inspection, it found that the Mogul was discharging significant amounts of water loaded with metals. Sunnyside, in a 2001 report to the state, noted that the increased flow could be caused by, "above normal levels of precipitation; natural flow regimes being restored as the mine pool rises and groundwater flows travel around the Sunnyside Mine workings instead of draining through the American Tunnel; or a fracture connection exists between the Mogul workings and the Sunnyside Mine workings."

We know now that option one is a nonstarter, probably thrown in there to further muddy the waters, so to speak. The distinction between the other two options is critical. If the waters in the Mogul and the Gold King rose as a result of "natural flow regimes being restored," then it's really not Sunnyside Gold's problem, is it?[59] After all, if the American Tunnel bulkhead just returned water to the Mogul that would have flowed through there had the American Tunnel never been dug in the first place, then it's not Sunnyside Gold's water, it's the Mogul's, and thus the owner of the latter is responsible. Yet it would be a far different story if the third explanation were correct, that Sunnyside mine pool water was migrating into the Mogul via a fracture or some other connection.

Hennis, who had hoped to either mine the Mogul or market it as a mining property, believed that the water emanated from the Sunnyside. He pointed to the 1993 hydrological models, which showed that it was possible that as much as 160 gallons per minute of mine pool water would migrate through the Brenneman Vein to the Mogul, and that it could happen within months of the bulkhead getting sealed. With this evidence in hand, Hennis hauled Sunnyside Gold to court.

In 2002, after Sunnyside Gold sealed off the American Tunnel's bulkhead #2, some three thousand feet into the mine, Gold King discharges kicked up to sixty gallons per minute, according to a letter sent by Fearn to the state. The state subsequently required that Fearn get a water discharge permit for the mine—something that had never been necessary in the past. The increased Gold King flows also seemed to be related to the bulkheads, but how the subterranean pieces of the puzzle might fit together was more mysterious. The 1993 study came up with no significant pathways for water to move from mine pool to the Gold King.

In any event, it was building into a hell of a quagmire for Sunnyside Gold, which in 2003 became a subsidiary of Kinross when the Canadian mining giant, with some $3 billion in annual revenue, acquired Echo Bay. Yet it found a possible escape hatch in a byzantine, property- and responsibility-shuffling deal involving Fearn and Hennis and their respective companies. It would, presumably, allow Sunnyside to leave, facilitate Fearn's effort to mine the Gold King, and get Hennis out from under the now-leaking Mogul and settle his gripes with Sunnyside.

Sunnyside would seal off the two newer bulkheads it had installed in the American Tunnel, thus stanching the flow of water that predated the tunnel's 1960 extension. Fearn would buy the Mogul from Hennis. Sunnyside would pay Fearn to bulkhead the Mogul and to complete some other pollution offset projects in the basin. Fearn would take over Sunnyside's discharge permits and the water treatment plant, and treat any water that might continue draining from the American Tunnel as well as the increasing discharges from the Gold King. Sunnyside would also give Hennis ownership of mining claims in Gladstone on which the treatment plant's settling ponds were located. That, in turn, required Fearn to lease that same land from Hennis in order to operate the plant.

The key was that the Sunnyside water, from wherever it issued forth, would continue to be treated by Fearn's company, even after all the offset projects had been completed. It looked like a win-win-win scenario, so the state signed off on the deal. The story of the Gold King blowout is filled with twists, turns, and "what if" moments. This is perhaps the most obvious place where a different decision—to simply require Sunnyside to stick around and live up to the terms of the consent decree, for example, or even to bulkhead the Gold King and kill the hope of ever mining it again—might have yielded a far different outcome.

But the convoluted agreement began disintegrating before the ink was even dry. In autumn 2003 Hennis dragged Fearn to court, alleging that Fearn, by not acquiring insurance for the treatment pond, was in violation of the lease. At the same time, Fearn's other mining ventures—along with his finances—were taking a nosedive. He lost the Pride of the West Mill to foreclosure in 2004. Unable to pay his power bill, the electricity to the American Tunnel water treatment plant was shut down for weeks that spring. Finally, in October 2004, Hennis evicted Fearn, shutting the treatment plant down for good.

THE TIMING COULDN'T HAVE BEEN WORSE. As required by the agreement, Fearn had bulkheaded the Mogul Mine. But as is often the case in highly fractured rock such as that found in many parts of the Silverton Caldera, it was not effective. Contaminated water continued to leak from the mine. Ditto with the lowest plug on the American Tunnel. The Gold King "started to belch out seriously," Simon told me, as did yet another nearby mine, the Red & Bonita.

For Simon and his fellow Stakeholders, not to mention the state water quality folks, this was turning out to be worse than the worst-case scenario. Everyone knew from early on that plugging the mine wasn't a clean-cut solution, and that some of the water backed up behind the plugs would someday make its way to the surface. But no one ever guessed that the water would emerge so quickly, at such high volumes, and with such high levels of acidity and metal-loading. It became abundantly clear that the discharge from neighboring mines was the result of one or more of the American Tunnel bulkheads. Not clear, though, was precisely where the water was coming from: Did the mine pool water back up, then find a pathway through to the other mine adits? Did the lower two bulkheads simply return Bonita Peak's hydrology to a pre-American Tunnel state of affairs? Or was it a little bit of both?

By 2009, the Gold King had a flow consistently above 120 gallons per minute, sometimes reaching 250 gallons per minute or more, and was carrying with it nearly two hundred thousand pounds of metals into the watershed per year. It was enough for the state to deem the Gold King "one of the worst high quantity, poor water quality draining mines in the state of Colorado." Together, the mines around Gladstone were spewing more than eight hundred thousand gallons into the watershed per day, loaded with hundreds of pounds of toxic metals. Water pH levels sometimes dropped as low as 2.1. "We were dealing with some seriously nasty stuff," Simon said.

And that nasty stuff made its way downstream, to deleterious effect. After water treatment shut down in late 2004, concentrations of zinc and other metals started climbing as far downstream as Durango. Trout and bug populations crashed.

At Elk Park, five miles downstream from Silverton, wildlife officials counted more than eighty fish per mile in 2005; within five years, the count was zero. Another dozen miles downstream, at Teft Spur, there were four hundred fish per mile in 2005; in 2010 there were fewer than one hundred. Where once mottled sculpins and brown, rainbow, and brook trout had been found in the Animas River gorge, only a few brooks remained. The water didn't turn crazy colors. Durango residents did not converge on the bridges to watch the fish die. No one sued anyone over it. Yet by all other measures, the slow deterioration of water quality beginning in 2005 was a far worse disaster than the Gold King blowout.

What was bad for fish, bugs, mining companies, and the folks living in the watershed, however, did have one upside: it provided empirical evidence that mine-related pollution was hurting fish and other aquatic life—stretches of stream unaffected by the woes at the Sunnyside remained healthier than ever. And it showed that while bulkheading and other remediation efforts can help, they don't hold a candle to active water treatment when it comes to improving water quality.

The Stakeholders knew that the most logical solution was another water treatment plant like the one that operated for years at the Sunnyside. But finding the $10 million or so to construct it, and another $1 million per year to operate it, wasn't easy. So they called in the big guns. "We'd spent all of our money, plus we knew that we had limited abilities," says Simon. "We didn't feel comfortable checking these out on our own, so we invited the EPA to help."

Goldfields

ON A FRIDAY MORNING IN EARLY JUNE 2005, after we had gotten the newspaper into machines and mailboxes, Wendy and I put our two bundled-up daughters into the car and headed south out of Silverton. Summer had stubbornly stayed away thus far, and patches of dirty snow clung to the north faces. As we climbed up Molas Pass, we hit a snow flurry—a near whiteout, in fact—and it felt like we had jumped back to January. It was a metaphor for a Silverton existence. It's a full life, and keeps you on your toes, but it's also a constant struggle.

By then, Silverton had two brand-new, million-dollar homes, no fewer than four real estate agents, three coffee shops, a sled manufacturer, a micro-distiller, a brewpub, a boutique ski manufacturer, and a snowboard maker was on its way. Silverton Mountain ski resort had become world famous for its extreme slopes, and sparked an inkling of a winter economy where there was none before.

Equity refugees from surrounding, over-inflated housing markets were buying up second homes in Silverton, thus inflating our little high-altitude housing market—home prices had tripled in just a few years. More hot air was blown into the market by speculating locals, who traded homes like the mine owners of old had done with claims. Two sets of affordable housing had been developed, with another one in the planning stages. Economic development folks were ramping up the pressure on the state to make it live up to its promise to extend fiber optic cable into the county. The science-as-economic-development seeds planted by the San Juan Avalanche Project back in the 1970s finally sprouted in the form of the Silverton-based Center for Snow and Avalanche Studies, which was investigating how dust affects snowmelt, and the Mountain Studies Institute, formed by folks from Silverton and Fort Lewis College in Durango to provide a hub for various forms of high-altitude science.

Happily, there was only one newspaper in town again. In 2002 we bought the *Silverton Standard & the Miner*, folding the *Mountain Journal* into the weekly.

Yet in spite of all this progress, some things hadn't changed. Many of the same power struggles that I had reported on a decade earlier still raged. A bitter war blazed over town street and public lands access, pitting snowmobilers and ATV riders against hikers and cross-country skiers. And political dysfunction reached new heights, in a small-scale, eerie foreshadowing of the Donald Trump phenomenon. After a U.S. senator had secured a large federal grant for the Mountain Studies Institute, the mayor, a notorious dispenser of "alternative facts" and no friend of science, thanked the senator's top aide by telling her that he'd "rather have a truckload of Taliban in here than MSI." When the comment came back to bite him, the mayor said his quote had been taken out of context by the media. That would be me. And for the record, I can't think of any context that would lessen the ugliness of that statement, made at that particular time in history.

Poverty rates remained high; the number of students in the school had, if anything, decreased. While per capita incomes were on par with the state average—due to the number of retirees and trust-funders in town—the average wage remained the lowest in the state, worse even than the chronically depressed counties out on the eastern plains. The absence of a "basic industry" was (and is) still deeply felt. Housing costs, meanwhile, were as high as they were in Durango, astronomical and out of reach to most residents. For those who weren't getting money from the outside, Silverton was still a hard place to make it. After driving through that June blizzard and ending up down in the lowlands where summer was in full bloom, Wendy and I decided finally to give up trying, and on the last day of 2005 drove a moving van down to the warmer, cheaper, and better-paying pastures of Paonia, Colorado.

In some ways, Silverton found itself in a 1950s-like situation. Mining had gone. Tourism and the amenities economy, with some help from cottage industry, had emerged to take its place. But it wasn't enough to fill the void left by the departure of the extraction industry and its high year-round wages and relative stability. There was something else about the New West economy that was also lacking: culture.

A few years earlier, during the time of dandelions, I had sat outside the Avalanche, eating key lime pie with Dolores LaChapelle. After the San Juan Avalanche Project was over, her husband Ed had left, and Dolores stuck around, building a career and reputation as an author, scholar, and pioneer of deep ecology. I asked her what it was like to be someone like her, writing books about sacred sex, the earth, and the rapture of deep-powder skiing, in a full-on mining town. "I just told people I was writing children's books," she replied, a nod to the dark, mean side of a working-class town. She was in her early seventies then, her face deeply lined, her trademark braid, long gone silver, hanging over her shoulder, her gray eyes bright as ever.

Then she started talking about the particular strain of culture that mountains foster, and about how, in Silverton, that culture was and still is tied directly to mining. Tearing ore out of the earth might mar the landscape, it might poison the water irreparably, but, like farming, it also creates an inextricable, visceral link between people and place. The entire community depended upon this relationship—abusive though it may be—with the earth. "It seems that mining was better than what we have now, in terms of culture," Dolores said. "Now, a lot of people just want to ruin Silverton by making it into a tourist trap." Yes, Aspen, Telluride, and Park City managed to move beyond mere tourism, to leave behind their mining pasts and embrace the New Western ethos, building their own version of community, culture, and institutions. But in so doing they also created a massive crevasse between rich and poor, with no middle class to speak of. Theirs is a community of and for the wealthy, one of hallowed homes that sit vacant for most of the year. It's no wonder Silvertonians cling to the past. And it's no surprise that in 2007 they jubilantly embraced an upstart company called Colorado Goldfields that came along with big promises to rejuvenate mining.

Originally based in Canada, Colorado Goldfields was first incorporated in 2004 in Nevada, for tax reasons, as Garpa Resources. Its scope and activities were small-scale until June 2007, when Todd Hennis took control of the company, bought all the existing shares of Garpa's stock, and changed the name to Colorado Goldfields Inc., or CGFI. By then, Hennis had acquired the Gold King and re-acquired the Mogul, both of which Fearn had lost in foreclosures. Colorado Goldfields entered into an agreement with Hennis to develop the Gold King and his other mining properties, hired Hennis as its CEO and president, and entered into a deal to purchase the Pride of the West Mill from Tusco. The company was moved to Lakewood, Colorado, a suburb of Denver.[60]

In early 2008, Colorado Goldfields hired Stephen Guyer, a seasoned executive, as its chief financial officer. It also began courting locals, and investors. Beverly Rich, a native of Silverton and San Juan County Treasurer at the time, was brought on as one of just three directors. A longtime leader of the San Juan County Historical Society, Rich has been a vocal proponent of revitalizing the mining industry of Silverton. The company made a short video starring a host of locals talking about how badly Silverton needed mining to come back, and released an optimistic investor's brochure about its bright prospects, with the Gold King as the flagship property.

CGFI, as they were known, soon captured the imagination of the locals, even those who had seen dozens of mining promoters come and go without ever pulling an ounce of gold out of the hills. Some were convinced, and desperate enough for economic development, to throw their savings into the venture. In hindsight, however, viewed through the lens of SEC filings, the whole thing appears to have been an unmitigated financial crap show almost from the beginning.

For starters, the company was putting most of its eggs into the Gold King, from which acid mine drainage discharges were increasing and which was becoming one of the worst polluters in the watershed. CGFI's other big asset, the Pride of the West Mill, was under a cease and desist order from the state, carried over from the previous owner. Even with no revenue coming in, and the prospect of any cash flow a long ways off, the company's two employees, Hennis and Guyer, were each making $12,500 per month beginning in June 2008.

At the same time, the biggest predatory lending scam in history was coming home to roost as sub-prime mortgages came due and the housing bubble imploded. It wasn't hard to see that Silverton's inflating market had been a bubble built upon a bubble that itself was an appendage of yet another bubble. Californians used equity from their homes to buy Durango homes, thus giving Durango homeowners enough equity to buy second homes in Silverton, thus driving up prices for the locals who were speculatively buying properties. When the national bubble finally popped, it brought Silverton's market down with it, hard. Houses lost fifty percent of their value or more. Foreclosures were rampant. Mining was more appealing than ever.

In September 2008, Hennis resigned from Colorado Goldfields. Lee R. Rice, a geological engineer, took his place as CEO, but Guyer appears to have been running the show. Later that year, CGFI failed to pay Hennis the annual $100,000 payment for the Gold King and other properties, and a few months later, Hennis, along with two other creditors, filed a complaint against the company for the back payment and other claims. The company counter-sued, launching a legal battle that would drag on for years, and would put the company's prime properties out of reach. Hennis ultimately won the suit.

In 2011, after investigating the Gold King and other leaky Cement Creek mines, the EPA went to Silverton and asked the citizens to support a Superfund designation in order to pay for a comprehensive cleanup, and construction and long-term operation of a water treatment plant. Many locals balked, worried about how a toxic waste site label would affect tourism and the already depressed property values. At the same time, there was a greater recognition than ever before that something needed to be done about water quality, and that the Stakeholders process, alone, wasn't adequate. Sunnyside Gold offered $6.5 million to build a treatment plant, then upped it to $10 million, on the condition that Superfund was held at bay. Colorado Goldfields argued that a designation would stifle their plans, though by then they had much bigger worries.

Regardless of the fact that the company apparently couldn't pay its bills, Guyer kept hiking his own pay, raking in $320,000 in salary and a bonus for 2011. Rich, the only local on the board of directors, resigned in late 2011, but Fearn and another longtime San Juan mining man, John Ferguson, were brought on as consultants. In order to replace the lost mining properties, Goldfields bought or leased others locally, including the Silver Wing group from Fearn's company, Jo Grant Mining. They also bought a group of uranium mining claims in southern Utah. At one point, the company even sent out a press release announcing that they were negotiating with Kinross to buy the now-flooded Sunnyside.

These appear to have been the dying gasps of a doomed gambit, and in 2013 Guyer filed the company's last SEC report. CGFI lost ownership of the Pride of the West Mill to Hennis in 2015, but continued to hold onto the state permit for the mill. In 2016, state regulators discovered that the mill's tailings pond had overflowed and spilled into the Animas River. They demanded that CGFI fix the problem or lose its permit. CGFI did not comply. The permit was revoked in December 2016.

WITHOUT STRONG COMMUNITY SUPPORT FOR SUPER-FUND, the EPA, along with the Colorado Division of Mining Reclamation and Safety, continued to investigate and do some remediation work on the leaky upper Cement Creek mines using money from the forfeited Gold King Mine bond as well as "removal" funds from the EPA.

Four separate mine portals, spread out over about one and a half miles along the western base of Bonita Peak, were discharging acid mine drainage into Cement Creek. The Gold King would be especially challenging to deal with. In the 1990s, the ceiling had collapsed inside the mine. Initially, that wasn't much of a concern, but as discharges increased, so did the potential of the debris acting like an ad hoc dam that could eventually give way. As early as 2007, Hennis, the state, and the EPA had all noted the potential for such a disaster. Blow-outs are not rare in the San Juans. One mine, near the Animas River headwaters, blew out in the 1990s, and then again in 2014. In 2000, Bill Simon was working his backhoe for the Forest Service on a waste removal and water diversion project at the Bonner Mine in the Mineral Creek drainage when it blew out, taking Simon's backhoe bucket, a bunch of his tools, and nearly his truck, with it. "It was damn near as big as the Gold King," he told me. In typical Simon fashion, he raced downstream to get ahead of the resulting plume so he could collect water samples.

In order to try to shore up the debris dam, the state back-filled the portal with dirt and debris, and installed drainage pipes to help ease some of the pressure of the mine pool. The EPA and its contractor started working on the Gold King Mine in 2014, intending to open up the portal and enter the mine to investigate the drainage situation. Drainage had *decreased* from over one hundred gallons per minute to just thirteen gallons per minute, a suspiciously large drop, and in hindsight a clear red flag indicating that water was being blocked somewhere inside the tunnel. The EPA, however, attributed the change to fluctuating "seasonal inflow to the mine." After just two hours of excavation on the blockage, work was stopped, according to EPA records, "when it was determined that the elevation of the adit floor was estimated to be six feet below the waste-dump surface elevation." This makes little sense and its veracity has been questioned widely: miners dump waste rock down the slope outside the mine portal, they don't pile it up in a way that would block their own ingress and egress. The workers back-filled the portal and ceased work for the year.

During the summer of 2015, crews working for the EPA and the state focused their work on the Red & Bonita, where they installed a bulkhead similar to those in the American Tunnel and the Mogul Mine. Bulkheads can effectively stop discharges altogether, as was the case at the Koehler Tunnel atop Red Mountain Pass. More often than not, however, the water finds a way out. Even so, the giant plug can help. Backing up water diminishes oxygen in a mine, slowing acid-mine-drainage-forming reactions, and it can also be used to control the flow of discharge in order to more easily treat it.

As the Red & Bonita project neared completion in July, workers headed up to the Gold King to start prepping the site for work there, which they knew would be challenging. Environmental Restoration, the St. Louis-based contractor chosen by the EPA to work on the Gold King, had issued a work plan noting, "Conditions may exist that could result in a blow-out of the blockages and cause a release of large volumes of contaminated mine waters and sediment from inside the mine

. . ." In order to mitigate the danger, the plan was to "gradually lower the debris blockage with the appropriate pumping of the impounded water to water management/treatment system."

The EPA's on-scene coordinator, Steve Way, was getting ready to take a vacation. And after eyeballing the situation at the Gold King, he called the Bureau of Reclamation to schedule a site inspection as soon as he returned, on August 14, because he was "unsure about the plans for the Gold King Mine."

On August 4, when Way was on vacation, Hays Griswold, who was filling in for Way, decided to start doing more work on the Gold King, including clearing out debris from the portal. The plan was to dig in through the debris from above the mine pool, creating an opening large enough to then slowly pump the water out. They still apparently were working on the erroneous assumption that the waste rock dump was six feet above the adit floor. In similar situations in the past, the workers had drilled into the adit from above so that they could size up the mine pool without the danger of busting the debris dam. But that would have been difficult, given the steep slope above the Gold King, so they bypassed this step. According to an investigation conducted later by the Department of Interior, the excavator started digging into the portal at around ten o'clock on a sunny, warm morning.

From the investigator's report: "As the excavator continued to dig on August 5, the operator reported hitting a 'spring.' He stopped, they removed the excavator, and the EPA OSC went up to look at the conditions. Within moments, the 'spring' began spurting upward 1.5 to 2 feet into the air."

Not in the report: "Oh. Shit."

Aftermath

Corns are thirsty and dying. Damn the EPA, damn the government, damn the industry!

—Duane "Chili" Yazzie, "Yellow River"

B ILL SIMON'S OLD MOP OF BROWN HAIR HAD BEEN SHORN GRAY, and he moved slowly and out of balance when I sat down with him in December 2015 at his home north of Durango, a stone's throw from what was my great-grandparents' farm near Hermosa Creek. Simon struggles with the physical ravages of Parkinson's, but as we talked for more than three hours, it became clear that his intellect hasn't suffered. It's as if he carries in his head a multi-dimensional map of the upper Animas watershed, its geology, hydrology, history, and even politics, and he's still intent as ever on solving the puzzles of the caldera.

Simon was quick to remind me that, in the grand scheme of things, Silverton's mining pollution problem, not to mention the Gold King spill, are relatively small on a global scale, paling in comparison to, say, the Bingham Canyon Mine outside Salt Lake City, which has created a seventy-square-mile underground plume of contaminated groundwater. A month earlier, a tailings dam at a copper mine in Brazil had burst, sending some forty million cubic meters of contaminated sludge, water, and debris down the Rio Gualaxo do Norte, blasting through villages, inundating homes, killing nineteen people, flooding fields, and wiping out aquatic life for more than three hundred miles downstream. The mine is owned by global mining giants BHP Billiton and Vale. The disaster got nowhere near the attention that the Gold King spill did. In the year before the Gold King blowout: A tailings pond breach in British Columbia sent 24.4 million cubic meters of waste into the salmon-rich Fraser River; 10 million gallons of acid mine drainage spilled from a copper mine's tailings pond in Mexico; and cyanide-contaminated waters spilled from yet another Mexico mine just weeks later. "So the problem of acid mine drainage is huge. It's worldwide," said Simon. "That's why I got involved. The problem is being ignored."

For years, Animas River downstreamers largely tuned out Simon and the Stakeholders and their efforts, as well. The *Durango Herald* ran articles on draining mines and the like, as did other media outlets, but for the most part environmental groups did not get involved. Nor did downstream municipalities, county governments, state health departments, or tribes, including the ones that would later sue the EPA over the Gold King spill and step up to push for Superfund or at least Good Samaritan legislation that would enable citizens' groups to start cleaning up draining mines themselves. Acid mine drainage is too complicated and subtle to be a sexy environmental topic, at least until disaster strikes, so it's hard to get people to rally around it. Anglers in Durango were still catching trout, even after the water treatment plant fiasco, though perhaps not quite as many. Besides, river users had other things to worry about: in the months leading up to the Gold King spill, studies revealed dangerously high levels of human fecal bacteria in the Animas River beginning near the New Mexico state line and continuing downstream to the San Juan River and onto the Navajo Nation.

Everything changed after the Gold King spill. Acid mine drainage became a regular part of the average Durangoan's vocabulary, and everyone from Colorado environmental groups to congresspeople demanded some sort of action and accountability. Congressional Republicans, many of whom had spent their careers trying to dismantle and defund environmental regulations, dragged EPA officials through hearing after hearing, Benghazi-like, in hopes of further diminishing the agency. Environmentalists called once again for reform of the General Mining Act of 1872, which remains in place almost as originally written, in order to create an industry-funded pot for abandoned mine cleanup. The Stakeholders Group was vilified for its role in keeping Superfund at bay for so long, even though the group had taken no official position on the matter.

The disaster renewed calls for a Superfund designation in the Upper Animas River Basin. At first, Silverton resisted. But that didn't play well in the low-country, where the town was portrayed as a backward-looking community so beholden to the mining industry that it had repeatedly refused to let the feds come in and clean up mining's massive mess. Silverton's tourism board called in a PR person to help strategize, and elected officials started realizing that the stigma of standing in the way of cleaning up a toxic dump might just be worse than that of officially being declared a toxic dump.

In February 2016, the Town of Silverton and the San Juan County commissioners voted unanimously to request Superfund designation for the area, slyly naming the site the "Bonita Peak Mining District," to divert attention from the town and thus mitigate impacts to the tourism industry. The EPA made the designation official in September of that year.

Simon knew all along that Superfund would eventually land in the Silverton Caldera—there's simply no other way to raise enough cash to tackle the problem at hand. Simon is an advocate for slowing down even more, and focusing on trying to solve the enigmas, to really understand how digging hundreds of miles of tunnels and shafts and adits in a mountain manifests itself on the surface, before throwing millions of dollars at imperfect fixes. "We're going too fast because we still don't know what's going on in there," he said, referring to the subterranean American Tunnel-Sunnyside Mine/Gold King puzzle.

When Sunnyside Gold installed the second and third bulkheads in the American Tunnel it made the first bulkhead unreachable. That effectively made it impossible to monitor the mine pool, which worries Simon. The level of the mine pool behind bulkhead #1 conceivably could have kept rising after it was thought to have reached equilibrium, and that's why water's dumping out of the neighboring mines. That would exert more pressure on the bulkhead than the plug was designed to withstand—the worst, worst case scenario would be a hundred-million-gallon blowout. Will the EPA spend its money trying to answer these questions and experimenting with innovative, more sustainable solutions? Or will they take the straightforward way out, setting up effective, but expensive, sludge-producing water treatment plants all over the basin?

Even as I write this, in early 2017, no one knows exactly what Superfund will mean for Silverton, the Upper Animas

River Basin, for Sunnyside Gold, for wannabe miners, or for the downstreamers. The Summitville Mine, in the southeastern San Juan Mountains, was declared a Superfund site in the early 1990s, after cyanide-tinted acid mine drainage defiled the Alamosa River. At least $200 million has been spent on that cleanup that so far has taken more than twenty years. The water treatment plant there will continue to run in perpetuity. That was a huge, open pit mine, far bigger than Silverton-area complexes, but it was also just one site; the Bonita Peak Superfund area includes forty-eight different mines, tailings piles, and other sites, scattered all over the Silverton Caldera.

Within weeks of the Gold King spill the EPA built a new water treatment system at the American Tunnel, at about the same place that the old Sunnyside plant sat, to deal with Gold King discharges. While acid mine drainage from the Red & Bonita, Mogul, and American Tunnel continues to dump into Cement Creek, the EPA hopes to start running those discharges through the plant, as well. That should help reverse some of the declines in water quality that followed the shutdown of the treatment plant in 2004.

Yet in an almost cruel twist, those gains may be offset by another mystery pollution plume that was noticed in 2013. Somewhere in the three-mile stretch between Silverton and Howardsville, large quantities of zinc and presumably other harmful metals are entering the Animas River. During spring months, the source has puked as much as 260 pounds of zinc into the river each day, more than all the draining adits in the Upper Animas River Basin combined. No one knows where the zinc is coming from. The obvious suspect is the Sunnyside/Mayflower Mill tailings piles, where the mill's tailings, water treatment sludge, and waste from other sites were dumped for

Sacrifice

MY FATHER WAS DYING. *The cancer, diagnosed the previous year, had fallen asleep over the winter. But it returned for springtime, leafing out and blooming mercilessly throughout his body and brain. He sat in his chair, by the window, and stared out at the Sleeping Ute, at the sky, and at the canyon in between. Which is something he did long before the sickness had invaded his body, and I could never quite figure out at what he so raptly gazed.*

They found the cancer in his lungs in the spring of 1997, when he was fifty-six years old. Cancer had taken his mother a decade earlier. It would take his younger sister fifteen years later. Victims and survivors of the disease are everywhere around here, it seems, in Silverton and Shiprock, Durango and Farmington. We look to the world around us for answers: the plume of fallout from the Nevada bomb tests, the junk pouring from the coal plant smokestacks, the smelters and the mines, the metals and radon wafting in the wind over our towns.

I put a garden into the earth outside his little house that spring, hacking away at the clay-like soil with tearful ruthlessness. I put the drops of morphine on his dried-up tongue, as though the sacrament. I pushed tiny seeds into soft, rich soil in the flats. I lit his cigarettes and dressed him to go to chemotherapy and could never get his shoes onto his swollen feet. And the seedlings thrived in the warm air of death.

The science and the statistics tell us we're looking in the wrong places. Sure, living next to an old uranium mill or gas well may elevate your cancer risk, but it's by an infinitesimally small amount. Studies of the folks living in uranium country at Grants, New Mexico, and Uravan, Colorado, have failed to turn up unusually high cancer rates, except among the miners, themselves, most of whom smoked like chimneys. The zinc, lead, cadmium, and copper spilling out of the mines will kill fish, but unless one drinks the chronically orange and acidified waters of Cement Creek every day, the acid mine drainage won't hurt the humans.

We are Westerners, pathologically independent, pragmatic people. We accept the science, and scold those who put giant, scaremongering signs atop the tailings piles. We scoff at the ones who cringe in fear when they see the river turn orange with iron hydroxides—the same stuff that gives that jar of curry sauce its burnished orange color. And we're happy to shoulder the blame for our own demise. The tailings piles didn't kill my father. He smoked too much, worked too hard, didn't use sunscreen, cared too much, and had bad genetics and just plain rotten luck. That's what killed him.

My father's body wilted away to a skeleton, his lips dried up and we doused them with sponges, and his arms were no more than loose skin draped on brittle bones. His teeth fell out, one by one.

But his hands remained the same. His hands, which had always seemed huge and powerful to me, had somehow been spared from the disease and its equally brutal treatment. His hands that had written thousands of words. His hands that could pull away dried, springtime grass on the edge of a mountain meadow to reveal the speckled eggs of a snowy plover. His hands that could coax a lush array of spinach and tomatoes; zinnias and radishes; cosmos and squash from the rocky, red soil in the garden in the backyard of our house in Durango.

I had always assumed it was his mind that gave him his power. But as his life faded, I realized it must have been his hands, for they, more than anything, connected him to his beloved earth. His hands spoke when his voice was silent.

Still, a seed of doubt remains, an inkling that something else is going on here, something the data cannot reveal.

Duane "Chili" Yazzie is a Diné activist, a politician, a musician. He's also a farmer, and he irrigates his fields of corn, squash, tomatoes, and hay with San Juan River water. On the day after the Gold King blew out, as word got out about the yellow river, he was out in these fields, tending to the earth: *"Farming is our life, water is our life, this is our culture, our spiritual way, it's who we are."*

In May 2016, Yazzie stepped up to the lectern at a conference in Farmington on the environmental conditions of the Animas and San Juan rivers. Most of the other speakers were scientists, engineers, or bureaucrats, presenting technical papers on sediment transport, bulkheads, and microbial communities. Yazzie, long, greying black hair pulled back into a traditional bun, recited a poem he had written titled "Yellow River." It's the story of his farm, the spill, and the aftermath— one of sadness, trauma, and desperation—and he read it with force and passion, beat style, an indigenous Ginsberg driving his point home.

"Nobody knows the impact, we don't know what will hap-

*pen, the water is being shut off. We are confused, anger starting
to boil, our elders have sad misty eyes, this is so surreal."*

Like all the other farmers downstream from the Gold
King spill, Yazzie had to shut off water to his fields and watch
them wilt beneath the rainless August sky. The EPA had giant
tanks of water sent to the area so the horses, sheep, and goats
wouldn't go thirsty. But the water arrived in old gas field tanks,
and it was tainted with whatever had been in the tanks before.

The plume passed by, the water got back to its regular
silty state, and a few weeks after the Gold King spill, the EPA
and state and county health departments assured everyone
living along the Animas and San Juan rivers that all was back
to normal. They had sampled the waters exhaustively, and the
data didn't lie: the water may not have been pure, but it was no
worse than before the spill, and was safe to swim in, fish in,
irrigate with, and, with proper treatment, drink.

*"Different testers test the river, no conclusions, can't say
extent of damage or if it's safe,"* Yazzie chanted under the fluo-
rescent lights. *"Government sez farmers will get compensated,
payday time, lawyers licking their chops. Water tests ok, Rez Prez
sez turn on water, EPA steps out, water must be ok, bye, bye."*

Nevertheless, Diné farmers in the Shiprock Chapter, Yazzie
included, refused to use the water. They decided to abstain
from irrigating their crops for an entire year, maybe more,
because they were uncertain about what toxins still lurked in
the depths. Their fields would fallow, and the corn would go
unplanted. The white scientists were baffled at this and, admit-
tedly, so was I. Even at its peak, the Gold King slug was not
especially dangerous. It didn't kill fish as far as anyone could
tell, and wasn't even distinguishable from the usual San Juan
River silt by the time it reached Utah. Why ignore science, at

the expense of your crops, maybe even your sustenance?

It may be because there are places where our version of science just can't reach. The quality of the water in the Animas and San Juan rivers is no different from what it was prior to the spill. Yet the Place—the interaction between the people here and the land and water—did change, somehow. The people who value the river the most, those who draw both physical and spiritual sustenance from its waters, were forever altered. Once a mountain is mined it's more, or perhaps less, than just a mountain with a hole in it—the whole Place is tossed out of balance, the ancient hydrologic regime forever transfigured. When the dynamite and the draglines chomp apart ancestral grazing lands, it takes away more than just grass, rocks, and shrubs, it also shatters a delicate harmony that had existed between humans and the land for ages. When a group of people in a community is murdered, such as the tragedy at Sacred Ridge so long ago, the Place gets tainted, as do all who remain there. The trauma gets into our psyches and then into our cells, maybe even our genes, affecting us both psychologically and physiologically.

About six months after the spill, the University of Arizona Institute of the Environment held a panel discussion entitled "Navajo Perspectives on the Gold King Spill." Yazzie was a panelist, as was Perry Charley, a professor at Diné College. He grew up in Waterflow, New Mexico, along the San Juan River and not far from the two giant coal power plants there, and has worked for years on uranium issues on the Navajo Nation. He was a witness to the slug coming down the San Juan, and he explained how its effects transcended the data and the science. "My first inclination as a scientist was to go out there and do sampling . . . but I started to back off, because I knew that this

Redemption

O N A WINTER'S EVE A WHILE BACK, a friend and I headed out for a drink at one of the Silverton bars. A blanket of snow covered the ground, and another storm had settled in, along with the giddiness that comes when you know the snow might close the passes, trapping you for hours, maybe days, transforming the town into the solitary domain of extremophiles. Just before darkness, the world went cerulean blue in a way that is only possible in the mountains in winter.

"The Miner's Tavern has got to be open," I said. It had been years, but I knew what it would be like: the dim light shining down through a haze of cigarette smoke; Judy, with her raven hair and stiletto heels, running the pool table to her rival's chagrin; Terry, who worked in the mines like his father, bellied up to the bar with his son, who never got the chance; Ernie holding court at the round table up front, with another elected official or three, tipsily deciding the fate of the town.

It was eerily quiet, and as we made our way down the empty main drag, all the shop windows were either boarded up or dark. Maybe everyone went home early, I thought. The last few years were tough, after all: Most of the cottage industries that sprouted before the national recession were gone, the community had been ripped apart by an ugly political battle and had its heart broken by a recent domestic homicide. To top it all off, the Gold King Mine blew out, and now the community was diving into the uncertain waters of Superfund.

We pulled up in front of the Miner's Tavern and started to get out of the car before we noticed something amiss. The neon beer signs were dark. Through the window, we saw pool tables piled with junk, and the door was padlocked from the outside. Turns out Silverton Mountain ski resort bought the entire Miner's Union Hall, including the tavern and theatre upstairs, and turned it into their office and, apparently, storage locker.

The symbolism was clear. Silverton had finally moved on, had embraced a future and livelihood that, for all its imperfections, is far less destructive to the land and the people and the water and the wildlife than mining. Yes, the hordes of sightseers will swarm the tundra every summer, they'll build their cabins in the high country, they'll love this place to the brink of death. But these mountains probably will never again be gouged open for the sake of gold or silver or copper or lead.

Still, as I stood there in the empty street, I felt an ineffable sadness. So much has been lost. We've learned nothing. One-hundred-and-fifty-year-old habits die hard. And when we venture outside of our little pockets of green—our Tellurides, our Durangos, and now our Silvertons—we'll find ourselves once again in the sacrifice zone. For every leaky mine we manage to restore to some semblance of "nature," we'll drill another oil well, burn another twenty million tons of coal, sully our sacred waters in ways that we aren't even yet aware of or can possibly understand.

Snowflakes swarmed the streetlights like a million falling moths.

Back in 2010 and 2011, hoping to study water contamination in Lake Powell, USGS scientists looked to the silt that builds up in huge volumes where the San Juan River runs into the still and stagnant reservoir. Here, they drove long metal tubes straight down into the silt to extract cylinders of sediment ranging from about five to fifteen feet long. They then analyzed the sediment, looking for metals, polycyclic aromatic hydrocarbons, radionuclides, and so on. As one might expect, they found "greater than reporting levels" of many elements and radioactivity in the sediments and the water nearby.

This might make you think twice about swimming or fishing in Lake Powell, but the silt core samples have more to tell us than just what kind of nasties are in the mud. The cores were far from homogenous in appearance. Down deep one core was described as tannish brown with fine black zones. Another layer had angular, reddish, bloody-looking banding. Near the surface was a "very strong red band, well delineated." The layers in the core sample's cross section were like the rings of a tree, or the layers of rock exposed in a road cut. The sediment is a calendar, a chronicle of water quality in the Animas and San Juan river basins.

Look deep enough in the silt and you'll see the Shiprock uranium mill's big spill, the Aneth Oil Field pipeline disaster, the coal combustion waste dumping, the Silverton tailings pond breaches, and the Lake Emma deluge. Go back and take a core sample now and you'll surely see the Gold King disaster, a distinct, iron-rich layer of orange. You'll see the history of the region, which, in so many ways, is a history of pollution. A history of sacrificing the sacred water.

Is there any hope for balance? Will we ever walk in beauty again? Perhaps.

About eight months after I stood despondently outside the Miner's Tavern on that snowy night, a team of scientists combed the streams of the Upper Animas River Basin doing research in preparation for Superfund efforts. One group made its way through the willows along the banks of the main stem of Mineral Creek, past deep red-orange iron fens in a V-shaped valley through which Highway 550 runs on its way toward Red Mountain Pass. This drainage was heavily impacted by mining, and fish had never been found in this particular stream segment. These were sacrificial waters. And even though the Stakeholders' remediation efforts had dramatically reduced levels of zinc and other metals here, aluminum and iron concentrations remained naturally high, so hopes that the stream would ever support life beyond the rock-eating, acid-loving, extremophilic bacteria were low.

But on that summer's day, one of the researchers cast his net into the water and pulled up a rainbow trout, its scales glimmering in the sun like a precious and intelligent metal. That day, they caught four more rainbows and five brookies, and at that moment they must have felt a bit like Olaf Nelson did when he chipped into the rich vein under the green-covered slopes of Bonita Peak 130 years ago.

Epilogue

I AM SIX. MY BROTHER'S HERE AND MY DAD AND MY MOM, here at the Sandbar, here where the Animas River runs slow.

I don't have a fishing pole. We're poor, and besides, you don't really need one. Instead, my dad cuts a long willow branch, removes the leaves, and ties twenty feet or so of fishing line with hook and lead sinker and red-and-white bobber to the small end. I carefully stab the hook into the wiggly worm, hold the line out to my side, and swing it as far into the murky green as I can. Then I wait, holding the line gently in my small, dirty hand.

I feel the tug on the line. It's the tug of life. Again, and I yank the line as hard as I can. I've got it. I grab the willow pole and sprint up the beach as fast as I can, until the trout, its scales shiny like mica, lies flopping in the sand, its eye looking skyward. I pick it up and feel its weight, its strength, its will to live, and I watch for a moment as its scarlet gills move desperately.

"Don't let it suffer like that," my dad says. Hold it tight, its scales rough on your fingers and its white belly soft on your thumb, and hit it hard on the driftwood log that juts out from the sand like a misplaced appendage. Blood trickles from its mouth. From the trees, cotton falls like snow.

When the sun sets behind Animas Mountain, the Sandbar gets cool quick, mosquitos hop across the water, and cliff swallows dart back and forth chasing them. The river takes on the exact pale-purple of the sky, like lilacs in a new lover's hair on a Sunday morning in May.

My dad lights a driftwood campfire and fries the fish and then we cook marshmallows on willow sticks and then it gets dark, the fire dies, and the stars shine marvelously bright. We throw our sleeping bags on the ground and crawl in, sand coming with us, but we don't mind. As I fall asleep I listen to the water. Silent during the day, it comes alive at night, its lost souls muttering to themselves in deep and ancient tongues, speaking to the trees, and answering the owl and its soft and wise whisper.

Endnotes

CHAPTER 1

1   Michael J. Gobla, Christopher M. Gemperline, and Leslie W. Stone, *Technical Review of the Gold King Mine Incident* (Denver: U.S. Bureau of Reclamation, 2015).

2   "Navajo Perspectives on the Gold King Spill" (panel discussion, University of Arizona Institute of the Environment, Flagstaff, AZ, March 2016).

CHAPTER 2

3   Steven G. Baker, *Juan Rivera's Colorado, 1765: The First Spaniards among the Ute and Paiute Indians on the Trails to Teguayo* (Lake City, CO: Western Reflections Publishing, 2016).

4   Joe S. Sando, *Nee Hemish: A History of Jemez Pueblo* (Santa Fe: Clear Light, 2008).

5   This section of Rivera's journal is especially muddled, geographically, so the modern reader cannot be certain about the location of *"un Pueblo tan grande que exude a la Poblacion de Santa Cruz de la Cañada"* atop a hill they called *el Tumichi*. But he's most likely referring to Sacred Ridge, the most significant settlement within the Ridges Basin community.

6   The "Pueblo people" are not a single tribe, but a group of people from various pueblos spread out across more than four hundred miles and speaking six different languages. Tewa is one of the language and cultural groups. The others are Hopi, Zuni, Tano, Tiwa, Towa, and Keres. Given the diversity of culture and language, some have questioned whether they should all be grouped under one name. In a 1994 essay, Ortiz argues that they should: "I do indeed believe that we can demonstrate that the peoples called Pueblos, despite their linguistic diversity and wide geographical range, have, at various times reaching into dim prehistory, shared a sense of cultural similarity, just as they have a common homeland." It is worth keeping this diversity in mind when thinking about the ancient Pueblo, or "Anasazi," world. Surely the ancient ones were not monolithic culturally, religiously, socially, or linguistically, either.

7   Alfonso Ortiz, *The Tewa World: Space, Time, Being, and Becoming in a Pueblo Society* (Chicago: University of Chicago Press, 1972).

8   Stephen H. Lekson, *The Chaco Meridian: One Thousand Years of Political and Religious Power in the Ancient Southwest* (Lanham: Rowman & Littlefield, 2015).

9   The Ridges Basin community had risen up, and collapsed, long before the pueblos at Chaco and the roads radiating out from them came to be. Still, the symbolic north-south line known as the Chaco Meridian may have also predated Chaco, itself. I haven't been able to find any archaeological theory on the possible significance to the early Pueblo people of the Hogback Monocline, but it is a prominent and, at places, dramatic landform. Two other Durango-area Pueblo I communities, one on the upper Florida River and another at Grandview, were located near the Hogback. The Chacoan Hogback Great House is on the New Mexico portion of the monocline, and the Chimney

Rock Great House is close to the formation in Colorado, as well.

10 The Pueblo people did capture rainwater with check dams and the like, and it appears that occasionally they stored rainwater in constructed reservoirs and basins. But they rarely if ever diverted perennial streams or rivers.

11 Rivera saw a large pueblo on a hill that apparently had been burnt and had remains of what looked like a tower. The location is unclear, only that he saw it after he had explored the Sierra La Plata, but it's almost certainly Sacred Ridge.

12 James M. Potter, *Animas-La Plata Project: Volume XVI — Final Synthetic Report.* SWCA Anthropological Research Paper No. 10. (Phoenix: SWCA Inc., 2010).

CHAPTER 3

13 The government offered bounties on all sorts of predators, and the settlers took advantage of it. Surviving "scalp records" from La Plata County (where Durango is located) include a heartbreaking tally. In 1880 and '81, 288 hawk heads (for twenty-five cents apiece) and three wolf hides were presented for bounties. Between 1889 and 1897, hunters collected bounties on 190 bears, 25 mountain lions, countless coyotes, and a handful of wolves. Southwest Colorado was a veritable killing field.

CHAPTER 4

14 The details of my family's arrival in the Animas Valley are sketchy. Some accounts say, for example, that the Hathaways arrived by themselves, and Julia and her son followed later. The information comes from stories passed down through the generations, historical newspaper accounts, Bureau of Land Management records, as well as from "Meads Make Pioneer History," written by Lena Knapp Stark in 1946, which appeared in *Pioneers of the San Juan Country Volume II*, Sarah Platt Decker Daughters of the American Revolution, Durango Chapter.

CHAPTER 5

15 The story of Olaf Nelson, aka Olof Arvid Nilsson, is elusive prior to 1879. His obituary doesn't say where he was born (though we can infer that it was Sweden, given his nickname), who his parents were, or when he came to Silverton. Searches of immigration records for the time have turned up nothing. This account of Nelson's life comes from various accounts in Silverton newspapers that appeared before and after his death, from San Juan County land records, and from a history of the Gold King Mine, written by Myrtle Nord, that appeared in the *Silverton Standard & the Miner* over several weeks in 1987 and 1988.

16 This account of Clayton Ogsbury's murder and the characters involved is informed mostly by Allen Nossaman's *Many More Mountains, Volume 3*, along with: various editions of the *San Juan Herald* and *La Plata Miner* newspapers; *The Story of Hillside Cemetery*, by Freda Peterson; *Pioneers of the San Juan Country, Volume 3*; *The Coe-Stockton Feud*, by Stan Zamonski, in *Wild West* magazine, 1992; the *Chicago Tribune*; and the San Juan County Historical Society Archive.

17 This inspired the "Mrs. Romney and the Outlaws" episode of the television series *Death Valley Days* in 1965. In TV world, Romney roused the townsfolk to kill the outlaws, thus allowing Durango to "mature and prosper." Romney is far less heroic in the real story.

18 *Chicago Tribune*, Dec. 15, 1883.

19 The railroad tracks lie at the bottom of numerous avalanche paths in the ten or so miles leading into Silverton, and the train was sometimes "blockaded" for days, weeks, and, in spring of 1906, for over one month while workers cleared the tracks. In 1906, a crew of two hundred Japanese Americans were brought on to do the hazardous and arduous job of clearing the tracks. During later blockades, Navajo people were often hired for the job.

CHAPTER 6

20 Pyrite's acid-forming properties are so strong that pyrite, itself, was mined in Rico, Colorado, to supply raw material for the sulfuric acid industry, which in turn provided its wares to—among many other things—uranium processing mills.

21 The process can occur naturally, as well, when storm discharge flows over pyrite, for example. Some natural springs, as we'll see later, can even be acidic and metal-loaded. But mining greatly exacerbates the problem, hijacks the groundwater system, and introduces more metals to the water.

CHAPTER 7

22 The Ames plant, which first generated power in 1891, holds a critical role in the history of America's electrical grid as the first large-scale commercial application of AC power, thus representing perhaps the final death blow in the War of the Currents that pitted Nikola Tesla (AC) against Thomas Edison (DC). The plant was built on the Howard Fork of the San Miguel River to power the Gold King Mill nearby (not related to the Gold King Mine near Silverton). Ames-generated power then lit up the town of Telluride and became part of a larger, regional grid. The Ames plant is still in operation today. The 300-kilowatt Silver Lake Mill hydropower plant, located just upstream from Silverton, was one of the first multi-phase alternating current plants in the region, and notable for sending electricity three miles to the mine and mill. It was eventually converted to coal power. Durango's coal-fired power plant, also alternating current, located on the banks of the Animas River in the heart of the town, was also an electrical pioneer.

23 *The Daily Journal* (Telluride), June 29, 1914.

24 Agnes Wright Spring, "Silver Queen of the San Juans," *Frontier Times* 45, no. 1 (January 1967).

25 Silverton had done this same thing back in the 1880s, drawing town water from Bear Creek and Boulder Creek, which were put off-limits to mining. The town still draws from these clean sources.

26 In 1895 the federal government "answered" the "Ute Question" by opening up the now-tiny Ute reservation to homesteading. Utes from the Moache and Capote bands were given first dibs on parcels (which became allotments), in the hopes of turning the nomads into sedentary farmers. What remained was then handed out on a first-come, first-served basis, prompting a mini land rush. Today the Southern Ute reservation south of Durango is a checkerboard of Indian and non-Indian land as a result. The Weeminuche band settled in the far corner of the state, on what is now the Ute Mountain Ute reservation.

CHAPTER 8

27 The historical record has been muddled, perhaps intentionally, around this transaction. In 1901, when recounting the history of the Gold King to a newspaper reporter, Kinney failed to mention Olaf or Louisa Nelson, who died in 1897, and indicated that he had control over the claim as early as 1890. He may have obfuscated the facts in order to make himself look a bit less weasel-like in his dealings with Louisa. The confusion has carried down to modern histories of the mine, which sometimes miss Olaf Nelson's 1891 death.

28 An underground mine can be a convoluted place, composed of miles of horizontal passageways (drifts, adits, crosscuts, tunnels) and vertical ones (shafts, lifts). Most mines have more than one level, with the first level being the highest, and the numbers increasing as one gets lower. So the Gold King Level #7 is six levels below Level #1 (and that much closer to the mill). Just to increase confusion: The Gold King Level #7 was originally called the American Tunnel. Later, however, yet another long haulage tunnel was dug far lower in the mountain, and it then took the American Tunnel name, which adheres today.

29 Miners generally worked their way through the rock by drilling cylindrical holes with power drills or hand steels and hammers, and then put explosives into the holes. This poor guy tried drilling into dynamite that hadn't yet been "shot" or exploded.

30 *Silverton Standard*, September 17, 1904.

31 *La Plata Miner*, February 21, 1885.

32 "James Dornan, a cook, formerly a pugilist, who is said to have been on bad terms with some of the men at the mine, has been arrested on suspicion of having started the fire." *Ouray Herald*, May 24, 1907.

33 This is the same portal—or opening—that blew out in 2015. The American Tunnel name would later be given to the tunnel dug from Gladstone into Bonita Peak.

CHAPTER 9

34 Colorado's Swedish immigrant community was large enough that it had its own Swedish-language newspaper, *Svensk-Amerikanska Western: The Swedish Weekly of the West*, based out of Denver, up until the late 1920s.

35 *The Bayfield Blade*, October 12, 1911.

36 Robert H. Webb et al., *Changes in Riparian Vegetation in the Southwestern United States: Floods and Riparian Vegetation on the San Juan River, Southeastern Utah; USGS Open File Report of 01-314* (Tucson: U.S. Geological Survey, 2001).

37 Bluff City, Utah, was an exception. The town had been settled in 1880 by the Hole-in-the-Rock pioneers who had been sent by the Mormon Church to colonize southeastern Utah. Year after year, high waters destroyed their irrigation diversion dams and sizable floods in 1884 and 1909 took out fields and homes. They finally gave up after 1911, and virtually abandoned Bluff. They became ranchers rather than farmers and moved up to what is now the town of Blanding and dug a tunnel through the Abajo Mountains to divert the much more harnessable waters of Indian Creek for their use.

CHAPTER 10

38 San Juan County total population, according to the U.S. Census, was 3,063 in 1910

and just 1,700 in 1920. It's not clear what the count was when the flu hit, but estimates put it at about 2,200 to 2,500.

CHAPTER 11

39 A consortium of mining interests owned at the time by the Guggenheim family. It included American Smelting and Refining Co., or ASARCo, which owned the smelter in Durango and would purchase the Silver Lake Mine near Silverton. Collectively, the companies would dominate the mining industry and lay waste to large portions of the West—and the rest of the globe.

40 Now a major Superfund site, and home of Butte's Berkeley Pit, where in late 2016 thousands of snow geese died after landing on the acidic, polluted waters that formed a lake in the abandoned pit.

41 *The Mining American*, Volume 49, 1904.

42 This would also go by the Shenandoah-Dives name, and later became the mill for the revived Sunnyside Mine. It's still standing northeast of Silverton and is open for tours from its owner, the San Juan County Historical Society.

43 William R. Jones, "History of Mining and Milling Practices and Production in San Juan County, Colorado, 1871-1991," in *Integrated Investigations of Environmental Effects of Historical Mining in the Animas River Watershed, San Juan County, Colorado: USGS Professional Paper 1651*, ed. Stanley E. Church, Paul von Guerard, and Susan E. Finger (2006).

CHAPTER 12

44 Palone and Todeschi's splitter still stands—and will for many years to come—on the slopes of Arrastra Gulch as a monument to the miners who toiled here. The splitter is not only remarkable for its stoutness, but also its craftsmanship and aesthetic appeal.

CHAPTER 13

45 John D. Rockefeller's notorious Standard Oil conglomerate was broken up into ninety companies under anti-trust laws in 1911. Standard Oil of Indiana, or Stanolind, bought Midwest Refining, the other major early San Juan Basin oil driller, and would go on to become Amoco, which was folded into BP in the 1990s. BP remains one of the biggest oil and gas operators in the San Juan Basin.

46 The most famous line in the 2007 film *There Will Be Blood* is that spoken by Daniel Day-Lewis's character, Daniel Plainview: "Sir, if you have a milkshake and I have a milkshake and my straw reaches across the room, I'll end up drinking your milkshake." After the film came out, writer and director Paul Thomas Anderson said he got the line from Albert Fall, who purportedly said it in a congressional hearing on Teapot Dome, to explain the phenomenon of "drainage" in oil fields. Drainage was, indeed, one of the reasons given for leasing out the Naval Oil Reserves, but there's no record of Fall making any sort of straw/milkshake statement. However, Sen. Pete Domenici, another New Mexican senator in the same ideological mold as Fall, did make a straw/milkshake statement in 2003 hearings on leasing the Arctic National Wildlife Refuge: "Here is a giant reservoir underground. It is many yards from where you have set out to manage and control the destiny of the tundra. There you are with this dramatic picture of how, just like a curved straw, you put it underground and maneuver it, and the 'milkshake'

is way over there, and your little child wants the milkshake, and they sit over here in their bedroom where they are feeling ill, and they just gobble it up from way down in the kitchen, where you don't even have to move the Mixmaster that made the ice cream for them."

47 New Mexico Advisory Committee to the United States Commission on Civil Rights, *The Farmington Report: A Conflict of Cultures* (New Mexico Advisory Committee to the United States Commission on Civil Rights, 1975).

CHAPTER 15

48 BP America created a produced water gathering and piping system to help reduce the need for trucks, although that has its own problems: in 2016 a BP-produced water pipe ruptured, spilling untold quantities of wastewater into a small stream.

49 Bureau of Land Management San Juan Field Office, *Coalbed Methane Development in the San Juan Basin of Colorado* (Bureau of Land Management San Juan Field Office, 1999).

50 Well, some homes were still contaminated. In 2005, a doublewide trailer exploded south of Durango after methane from a leaking, long-abandoned gas well had built up inside. The seventy-year-old occupant was badly burned, but survived. The COGCC spent hundreds of thousands of dollars trying to understand and mitigate the problem.

CHAPTER 16

51 Uravan, which was a U.S. Vanadium Corporation company town constructed for the boom, would ultimately be demolished and reclaimed as a Superfund site due to extensive radioactive contamination.

52 Durango drew its drinking water from the Florida River, not the Animas River, due to the earlier problems with hardrock mine and mill waste.

53 Keep in mind that this water still would have been tainted by the Silverton-area mines and tailings, and may have even had radioactive material in it from the aforementioned Graysill Mine. Another control station was set up on the Florida River, Durango's water source, before it entered the Animas.

54 To be fair, two renegade USPHS scientists, Duncan Holaday and Victor Archer, did research the high incidences of cancer in Navajo uranium miners during the 1950s, but the Atomic Energy Commission ignored or suppressed their findings. It wasn't until the mid-1960s that the two were allowed to go public with their results, which did show a conclusive link between uranium mining and cancer, particularly of the lungs.

CHAPTER 18

55 Duncan Oil had a less than stellar environmental record. In the late 1980s researchers found that tanks and pits at the company's Hogback oil field next to the San Juan River were leaking, and polycyclic aromatic hydrocarbons were getting into the groundwater at high levels. Oil also leaked from the site. In 1992, the EPA and Navajo Nation oversaw a massive cleanup, conducted by Duncan Oil.

CHAPTER 21

56 In this method, ore is crushed, piled up on a pad, and sprinkled with sodium

cyanide, which slowly penetrates the ore and adheres to the gold. The gold-infused cyanide tea is then collected and the gold is removed by electrolysis. This method is common today, but was never used in the Silverton area. However, small amounts of cyanide were used by Silverton-area mills employing non-heap-leaching extraction methods and for other purposes. Cyanide has contributed to some of the worst mining disasters in history.

57 The Idarado is a state-administered Superfund site, not an EPA-administered one.

CHAPTER 23

58 Simon Hydro-Search, *Preliminary Characterization of the Hydrology and Water Chemistry of the Sunnyside Mine and Vicinity, San Juan County, Colorado* (Silverton, CO: San Juan County Mining Venture, 1992). Accessed via Colorado Department of Reclamation, Mining, and Safety.

CHAPTER 24

59 Think about it like this: Say you have a wetland on your property that's a nuisance. When your neighbor drills a water well on her property, your wetland dries up. Twenty years later, the neighbor plugs the well, and your wetland returns. Can you hold the neighbor accountable for wrecking your lawn?

CHAPTER 25

60 Colorado Goldfields Inc. filings with the U.S. Securities and Exchange Commission, 2007-2014.

Bibliography

Abell, Robin. *San Juan River Basin Water Quality and Contaminants Review*. Albuquerque: University of New Mexico, 1994.

Agricola, Georgius. *De Re Metallica*. Translated by Herbert and Lou Hoover. New York: Dover Publications Inc., 1950.

Armstrong, Betsy R. *Century of Struggle against Snow: A History of Avalanche Hazard in San Juan County, Colorado*. Boulder: Institute of Arctic and Alpine Research, University of Colorado, 1976.

Baker, Steven G. *Juan Rivera's Colorado, 1765: The First Spaniards among the Ute and Paiute Indians on the Trails to Teguayo*. Lake City, CO: Western Reflections Publishing, 2016.

Bellorado, Benjamin A., and Kirk C. Anderson. "Early Pueblo Responses to Climate Variability: Farming Traditions, Land Tenure, and Social Power in the Eastern Mesa Verde Region." *Kiva* 78, no. 4 (2013): 377–416. doi:10.1179/0023194013z.0000000007.

Benally, Clyde, with Andrew O. Wiget, John R. Alley, and Garry Blake. *Dinéjí Nákéé' Nááhane': A Utah Navajo History*. Monticello, UT: San Juan School District, 1982.

Bureau of Land Management San Juan Field Office. *Coalbed Methane Development in the San Juan Basin of Colorado*. Bureau of Land Management San Juan Field Office, 1999.

Courlander, Harold. *The Fourth World of the Hopis: The Epic Story of the Hopi Indians as Preserved in Their Legends and Traditions*. Albuquerque: University of New Mexico Press, 2000.

Curtis, Kent A. *Gambling on Ore: The Nature of Metal Mining in the United States, 1860–1910*. Boulder: University Press of Colorado, 2013.

Frodeman, Robert. *Geo-Logic: Breaking Ground between Philosophy and the Earth Sciences*. New York: State University of New York Press, 2003.

Gobla, Michael J., Christopher M. Gemperline, and Leslie W. Stone.

Technical Review of the Gold King Mine Incident. Denver: U.S. Bureau of Reclamation, 2015.

Hayden, F. V. *Ninth Annual Report of the United States Geological and Geographical Survey of the Territories: Embracing Colorado and Parts of Adjacent Territories; Being a Report of Progress of the Exploration for the Year 1875*. Washington, DC: G.P.O., 1877.

Hornewer, N.J. *Sediment and Water Chemistry of the San Juan River and Escalante River Deltas of Lake Powell, Utah, 2010–2011: Open-File Report 2014-1096*. Reston, VA: U.S. Geological Survey, 2014.

Jacobs, G.C. "The Phantom Pathfinder: Juan Maria Antonio de Rivera and His Expedition." *Utah Historical Quarterly* 60, no. 3 (Summer 1992): 200–23.

Jones, William R. "History of Mining and Milling Practices and Production in San Juan County, Colorado, 1871–1991." In *Integrated Investigations of Environmental Effects of Historical Mining in the Animas River Watershed, San Juan County, Colorado: USGS Professional Paper 1651*, edited by Stanley E. Church, Paul von Guerard, and Susan E. Finger, 39–86. Reston, VA: U.S. Geological Survey, 2006.

Jordan, David S. "Report of Explorations in Colorado and Utah during the Summer of 1889, with an Account of the Fishes Found in Each of the River Basins Examined." In *Bulletin of the United States Fish Commission Vol. IX for 1889*, 1–40. Washington, DC: G.P.O., 1891.

King, William H., and Paul Trekell Allsman. *Reconnaissance of Metal Mining in the San Juan Region: Ouray, San Juan, and San Miguel Counties, Colo*. Washington, DC: U.S. Bureau of Mines, 1950.

Lavender, David. *One Man's West*. Lincoln: University of Nebraska Press, 1977.

Leblanc, M. "4,500-Year-Old Mining Pollution in Southwestern Spain: Long-Term Implications for Modern Mining Pollution." *Economic Geology* 95, no. 3 (2000): 655–62. doi:10.2113/95.3.655.

Leithauser, Jennifer. "The Spanish Influenza - Terror and Heroism in Silverton, Colorado." *The Blue Spruce Almanac*. http://www.grandturk.org/almanac/influenza.html.

Lekson, Stephen H. *The Chaco Meridian: One Thousand Years of Political and Religious Power in the Ancient Southwest.* Lanham: Rowman & Littlefield, 2015.

Matthews, Washington. "Ichthyophobia." *The Journal of American Folklore* 11, no. 41 (1898): 105. doi:10.2307/533215.

Medine, Allen J. *Water Quality Assessment: Animas River Basin.* Denver: U.S. Environmental Protection Agency, 1990.

Moore, George, and Berwyn Moore. "Public Health Initiatives in the Four Corners of Colorado, 1955–1957." *Public Health Reports* 123, no. 3 (2008): 376–81. doi:10.1177/003335490812300318.

Naranjo, Tessie. "Thoughts on Migration by Santa Clara Pueblo." *Journal of Anthropological Archaeology* 14, no. 2 (1995): 247–50. doi:10.1006/jaar.1995.1013.

"Navajo Perspectives on the Gold King Spill." Panel discussion at the University of Arizona Institute of the Environment, Flagstaff, AZ, March 2016.

New Mexico Advisory Committee to the United States Commission on Civil Rights. *The Farmington Report: A Conflict of Cultures.* New Mexico Advisory Committee to the United States Commission on Civil Rights, 1975.

Nordstrom, Darrell Kirk, Charles N. Alpers, Carol J. Ptacek, and David W. Blowes. "Negative pH and Extremely Acidic Mine Waters from Iron Mountain, California." *Environmental Science & Technology* 34, no. 2 (2000): 254–58. doi:10.1021/es990646v.

Norvelle, Norman. "Animas River Environmental Contamination from the Durango Mill Site." Presentation at the Conference on Environmental Conditions of the Animas and San Juan Watersheds, Farmington, NM, May 2016.

Nossaman, Allen. *Many More Mountains: An Illustrated History of the Earliest Exploration in the High San Juans of Southwestern Colorado and the Settlement and Founding of Silverton, Colorado.* 3 vols. Denver: Sundance Publications, 1989–98.

Oldaker, Paul. "The Story of Moving Mountain: An Historic Gas Seepage and Mass Wasting Event." Presentation at the AAPG Rocky Mountain Section 58th Annual Rocky Mountain Rendezvous, Durango, CO, June 13–16, 2010.

Ortiz, Alfonso. *The Tewa World: Space, Time, Being, and Becoming in a Pueblo Society*. Chicago: University of Chicago Press, 1972.

Osterholtz, Anna J. "Hobbling and Torture as Performative Violence." *Kiva* 78, no. 2 (2012): 123–44. doi:10.1179/kiv.2012.78.2.002.

Peterson, Freda Carley. *The Story of Hillside Cemetery: Burials 1873–1988*. Oklahoma City: Freda Carley Peterson, 1989.

Potter, James M. *Animas-La Plata Project: Volume XVI — Final Synthetic Report*. SWCA Anthropological Research Paper No. 10. Phoenix: SWCA Inc., 2010.

Potter, James M., and Jason P. Chuipka. "Perimortem Mutilation of Human Remains in an Early Village in the American Southwest: A Case for Ethnic Violence." *Journal of Anthropological Archaeology* 29, no. 4 (2010): 507–23. doi:10.1016/j.jaa.2010.08.001.

Potter, James M., and Thomas D. Yoder. "Space, Houses, and Bodies: Identity Construction and Destruction in an Early Pueblo Community." In *The Social Construction of Communities: Agency, Structure and Identity in the Prehispanic Southwest*, edited by Mark Varien and James Potter, 29–31. Lanham, MD: AltaMira Press, 2008.

Quintana, Frances L. *Pobladores: Hispanic Americans of the Ute Frontier*. Aztec, NM: Frances Leon Quintana, 1991.

Ransome, Frederick Leslie, and Whitman Cross. *A Report on the Economic Geology of the Silverton Quadrangle, Colorado*. Washington, DC: G.P.O., 1901.

Ross, Harold Wallace, and Thomas Kunkel. *Letters from the Editor: The New Yorker's Harold Ross*. New York: Random House, 2001.

Sando, Joe S. *Nee Hemish: A History of Jemez Pueblo*. Santa Fe: Clear Light, 2008.

Sarah Platt Decker Chapter Daughters of the American Revolution. *Pioneers of the San Juan Country: A Reprint of Volumes I, II, II, and IV*. Bountiful, UT: Family History Publishers, 1995.

Shuey, C. "Policy and Regulatory Implications of Coalbed Methane Development." In *International Symposium on Oil and Gas*

Exploration and Production Waste Management Practices, Proceedings, New Orleans, 757–69. 1999.

Simon Hydro-Search. *Preliminary Characterization of the Hydrology and Water Chemistry of the Sunnyside Mine and Vicinity, San Juan County, Colorado*. Silverton, CO: San Juan County Mining Venture, 1992.

Smith, Duane A. *The Trail of Gold and Silver: Mining in Colorado, 1859–2009*. Boulder: University Press of Colorado, 2010.

Southern Ute Indian Tribe. "History of the Southern Ute." *Southern Ute Indian Tribe*. https://www.southernute-nsn.gov/history.

Spring, Agnes Wright. "Silver Queen of the San Juans." *Frontier Times* 45, no. 1 (January 1967).

Stratton, David H. *Tempest over Teapot Dome: The Story of Albert Fall*. Norman: University of Oklahoma Press, 1998.

Thompson, Ian M., Mark D. Varien, Susan Kenzle, and Rina Swentzell. "Prehistoric Architecture with Unknown Function." In *Anasazi Architecture and American Design*, edited by B.H. Morrow and V.B. Price, 149–58. Albuquerque: University of New Mexico Press, 1997.

Webb, Robert H., Diane E. Boyer, Lynn Orchard, and Victor R. Baker. *Changes in Riparian Vegetation in the Southwestern United States: Floods and Riparian Vegetation on the San Juan River, Southeastern Utah; USGS Open File Report of 01-314*. Tucson: U.S. Geological Survey, 2001.

White, Jim. "Animas River Report." Durango: Colorado Division of Wildlife, 2010.

Yazzie, Duane "Chili." "Yellow River." Poem recited at the Conference on Environmental Conditions of the Animas and San Juan Watersheds, Farmington, NM, May 2016.

Zolbrod, Paul G. *Diné Bahané: The Navajo Creation Story*. Albuquerque: University of New Mexico Press, 1987.

Newspapers and magazines, dating from 1874 to the present: *The Silverton Standard, Silverton Standard & the Miner, La Plata Miner, Silverton Democrat, Durango Herald, Durango Democrat, Durango Wage Earner, Silverton Mountain Journal, San Juan*

Mountain Journal, High Country News, Leadville Democrat, Aspen Tribune, Colorado Transcript, Dolores News, Telluride Journal, Fort Collins Courier, Aspen Daily Times, Grand Junction Sentinel, The Mining American, Eagle Valley Enterprise, Record Journal of Douglas, Rocky Mountain News, Denver Post, Durango Herald Democrat, Steamboat Pilot, Bayfield Blade.

About Jonathan P. Thompson

Jonathan P. Thompson is a native Westerner with deep roots in southwestern Colorado. He has been an environmental journalist focusing on the American West since he signed on as reporter and photographer at the *Silverton Standard & the Miner* newspaper in 1996. He has worked and written for *High Country News* for over a decade, serving as editor-in-chief from 2007 to 2010. He was a Ted Scripps fellow in environmental journalism at the University of Colorado in Boulder, and in 2016 he was awarded the Society of Environmental Journalists' Outstanding Beat Reporting, Small Market. He currently splits his time between Colorado and Bulgaria with his wife Wendy and daughters Lydia and Elena. Visit riveroflostsouls.com for his most recent photos, blog posts, and more.

Torrey House Press

Voices for the Land

The economy is a wholly owned subsidiary of the environment, not the other way around.

—Senator Gaylord Nelson, founder of Earth Day

Torrey House Press is an independent nonprofit publisher promoting environmental conservation through literature. We believe that culture is changed through conversation and that lively, contemporary literature is the cutting edge of social change. We strive to identify exceptional writers, nurture their work, and engage the widest possible audience; to publish diverse voices with transformative stories that illuminate important facets of our ever-changing planet; to develop literary resources for the conservation movement, educating and entertaining readers, inspiring action. Visit www.torreyhouse.org for reading group discussion guides, author interviews, and more.